HAPPY LIVES, GOOD LIVES

HAPPY LIVES, GOOD LIVES

A Philosophical Examination

Jennifer Wilson Mulnix
& M.J. Mulnix

broadview press

Library and Archives Canada Cataloguing in Publication

Mulnix, Jennifer Wilson, author
    Happy lives, good lives : a philosophical examination / Jennifer Wilson Mulnix and M.J. Mulnix.

Includes bibliographical references and index.
ISBN 978-1-55481-100-7 (paperback)
    1. Happiness—Philosophy. I. Mulnix, Michael Joshua, author II. Title.

B187.H3W44 2015   152.4'2   C2015-902185-5

Broadview Press is an independent, international publishing house, incorporated in 1985.

We welcome comments and suggestions regarding any aspect of our publications—please feel free to contact us at the addresses below or at broadview@broadviewpress.com.

North America:
PO Box 1243, Peterborough, Ontario K9J 7H5, Canada
555 Riverwalk Parkway, Tonawanda, NY 14150, USA
Tel: (705) 743-8990; Fax: (705) 743-8353
Email: customerservice@broadviewpress.com

UK, Europe, Central Asia, Middle East, Africa, India, and Southeast Asia:
Eurospan Group, 3 Henrietta St., London WC2E 8LU, UK
Tel: 44 (0) 1767 604972; Fax: 44 (0) 1767 601640
Email: eurospan@turpin-distribution.com

Australia and New Zealand:
Footprint Books
1/6a Prosperity Parade, Warriewood, NSW 2102, Australia
Tel: 61 1300 260 090; Fax: 61 02 9997 3185
Email: info@footprint.com.au

www.broadviewpress.com

Copy-edited by Martin R. Boyne

Broadview Press acknowledges the financial support of the Government of Canada through the Canada Book Fund for our publishing activities.

Book design and composition by George Kirkpatrick
PRINTED IN CANADA

For our mentor, RAF,
who taught us to be better philosophers.

Contents

Preface

THIS BOOK, *Happy Lives, Good Lives: A Philosophical Examination*, is intended to accompany our anthology, *Theories of Happiness: An Anthology*. Yet it also designed to stand on its own as a source for important philosophical perspectives on the nature of happiness as well as an overview of the current science of happiness. Our goal is to discuss central questions within the field of happiness studies. In addition to exploring the nature, causes, and correlates of happiness, we also investigate its value to life, its connection to well-being, its relationship to morality, whether it can be accurately and meaningfully measured, whether the standards of the happy life are universal or relative to the individual, and whether governments ought to use measures of happiness to steer public-policy decisions. These are just some of the many issues surrounding the concept of happiness that this book endeavors to address.

We do not discuss historical views of happiness in chronological order, but instead order them topically so as to reflect a dialogue between ideas. This allows for a deeper exploration of the key features of each view and opens the door for data from the social sciences to speak to views expressed much earlier in history. This provides, we think, for a richer conversation and will bring out the key insights and strengths, as well as the most challenging aspects, of each view. After some introductory chapters that lay out the framework for the important questions surrounding an investigation into happiness, this book focuses primarily on the three major philosophical theories of happiness: *hedonism*, *desire satisfactionism*, and *eudaimonism*. Along the way, the book incorporates information gathered from the social sciences that especially speaks to the issues of measurement and error. We also include some practical advice that one might follow in pursuit of happiness.

Ideally, this book is suited for courses on the philosophy of happiness or well-being. It could also be used in courses on the meaning of life, morality and the good life, or related topics. Due to considerations of space, however, we are unable to discuss all the positions one might take with respect to happiness. While we believe that this book represents a thorough treatment of the paradigmatic approaches within the philosophy of happiness, we do not intend our discussion to be an exhaustive one.

We are especially grateful to helpful comments we received on an earlier draft from Richard Fumerton, Matthew Lewis, and an anonymous referee. We also very much thank our editor Stephen Latta and the staff at Broadview Press. Additionally, we would like to acknowledge and express thanks to our home institutions: work on this book was supported by a sabbatical leave from the University of Massachusetts at Dartmouth and an alternative professional release from Salem State University. Finally, we would like to express much gratitude to our students for many fruitful conversations.

HOW LONG DO YOU put off thinking yourself worthy of the best things, and never going against the definitive capacity of reason? You have received the philosophical propositions that you ought to agree to and you have agreed to them. Then what sort of teacher are you still waiting for, that you put off improving yourself until he comes? You are not a child any more, but already a full-grown adult. If you now neglect things and are lazy and are always making delay after delay and set one day after another as the day for paying attention to yourself, then without realizing it you will make no progress but will end up [ignorant] all through life and death. So decide now that you are worthy of living as a full-grown adult who is making progress, and make everything that seems best be a law that you cannot go against.

– Epictetus, Enchiridion c. 51

Online Materials

EVERY COPY OF *Happy Lives, Good Lives: A Philosophical Examination* includes access to a companion website for both students and instructors. This website includes

- Study questions for each chapter
- Additional case studies to consider
- Recommendations for further reading
- Links to videos and other related online content

To access these online materials, visit **sites.broadviewpress.com/happiness**.

Part I: Thinking about the Nature and
               Value of Happiness

Chapter 1:   Introduction

WE ALL WANT TO be happy. But what does this mean? We certainly care about it, thinking it is deeply important to life. We believe that to pursue it is a basic right. We plan our lives around getting as much of it as we can. We wish it for our loved ones. Yet how many of us ever spend any serious time trying to figure out what happiness is and what leads to it? This high-lights a particularly strange tension. On the one hand, happiness seems to occupy a central place in our lives, as it is one of our most cherished values. On the other hand, we rest content with vague and hazy notions of what it might be, and we spend little time or energy making sure we are right. If we continue on this path, delaying paying attention to our happiness, then as the Greek Stoic philosopher Epictetus warns, we are destined to make no progress in improving ourselves and achieving happiness in our lives.

We need to decide right now that we are worthy of happiness and that we will dedicate our lives to being the best version of ourselves that we can be. But to do this will require careful thought and examination of arguments and evidence. It will require the determination to figure out for ourselves what happiness is and what causes it, and then the resolve to apply these lessons to our own life. After all, there is no point in embarking on this journey if we are unwilling to change the way we live as a result of our newfound knowledge. And if we do not live in a way that will bring us happiness, in what sense can we be said to love our lives? Life is valuable; we should not waste it.

When people are asked what they think happiness is, there's almost no limit to the range of answers. Common answers focus on things such as having a generally positive attitude or being content with life, while other popular answers specify the central elements of a happy life, such as having good health, a loving family, a suitable quality of life, and meaningful relationships. Others include various things such as eating gourmet foods, having one's favorite sports team win, or listening to music. What is interesting about these different answers is that they pick out very different kinds of things. Some mention attitudes and emotions, while others are more about possessing a life with certain desired features like family and health. Still others are about very specific events turning out the way we want. Yet, if we look carefully, at least some of these answers (like having our favorite team win a big game) seem to be concerned more with what *causes* happiness, rather than with what happiness itself actually *is*. When we explore different views of happiness, it is important to keep this distinction clear. Though these are different questions, they are frequently run together.

Seeking to determine the causes and correlates of happiness is primarily a task for empirical science. Still, many psychologists and economists working on this project write in ways that imply they believe they are talking about what happiness is – as if they are discovering the nature of happiness through their empirical studies. But, of course, questions about the nature of happiness cannot be answered by empirical observation alone. After all, how would the scientist know that she was observing and measuring happiness if she had not already determined in advance of her study what happiness *is*? Questions about the *nature* of happiness are the subject matter of the *philosophy* of happiness. Philosophers take it as their special project to discover the nature of things. On the other hand, what *causes* happiness is a question for the empirical sciences. Once we have settled on the nature of happiness, we must then use the scientific method to figure out what other sorts of things correlate with and cause it.

This is a book primarily on the *philosophy* of happiness, about the very *nature* of that thing we refer to as "happiness" or "being happy," as well as the attainment of it. Our principal aims are to clarify the concept of happiness and to consider its value. "Philosophy" comes from the Greek root words *philo* and *sophia*, which together mean "the love of wisdom." Wisdom, though, is not mere intelligence. There are plenty of smart, yet unwise, individuals. Wisdom is the ability to use intelligence to live well, and philosophy is the art of living well: it is a way of life, and it involves building ourselves into what it is that we want to be. Happiness is one aim of such a project. Before we start the work of improving ourselves, our very first task is to decide what it is that we are aiming at – what exactly *is* happiness? We are not interested in answering this question only as an academic exercise, but also so that we can gain practical insight into how to more successfully pursue a happy life. The whole point of gaining such knowledge is to put it to use in living better lives. This leads to the second task: to lay down a plan for getting happiness, which will involve a consideration of what sorts of things cause and correlate with happiness. In this vein, we will also need to consider evidence from empirical science. And finally, the third task is to live according to that plan. As Epictetus advises in the epigraph at the start of this book, once we come to know and accept what happiness is, and what causes it, then we need the resolve to live according to that knowledge. If we don't follow through with our plan for happiness, we will not make progress but will instead waste away our days in fruitless endeavors.

So where do we start? Partly complicating the problem is that it isn't even clear when we talk about happiness in various contexts that we are talking about the same thing in each case. Sometimes we express that we are happy with some specific aspect of our lives, which suggests that happiness is a distinctive kind of attitude that we can have toward a particular situation, and where we find that we can be happy with some things, but unhappy with others. For example, it is quite natural for someone to say, "Well, I am happy with my marriage and I am happy with my friendships, but I am unhappy with my career and my leisure time." On this kind of view, a person's happiness might fluctuate from day to day, depending on the circumstances. Of course, while sometimes we do say things like "I am happy today but I wasn't yesterday," we *also* say things like "My *life* is a happy one." It is natural, for example, for people to remark, "While I am unhappy with my situation of the last several months, I am nonetheless happy overall." This then might suggest that happiness is less about particular aspects of our lives than about our life in total.

So how do we make sense of these claims? Is happiness something specific, attaching to certain domains or experiences in our lives, or is it more appropriately something general, applying to our life as a whole? And is happiness something stable that endures over a long span of time, or is it something that comes and goes in our experience, yearly, weekly, daily, or even hourly? Can happiness be *all* of these things? What these brief considerations reveal is just how important it is for us not to rely on our vague notions of happiness. Rather, we need to carefully deliberate about what it is. We do not want to begin to pursue happiness before we are sure what it is, since if we go after the wrong things in life, we might do more to harm than help our happiness.

Who Is the Happy Person?

One nice feature of deliberating about happiness is that we can learn vicariously through the way others live. We do not have to experience every life for ourselves in order to know whether or not some choices will make us happy. We can get instruction in how to live by studying examples of lives we have never lived. We see, for instance, that the life of a heroin addict is not happy, even though we have never tried on such a life to see how it feels. The examples that others set for us can be useful in our pursuit of happiness, guiding us on what to do and what to avoid in order to attain our own happiness.

So a useful place to start in our exploration of happiness is to consider many different kinds of lives. This book will do just that. These lives may be either real or fictional. In Chapter Two, for example, we will consider the fictional life of Truman Burbank from the popular 1998 movie *The Truman Show*, and in Chapter Three we will think about the real life of American serial killer Ted Bundy. Each life is introduced so as to isolate for us a particular question such as, in the case of Truman, is happiness just a mental state? Or, in the case of Bundy, can an immoral person be happy? The aim of considering these various kinds of lives is to draw on our understandings and intuitions about these cases in order to clarify our reasons for thinking that the person in question is happy or not. Asking ourselves whether the person described is happy will help us not only to refine our understanding of what happiness is, but also to realize which specific commitments or values about happiness we hold. We might even see that there are some inconsistencies in our commitments. In order to resolve this conflict, it will be important for us to carefully deliberate over the reasons for choosing one commitment over another.

There are several ways in which to determine whether a life in question is happy. First, you could endorse one of the theories of happiness explored in this book, and then apply it to the particulars of the situation to ascertain whether that person is happy. On this approach, answering whether the person is happy depends on your favored theory of happiness. A second way is to use your intuitions about a case to make the judgment as to whether the person in question is happy, and then afterwards to look for which theory best respects and accommodates this judgment, thereby using your intuitions as support for accepting one of the theories of happiness over the others. The best approach is to utilize both of these methods cooperatively to achieve a kind of balance among our intuitions and judgments. One benefit of these case studies or thought experiments is that they allow us to test our views of happiness by seeing how a particular view would answer the question and then checking whether our own intuitions match up with that view's conclusion. Of course, our judgments about whether or not a person is happy never take place wholly devoid of some theoretical commitment on our part. Whether we notice it or not, we always assume a theory of happiness more or less explicitly when judging a particular person to be happy or unhappy. It seems that our choice of theory and our intuitions about whether a person is happy work in tandem, each informing and refining the other. If we carefully attend to each, we can achieve a sort of equilibrium between our convictions about particular cases and our general theory of happiness.

Additionally, when we consider many different kinds of lives, we want to make sure that our judgments in these various cases are consistent with each other. The reasons we may offer for thinking that one particular person is happy or unhappy should not directly conflict with the reasons we might give for why another person is happy or unhappy. As an example, if we think Truman is happy for the *sole* reason that he experiences lots of pleasure, then we cannot turn around and say that Bundy is *unhappy* in spite of experiencing great amounts of pleasure just because he is immoral. However, we *could* say that Truman is happy both because he experiences lots of pleasure *and* because he is a moral person, and then say that Bundy is unhappy because, although he experiences pleasure, he is immoral. So one project throughout the book will be for you to try to isolate and clarify your specific reasons for why you think each person in question is or is not happy. This will then help you to settle on which account of happiness you endorse.

Three Theories of Happiness

There are three broad categories into which philosophical theories of happiness can be classified: *hedonism*, *desire satisfactionism*, and *eudaimonism*. Each category includes distinct versions that differ from each other, yet they can all be classified together by way of sharing some common central features.

Broadly speaking, hedonism thinks of happiness as a kind of good feeling, and this would include experiencing what psychologists call *positive affect* (an affect is any mental state that is essentially a feeling). Examples of positive affect include pleasures and certain emotions and moods. Although there are different versions of hedonism depending on how one understands the nature of pleasure and which positive affects are central to happiness, varieties of hedonism nevertheless share the notion that happiness describes a feel-good mental state, which is the only important element in a happy life.

Desire satisfactionism holds that happiness describes a positive attitude, such as being satisfied with, gratified about, or approving of something. Generally, an attitude is a psychological stance you take about something, whether it be positive or negative. Unlike pleasure, which feels to us a certain way, an attitude like approval seems to lack any distinct feeling. Happiness is a cognitive appraisal, a positive evaluation of some facet of your experience – such as your life as a whole, or some aspect of it. In this way, happiness is less about feeling a certain way and more about whether our desires or preferences are satisfied. There are several varieties of desire satisfactionism. One type of desire satisfaction view, called *local desire satisfactionism*, takes happiness to be the satisfaction of our *local* desires. We have all sorts of local desires, such as a desire to eat pizza, to go shopping, or to watch a football game. These desires are local because they have a sort of specificity; they are not about our life in general, but instead are concerned with particular aspects of it. On this view, to be happy is to experience a sufficiently high ratio of satisfied to unsatisfied local desires, whatever these local desires may be. On the other hand, local desire satisfactionism treats all of our local desires as equally important to our happiness, and some have found this to be a fault with the view. Instead, perhaps happiness results from having our important desires satisfied. This, of course, would require that we organize our desires according to their importance. Such a view, *whole life satisfactionism*, captures this central claim by focusing on the satisfaction of a single general desire: the desire for our life overall to go as we want. To be happy is therefore to be satisfied with our life as a whole.

Finally, eudaimonism holds that happiness consists in fully actualizing yourself or fulfilling your positive potential as a human person. Your potential is not limited only to your ability to experience pleasures and satisfactions, but also includes your ability to reason, to be morally virtuous, and to exercise autonomy, among other things. So there are things independent of your first-hand experience of life that can make your life go better and that are part of your happiness, whether you recognize them or not and whether you value them or not. To be happy, then, is to live a complete life that lacks nothing of value – to flourish as a human person.

The Value of Happiness

As already noted, it seems clear that we all want to be happy. However, when we think about different kinds of lives (such as Truman's or Bundy's), we see that sometimes we are willing to call the person in question happy in spite of that person's life failing or going poorly in certain respects. We might even be unwilling to switch places with that happy person on account of their life not going well. In those cases, we don't think that the person is living a "good life" or experiencing "well-being." "Well-being" refers to what is good for a person, or to how well a person's life is going. So a good life is a life that is worthwhile and of value for the person who lives it. Theories of the good life or well-being specify what is valuable in life; it is an open question how large a role, if any at all, happiness plays in living a good life. Perhaps there are other things of value to a good life that are separate from our own happiness. These things might even be intrinsically valuable: having value on their own, for their own sake, independent of any potential contribution to our happiness. These might include agency, love of others, and moral commitments, for example.

Additionally, it seems quite clear that these other values can sometimes come into conflict with our private happiness. For example, there seem to be situations in which it is morally problematic to pursue our own happiness, such as when our happiness depends on harming others. This highlights the trade-offs that might be involved in the pursuit of a good life. In cases of conflict, we will need to make a decision between our private happiness and something else we might value. In these cases, we might be willing to forgo our own personal happiness in the service of perceived moral commitments or for the sake of the happiness of others, such as our children or even society at large. Indeed, there are many real-life situations in which people knowingly sacrifice their own private happiness for some other thing they value. But if happiness can be in conflict with these other valued things, then perhaps happiness might have very little value at all. And if the pursuit of happiness *precludes* living a good life, would we still choose happiness? We *think* we all want happiness, but do we *really* want a good life?

So we need to determine what relationship there is, if any, between being happy and living a good life. Perhaps the two are not at all related. Or, perhaps, happiness is one intrinsic value among many, all contributing to a good life (perhaps it is even a *necessary* element). Or happiness may even be the *only* thing of intrinsic worth, and thus to live a happy life *just is* to

live a good life. We therefore have on our hands two very legitimate questions: What do we mean by "happiness," and just how valuable is it? In the
remainder of this book we will attempt to answer these questions.

Overview of the Book

Chapter Two, "Intuitions about Happiness," and Chapter Three, "Happy
Lives, Good Lives, and Moral Lives," start us out with a discussion of some
of the principal questions surrounding the concept of happiness. These
questions include the following:

- Is happiness a mental state?
- Is it a feeling?
- Can we be mistaken about whether we are happy?
- Is happiness under our control?
- Are there universal ingredients in a happy life?
- Is happiness descriptive or evaluative?
- What is the value of happiness?
- Is the happy life the same as the good life?
- What is the relationship between happiness and morality?
- Is it sometimes morally problematic to pursue happiness?

The purpose of these introductory chapters is to provide a brief overview of
the important questions in the investigation of the nature of happiness that
will then be discussed, in later chapters, in connection with a fuller exploration of the main theories of happiness. The idea is to raise these questions
at the start of our inquiry so that we can keep these issues in mind as we
progress throughout the book and examine views of happiness in more
detail. Chapters Four through Ten then explore these main theories of happiness in depth, carefully examining the elements of the respective views
and how they answer the questions posed in these beginning chapters.

More specifically, in the second part, Chapter Four, "The Feel-Good
Feature of Happiness," and Chapter Five, "Taking Pleasure in Things and
Feeling Joy," analyze the views classified as forms of hedonism. Chapter
Four centers primarily on the classical hedonism of Jeremy Bentham and
John Stuart Mill, who endorse the claim not only that happiness consists in
experiencing pleasure, but also that happiness is the fundamental element
in well-being. Chapter Five surveys some contemporary alternative forms
of hedonism put forward by Fred Feldman and Daniel Haybron, which

broaden the understanding of pleasure to include attitudes (in Feldman's case) and emotional states (in Haybron's account). Additionally, both Feldman and Haybron treat happiness as primarily a descriptive term but think that the psychological state of happiness might correlate with, and therefore be used as an approximation for, a good life.

Next, in the third part, Chapter Six, "Satisfied with What?", and Chapter Seven, "It's All about Perspective," evaluate the views grouped within desire satisfactionism. Chapter Six begins by overviewing some problems with local desire satisfaction accounts of happiness before moving on to explore the whole life satisfaction view of Władysław Tatarkiewicz. Tatarkiewicz calls attention to the ways in which the past, present, and future each influence our satisfaction with life. This chapter also considers several objections to whole life satisfaction views, including using findings from empirical psychology to question whether we are able to form reliable life satisfaction judgments. In light of these concerns, the focus of Chapter Seven is on two formulations of whole life satisfactionism – one offered by Valerie Tiberius and Alicia Hall, and the other by John Kekes – which build in constraints to our life satisfaction judgments, such as the need to adopt a reflective perspective and the need to gather adequate information about one's values and one's plans. Doing so helps us to make more reliable judgments of life satisfaction, which in turn helps us to better plan for a good life.

In the fourth part of the book, Chapter Eight, "Is Ignorance Bliss?", Chapter Nine, "Happiness, Moral Virtue, and the Purpose of Life," and Chapter Ten, "Finding Equanimity in the Face of Suffering," together assess and apply the views known as eudaimonism. Chapter Eight considers the question of whether we prefer other things to happiness, such as agency or authenticity for example, and also whether we can be happy even while radically deceived. This chapter also examines arguments for thinking that the happy life and the good life refer to the same thing. Chapter Nine surveys two paradigmatic forms of eudaimonism offered by the ancient Greek philosophers Plato and Aristotle, each of which gives moral virtue an especially important, though different, role to play in happiness. Both philosophers hold that happiness, as a complete end, is a skillful way of living and that the happy life will lack nothing that could make it better. Chapter Ten then explores the practical advice offered in the eudaimonistic philosophies put forward by the ancient Stoic Epictetus and the contemporary Buddhist His Holiness the Dalai Lama. Given that happiness is a skillful way of living, it will involve the development of practical wisdom: knowing how to live well, and succeeding at doing so. Both Epictetus and the Dalai Lama suggest how one can develop practical wisdom, or "train the mind for happiness." The chapter pays special attention to their advice on how to deal with suffering so that we can achieve some measure of happiness even in less than ideal circumstances.

In the final part, Chapter Eleven, "Justice and National Happiness," focuses on the topic of national happiness and the happiness indexes used to measure the happiness of a nation. The chapter also considers what role these national happiness measures should play, if any, in public policy. A rather common view is that one purpose of social institutions is to increase the happiness of the people. However, some public-policy measures designed to increase general happiness could very well end up violating an individual's right of self-determination or liberty of conscience, depending on whether those measures force conformity to a particular view of the good life. Given these concerns, nations might want only to make available to citizens information gathered about the causes and correlates of happiness so that they themselves can make more fully informed choices about how best to live. Thus, we might think that developing the science of happiness is a valuable collective end, as it has the possibility to help each of us achieve happiness more fully.

Chapter Twelve, "Concluding Reflections," ends the book by summarizing and highlighting the main issues in our discussions about the nature and value of happiness and about how to most effectively pursue it in our own lives. It also suggests what questions we might want to answer in our continued pursuit of happiness.

Through a careful exploration of the different theories, arguments, and concerns that philosophers, psychologists, and economists alike have raised in regard to our concept of happiness, we can begin to piece together a more thorough and informed account of our own happiness. It is not until after we have done this that we will actually have a target at which to aim. Of course, for this exploration to be useful, we have to be careful, sincere, and honest in how we approach each position. If we want a more fully informed view of what happiness is so that we can plan our life accordingly, we need the courage to be open-minded and the willingness to change our view if the evidence suggests we should. In the end, we can hope to come away a bit wiser – and a bit more effective at pursuing happiness.

Chapter 2: Intuitions about Happiness

IN THE 1998 FILM *The Truman Show*, the lead character Truman Burbank lives a seemingly idyllic life. He has a nice house on Seahaven Island complete with a white picket fence. He is married to a cheerful wife and has kindly neighbors. Truman, played by Jim Carrey, has a best friend he has known since grade school and in whom he often confides and trusts to offer life advice. He is respected at his job as an insurance salesman. All in all, his life is peaceful and joyful. Yet, unbeknownst to him, Truman is the star of a reality TV show broadcasting his life to the world. Abandoned as an infant, he was adopted by the show's director Christof. The entire island on which he lives is a massive set. It is surrounded by a sophisticated enormous dome that looks and acts like the natural sky. Truman's entire life is a fabrication. His wife, his friends, his neighbors, even his mother and father, are all actors. Truman has never experienced an honest human relationship. Over time and because of some untimely coincidences, he begins to be suspicious that he is trapped. He sets sail from the island to escape and eventually learns the truth when his sailboat collides with the edge of the dome. As Truman stands at the threshold to a door that will take him to into the "real world," Christof attempts to persuade him to stay, claiming that by staying he can live happily and without fear. He says: "Truman, there's no more truth out there than in the world I created for you – the same lies and deceit. But in my world you have nothing to fear." In the end, though, Truman chooses the true over the artificial and walks away from his false life.[1]

---

1   As we will see in Chapter Eight, Truman's life parallels in many ways the (continued)

The case of Truman Burbank raises some very interesting questions with respect to happiness. For instance, do you think that before he found out his life was a sham, Truman was happy? He seemed to experience many positive emotions, with an apparently loving spouse and respect from his friends and acquaintances. Moreover, Truman seemed psychologically healthy. He did not suffer from clinical depression or intense bouts of anxiety. Though his desire to go to Fiji was, as of yet, unfulfilled, many of his other desires appeared to be satisfied. Still, his life was a fake; it was a charade. All of the emotions he felt and the satisfactions he experienced were based on fiction. He lived in a simulated reality, and his relationships were not genuine. And while he experienced his life as free, his choices were manipulated by others. Can one truly be happy in such a setting? Though the example of Truman is fictional, it raises concerns that are similar to many real-life cases. Think, for example, of spouses who once believed that they were involved in fulfilling, faithful, and loving marriages only to find out many years later that their partner was a recurrent adulterer. In these situations, are we willing to say that the spouse was happy while living in a sham marriage? Our intuitions concerning Truman and related cases pull us in opposite directions. Some think he is happy before he finds out what is going on, while others reject this, arguing he is unhappy. Let's explore the reasoning behind each of these reactions. What assumptions underlie and inform them? Examining these assumptions will also give us a chance to briefly survey the three main theories of happiness that will be the focus of discussion throughout the book.

Is Happiness Only a State of Mind?

Those who are inclined to say that Truman's life was happy before he found out the truth are probably thinking of happiness as some sort of conscious mental state. Truman experienced his life as being a certain way and was pleased, satisfied, and fulfilled by that. On this line of thought, to be happy is to experience life first-hand as going a certain way. Still, what sort of experience of life is it to be happy? There are many common synonyms for happiness: enjoyment, peace of mind, fulfillment, cheer, pleasure, euphoria, as well as being content, satisfied, serene, blissful, joyful, elated, and in high spirits. There are many others. All of these possible synonyms for

---

Experience Machine thought experiment discussed by Nozick. A fuller discussion of deception and its connection to happiness will be explored in that chapter.

happiness are mental states, yet they are not the same. In the case of plea-sures, some are sensations, roughly the opposite of pain, such as the pleasure we get from a massage. Other pleasures, such as more intellectual pleasures, include an intentional component – they are about or represent things in the world – such as the pleasure we might get from reading a book by our favorite author. Even so, what all of these different kinds of pleasures have in common is that they all feel a certain way when we are in them. The same is true of many emotions and moods, such as joy, euphoria, and bliss, which are roughly opposites of depression, sadness, or melancholy. On the other hand, perhaps happiness is more like an attitude, such as being satis-fied, gratified, fulfilled, or pleased with something or other in particular, or with our life as a whole; this would be more or less opposite to being dissatisfied, frustrated, or displeased with these things. These attitudes are also intentional in that they are about or represent things in the world, yet such attitudes may not have any associated feeling accompanying them. In other words, unlike pleasure, which feels to us a certain way, the attitude of approval seems to lack any distinct feeling; it is more like a positive judg-ment or evaluation of something or someone.

This, then, highlights one distinction among our different mental states: some of them have noticeable *phenomenological feels*. That is, some mental states, such as pleasure or pain, elation or grief, *feel* a certain way to us – there is an essential "what it is like" feature that attends being in such mental states. So maybe happiness is a kind of good feeling or positive af-fect like pleasure, or like certain emotions and moods. Broadly speaking, any view that thinks of happiness as a feel-good mental state – whether that be physical pleasure, intellectual pleasure, emotional pleasure, a more stable mood state, or some combination of these – could generally be called *hedonism*. Hedonism will be the first main theory of happiness explored in the book, and it accords with the commonsense idea that being happy *feels* good. Perhaps the most common form of hedonism holds that pleasure (or the avoidance of pain) is the only important element of a happy life.

Still, even saying that happiness is a good feeling or positive affect is a bit vague, since pleasures, emotions, and moods are all different from each other. Broad varieties of hedonism include all kinds of positive affect as constituents of happiness. Alternatively, as we will see in the coming chapters, some versions of hedonism specify a type of feel-good mental state as happiness. For example, according to philosopher Jeremy Bentham, happiness is just the same as experiencing sensory pleasure, and the more sensory pleasure one experiences, the happier one is. On this sort of view, one can be made happy by eating a tasty meal, listening to a beautiful song, or even feeling a short-lived cool breeze on a hot and humid day. On the other hand, according to philosopher Daniel Haybron, happiness refers only to our experience of positive emotions and moods, since sensory pleasure is too superficial to matter to one's happiness. He explains that although it is obvious that we would experience pleasure from the cool breeze, it is not straightforwardly clear that we would be made *happier* by it. For Haybron, happiness is not a fleeting and fickle phenomenon that can come and go several times in an hour. Pleasures come and go quickly: now we experience a cool breeze, next a stagnant heavy heat. On the other hand, moods and emotions tend to last for a while. When someone is depressed or anxious, this can often last for days, weeks, or even longer. The same is true with positive emotions and moods such as joy or serenity. The durability of our emotions and moods suggests that they play a larger role in our happiness than do the transient experiences of pleasure. According to Haybron, happiness is not about pleasurable sensations so much as it is about our deeper psychological health. This understanding of happiness has the strength of accounting for its stability: we tend to think that when a person is happy, this will persist for some time.

Of course, some of our mental states are not feelings; they are not affects of any kind. Beliefs, judgments, and many attitudes have no associated feeling. For example, believing that Roger Federer is the greatest tennis player in history, or judging that today will be cloudy, lacks a distinct feel. The same is true with many attitudes. For instance, pride and gratification are positive psychological attitudes toward some facet of your experience, such as your life or an aspect of it, but they also seem to lack any well-defined feeling. Taking pride in one's accomplishment after a hard day of physical labor in the garden is one such example. So too is approving of how your town council handles property assessments.

The second main theory of happiness, *desire satisfactionism*, takes happiness to be an attitude, not a feeling. In particular, it is the positive attitude of *satisfaction*. Happiness is less about feeling a certain way and more about whether we are satisfied with how things are going for us. To be satisfied is akin to making a cognitive evaluation that things are turning out as we had hoped. It is to judge that our life, or some aspect of it, is going the way we want it to. There are many people who experience little in terms of positive affect and yet who nevertheless are satisfied with their accomplishments in life. For instance, philosopher Ludwig Wittgenstein was a notorious curmudgeon. He preferred seclusion, building a remote hut in Norway to isolate himself from others. As a teacher he had a reputation for cruelty among his students. And yet his last words were, "Tell them I've had a wonderful life."[2] Is it possible that Wittgenstein lived a happy life? Though he appears to have experienced little in terms of positive emotionality and to have endured a significant amount of negative emotionality, he nevertheless approved of his life as a whole. He appraised it as wonderful; he seems to have been satisfied with how things went overall. Desire satisfaction views of happiness can make sense out of thinking that such lives as Wittgenstein's can be happy for those who live them.

Of course, to say that happiness is the same as satisfaction leaves open what exactly we must be satisfied about in order to be happy. There are two main responses. One type of desire satisfaction view takes happiness to be the satisfaction of our *local* desires. We have all sorts of wants: we want to be healthy, wealthy, and wise; we want to feel pleasure and avoid pain; we want a promotion at work; we also want the person two rows behind us at the movie theater to put his cell phone away. In other words, we can have desires about pretty much anything we can imagine. These wants are local; they have a sort of specificity. They are not about our life in general, but instead are concerned with particular aspects of it, like our current daily activities, or our material wealth, job, relationships, health, and tastes. To be happy according to *local desire satisfactionism* is to experience a sufficiently high ratio of satisfied to unsatisfied desires.

The second desire satisfaction view takes happiness to be a satisfaction of a single *general* desire: the desire for our life overall to go well. This kind of desire is global, rather than local, because it is a desire that our life as a whole be going as we want. The global or general desire that life go according to plan integrates all of our local desires into a larger picture that reveals how we want our life to be overall. Rather than count the satisfaction of all local desires as equally important to happiness, we weigh some as more valuable than others. For example, the desire for a loving spouse might be more centrally important to one's happiness than would the desire to watch an episode of one's favorite television show. In this way, a person might be happy even if she has more desires left unsatisfied than satisfied, provided that the desires that are satisfied are those important to her. This view, often referred to as *whole life satisfactionism*, seems to capture the intuition that happiness is about our life in total, and not merely some small segment of it. It also makes sense of how we live our lives. Most of us have a more or less

---

2   Monk (1990: 579).

thought-out plan of important or essential goals or accomplishments we would like to achieve in the course of our lifetime, such as getting a college degree, finding a fulfilling career, getting married and having children, having leisure time for hobbies and vacations, possessing good health, and enjoying a comfortable retirement. We also judge our lives as more or less happy according to how close we are to achieving or being able to achieve these things.

Notice that one feature of the view that happiness is satisfaction is that it broadens what can influence a person's happiness beyond mere feelings. Of course, feelings still have an impact upon our happiness on this view, since all things being equal, we still prefer feeling good to feeling bad. We take great satisfaction in a life that is full of many pleasures and positive emotions. Yet other things beyond our feelings can be objects of desire as well: holding certain titles, making a certain amount of money, being educated, possessing political freedoms, succeeding at a difficult task – these are all things we might want, but they are not the same as feeling pleasure or positive emotionality. In other words, we might desire these things for reasons other than simply how they make us feel, if they make us feel any way at all. We may take tremendous satisfaction in having accomplished our desire to write a book, even if the process of writing was itself arduous and stressful. In this way, the sorts of events that can influence a person's happiness are far larger in number and far more varied in kind than hedonism suggests.

Returning to the case of Truman, it seems that he could be considered happy, even while being massively deceived, whether we think that the relevant mental state is pleasurable experience or satisfaction with one's life. Truman experiences a lot of positive affect in his life up until the time at which he starts to suspect the deception. Certainly, he seems to be perpetually in high spirits, and we find him often enjoying merry daydreams where he plays amusing characters in front of his bathroom mirror. Truman possesses great vim and vigor, as encapsulated in the daily morning tagline with which he greets his neighbors: "Good morning! Oh, and in case I don't see you, good afternoon, good evening, and good night!" Hence, according to hedonism, Truman is happy. The same holds for desire satisfaction theories. Truman is satisfied with many elements of his life, whether it is his desire for a good job, a loving spouse, a best friend, friendly neighbors, enough material wealth to be comfortable, and so on. Moreover, it is likely that if Truman were to reflect on how his life was going so far, he would conclude that, all in all, things were pretty darn good (his desire to vacation in Fiji notwithstanding). So if happiness is a mental state of experiencing life first-hand as going a certain way, then it is quite plausible to conclude that Truman is happy before learning of his fabricated life.

Thinking of happiness as a mental state has much appeal. After all, how can things of which you are unaware affect your happiness? It seems counterintuitive to believe that the level of your happiness could be affected by events that you don't even know about. For instance, suppose that last Wednesday night, Richard, as he does every Wednesday, put five dollars on the Powerball jackpot. He has been really busy, so even though it is already Thursday, he has not yet had time to check his numbers. He heard that there was a winner, but because it is unlikely to be him, he has not been overly motivated to check his ticket. What are the odds, after all? Suppose, though, that Richard is holding the winning ticket in his wallet. Would you think that his happiness has already increased, even though he does not know he has won? Or do you think that it is not until he checks the ticket and realizes that he is a newly minted millionaire that his happiness will elevate? Many think that Richard cannot be made happy by the fact of his winning the lottery until he becomes consciously aware of that fact. This implies that only those things of which we are aware can influence our happiness. Applied to Truman, this suggests that he might well have been happy before discovering his life was a ruse. After all, he was not aware that he had been confined to a television set for his entire life, so how could this affect his happiness? On the other hand, certainly, there were many important elements that were missing in Truman's life, suggesting perhaps that happiness is more than just how we experience our lives.

Is Happiness More Than a Mental State?

Maybe happiness is neither a feeling nor an attitude; or, at least, maybe it requires more than these. Some might think that Truman could not be happy living on Seahaven Island because his life is missing central elements. What if there are things that matter to our happiness other than just our first-hand experience? For instance, Truman did not have genuine attachment to others. All of Truman's relationships were inauthentic: his wife and best friend, his neighbors, his coworkers – they were all actors. According to this intuition, it does not matter how Truman views his life; what matters is how his life is actually going. This suggests that in order to be happy, we need more than just to be in certain mental states. Happiness requires that our experiences authentically reflect the conditions of our lives.

Others might point out another feature of Truman's life that undermines his happiness regardless of whether he feels good or is satisfied: namely, he lacks the liberty to do as he wants. Though his choices might seem free to him, he is surrounded by people who restrict his choices. He is a prisoner, trapped on Seahaven Island. When he tries to leave in order to get to Fiji for a vacation, he is literally blocked at every turn. Cars dart out of side streets and driveways to create impassable traffic when he attempts to get out of town. When Truman tries to escape by boat, Christof conjures a tempest so violent that Truman almost drowns. Can a person who has no real control over his life be happy? If not, then happiness requires more than mere subjective experience; it also requires certain things external to our mental life. Accordingly, Truman's lack of liberty has a negative effect on his happiness, whether he realizes it or not. His life would be happier were he able to exercise control over it.

We can thus draw a difference between Truman's first-hand experience of his own life and how his life is actually going. If we believe that happiness has more to do with how one's life is actually going, then we think of happiness as including more than just mental states. If external conditions such as authenticity and liberty are a part of happiness, then this means that your private desires, values, and beliefs do not completely determine whether you are happy. Rather, there are certain things that make your life go better, independent of mental states. And these elements are part of your happiness, whether you recognize them or not, and also whether you value them or not.

These considerations point to a third main conception of happiness, one that takes happiness to consist in things beyond our simple first-hand experience of life. This view is called *eudaimonism*, derived from the Greek word *eudaimonia*, which is often translated as either "happiness" or "flourishing." According to eudaimonism, to be happy is to fulfill your positive potential or to flourish as a human person. To be happy in this sense is to live a complete life in which you fully actualize yourself. Beyond the mere experience of pleasures and satisfactions, your life can also go better or worse with regard to your ability to reason, to be creative, to be morally virtuous, to exercise autonomy, to engage in meaningful relationships, to live authentically, to possess good health, to be respected by others, and so forth. These other constituents go above and beyond our first-hand experience of life. Happiness consists not simply in how we view our lives, but rather in how our lives are *actually* going. On this view, happiness is an achievement, one that requires great effort. You have to earn it. And when you do, it is always good for you.

For example, disagreeing with the previous mental-state views of

hedonism and desire satisfactionism, eudaimonism asserts that sometimes pleasures or satisfactions are elements of *unhappiness*. We all know
that some experiences that feel good are actually bad for us, and likewise,
some experiences that feel bad are actually good for us. Addictive drugs,
such as crystal meth, are a case in point: while they might feel good, they
are quite bad for us. So too is the taste of sugary soda. Additionally, some
people experience *Schadenfreude*: feeling joy at seeing others harmed. Still,
we might be reluctant to say that *Schadenfreude* is a "positive" emotion.
The same worries can be expressed concerning the attitude of satisfaction.
Sometimes, being satisfied is not good for us. People can be satisfied with
their circumstances even when they are actually quite dire, because they
have resigned themselves to the belief that they have no other option. For
example, some women become accustomed to and accept being treated as
second-class citizens, even expressing satisfaction with the fact that they
receive less education or are less able to participate in politics. People can
also experience satisfaction as a result of a mistaken view of reality, such as
the case of a person whose spouse is secretly unfaithful. It seems, then, that
both pleasures and satisfactions can sometimes be bad for us. What is more
important is *how* those pleasures or satisfactions are achieved, rather than
the mere experience of them.

In contrast, we have the intuition that being happy, whatever else it
might be, is good for us. We organize and plan our life around getting it,
we take it as obvious that we have a right to pursue it, and we think that
achieving it would be one kind of success in life. Rarely, if ever, do we
think that being happy is a bad thing. So, if we think happiness is good for
us, then there appear to be problems with reducing it to the experience of
pleasure or satisfaction. In other words, maybe there is more to the story of
happiness than simply being in certain mental states. According to eudaimonism, happiness cannot merely be identified with the mental experience
of life. It requires that those experiences genuinely reflect the circumstances
of our lives, that they are not ill-gotten, and that they are good for us.

But now we are in a pinch. We seem to have both of the following
intuitions concerning the nature of happiness: first, happiness is simply experiencing life in a certain way; and second, happiness is *more* than just how
we experience our life. These intuitions about happiness conflict with each
other, so at least one of them must be wrong. But which one? To answer
this question we need to carefully examine arguments for and against each
intuition, which come in the chapters to follow. Nevertheless, here we see
how thinking about others' lives can help us to clarify our thoughts about

happiness. It can even point to ways in which our ideas about happiness are inconsistent with one another. We can use these sorts of examples to more carefully hone our theory of happiness. In addition to revealing a sort of tension within our idea of happiness, the considerations surrounding the example of Truman also suggest that sometimes we might be wrong about whether we are happy. Is that really the case? Can we be mistaken about our own happiness?

Can We Be Wrong about Our Own Happiness?

Imagine a sequel to *The Truman Show*. We cut in to a scene on a beach. After learning that the first 30 years of his life were a manufactured narrative of lies and deception, Truman has since escaped and retired to Fiji. We find him on the beach sipping rum. He appears content and fulfilled, with the broad smile that only Jim Carrey can produce. Then a reporter intrudes, asking a simple question: "Truman, knowing what you know now about your life then, were you happy on Seahaven Island?" Truman responds, "Well, I thought I was, but now I realize it was all a lie and that I was mistaken." Wait. Does this response even make sense? Is it possible that we could be wrong about whether we are happy now? In the future, when we look back at our present situation, might we realize that although we thought we were happy or unhappy, we were actually mistaken? Can we understand Truman's answer to the reporter's question, or is his answer just veiled nonsense? Or consider the example from earlier about Richard who likes to play the lottery. Imagine that on his birthday his children decide to play a prank. They give him a fake winning lottery ticket. After scratching the ticket Richard thinks he has won big money. Is he happy during the time he is unaware of the hoax and believes he has won the lottery? Upon learning of the joke, would Richard say that though he thought he was happy, he was actually wrong about that? And what does our reaction to these scenarios imply about the nature of happiness?

If we believe that happiness is pleasurable experience, we are going to have trouble understanding Truman's claim to have been mistaken about his own happiness. How could he have been wrong about feeling pleasure? After all, though we may be wrong about what causes our pleasure, it seems that when we experience pleasure, we are naturally aware of it. The same is true with pain. When a doctor gives a patient anesthesia so that she does not feel the pain of having a wisdom tooth removed, it would be an abuse of language to describe her as "in pain but just not feeling it." As such, if happiness is about pleasurable experience, Truman would not be able to answer that although he thought he was happy then, he was wrong. He *could* conceivably say that he was happy then, but *also* that he is happier now. He might maintain that he is happier now because he derives added pleasure from knowing that he is no longer trapped on Seahaven Island. But it would be insincere for Truman to revise his past experience claiming that, while it was happening it felt good, but now that he thinks about it, it really felt bad. This would be like someone saying: "Although I thought my massage yesterday felt good, in fact, it was really painful." And that just doesn't make sense.

Moreover, we are typically aware of whether we are satisfied or dissatisfied with our situation, though we might not be as confident about the degree or extent of our satisfaction or dissatisfaction. Judgments of satisfaction are characteristically comparative judgments. In other words, being satisfied is relative to what one is used to and what one expects. Of course, given the relative nature of these judgments, you might change your mind later about whether or not your current situation remains satisfactory, but that does not change the fact that in this moment you experience the attitude of satisfaction. For example, suppose you land a new job and you are completely satisfied with what you take to be a nice salary. However, imagine you later learn that everyone else in the office, even those hired the same day as you to do similar work, are being paid significantly more. At that point, you may no longer be satisfied with your salary. Your attitude might change. Nevertheless, although your level of satisfaction with your salary might go down, this does not mean that you were not previously quite satisfied with your salary.

On the other hand, perhaps we can make sense of Truman's claim that he was not happy if happiness requires not only the belief that his desires are satisfied, but also the fact that they *actually* are satisfied. While most of us are pretty reliable at knowing what we want and whether we are getting it, it is still possible that we can want something, believe we are getting it, and yet not actually be getting it. Recall again the spouse who wanted and believed he or she was getting a faithful and loving marriage, but who was wrong. Or we might want and think we are getting the respect of our colleagues, but be oblivious to the fact that they are simply being polite. So it is at least possible for Truman to falsely judge himself happy, since although he believes his desires are being satisfied, this is not actually the case. Someone else may even be able to prove to him that he is mistaken by pointing out the lie. Or, later in life when he has more information, Truman might realize that even though he believed things were going as he wanted them to, his belief was false, and so he was wrong about being happy.

What about eudaimonistic accounts of happiness? Would they be able to accommodate our being wrong about our current happiness? The short answer is yes. Again, once we introduce external constraints or conditions as part of happiness – once we maintain that happiness includes things that are beyond the first-hand experience of one's own conscious mental states – then it is no longer clear that the best source of information is Truman himself. A belief that we possess liberty, authenticity, and meaningful relationships is not definitive of whether we actually have these things. Indeed, it is easy to have false beliefs about the world and other people. Truman believed his relationships were honest, his experience authentic, and he was free. But he was wrong about all of these. If, then, Truman claimed to be happy, he was wrong about that too, since he was missing these crucial elements. In fact, in the film, some former actors actually sneak back onto the set to try to warn Truman about what his life is missing so that, in their eyes, Truman can become *truly* happy and not just think he is happy. So, if happiness has more to do with how our lives are actually going and not just with how we experience them from the inside, then it is more likely that we could be mistaken about whether we are in fact happy. On this view, we can therefore interpret Truman's claim that he was mistaken in thinking he was happy as meaning that although he experienced pleasures and satisfactions then, he now sees how much of his life was a lie and how many centrally important aspects it was missing. Thus, he was unhappy even while he thought otherwise.

Is Happiness under Our Control?

Of course, if we can be mistaken about our happiness, misjudging ourselves to be happy when we are not, how much do we really control it? To be sure, it will be difficult to improve our level of happiness if we are widely off the mark with respect to our evaluations of our current happiness. Yet, even assuming we can correctly identify whether or not we are happy, can we willfully influence our happiness level in spite of the many things that may happen to us that fall beyond our control? Perhaps our happiness is just a matter of luck. In fact, the root word in Middle English for "happiness" – "hap" – refers to good luck or good fortune, which implies that a central element of happiness is left to chance: happiness is happenstance. This seems to apply particularly nicely to some of the ways in which we use the word "happy." For example, we sometimes say that something was "a happy turn of events" or a "happy accident." But if happiness is so closely tied up with chance and luck, does this mean it is beyond our control? Not necessarily.

On the view that happiness is a type of good feeling, while we cannot completely control what we find pleasurable or painful, we can exercise some control over it. For instance, we can come to acquire certain tastes, and thus take pleasure in sensations we once did not. We might even find that these acquired tastes give us more pleasure than our previous ones. Or, upon carefully noting which activities seem to lead to the most enjoyment, we can attempt to order our lives so that we can continue to do those things, while avoiding what we find disappointing or painful. On the other hand, the experience of pleasure seems to be subject to an odd phenomenon sometimes referred to as the "treadmill effect."[3] Basically, when we experience a given pleasure, we grow accustomed to it and will need more of the same experience in the future to get to the same degree of pleasure. In this way, we are like the donkey compelled to pursue the carrot he will never quite reach. The rate at which we adapt to pleasurable experiences and the strength of the treadmill effect are not things we have the power to change. So, although we can pursue pleasure and attempt to find new pleasures to enjoy, there are many things that fall beyond the scope of our will if we think of happiness as a feeling.

On the view that happiness is an attitude of satisfaction, it seems that we should be able to exercise a large amount of control over our happiness. One way to control our satisfaction is through the desires that we choose to emphasize in our life. Certainly, if we take our important desires to be things such as living forever or being greatly admired around the world, then we are bound to be frustrated. On the other hand, if we pursue desires that are within our own power to satisfy – those that do not require others to oblige us or the world to operate in a specified way – then we stand a much better chance of being happy. For example, we might restrict our desires to being compassionate or doing the best that we can, both of which are entirely under our control.

Additionally, given that judgments of satisfaction involve comparisons, we can choose which comparisons we make. Thus, we can also influence our level of satisfaction by switching our perspective. For example, when we evaluate our lives, we need some benchmark against which to compare it. So if we always compare ourselves with those who are doing better than us – the Forbes Richest Americans, for example – we are likely to be

---

3   Brickman and Campbell (1971) first suggested the idea of a treadmill effect.

unhappy. After all, how can we measure up to *that* standard? On the other hand, if we make a downward comparison, comparing our lives to those who are less fortunate, we will note all the things we have to be grateful for, and this will likely increase our level of satisfaction with life.

Still, whether we have a tendency to look at things from an optimistic or a pessimistic perspective seems a matter of personality. It might well be based in our biology, our genetics. To the extent that it is, our level of happiness seems partially determined, and beyond willful manipulation. Some people seem by nature neurotic and others not. Some people are extroverted, while others are introverted. In fact, neuroticism is one of the most highly correlated predictors of unhappiness, while extroversion is for happiness. In a study conducted by Nettle and his colleagues, scoring high on an extroversion scale closely correlated with also scoring highly on a happiness scale.[4] But whether one is neurotic or extroverted is a personality trait. Whether it is a matter of genetics or the circumstances one faces in life, our deeply ingrained personality traits are not easy to undo. In spite of our inability to easily alter our personality traits, they seem to have a large impact on our happiness.

Additionally, there seems to be for each of us a happiness "set point" – a default level of happiness to which we tend to return naturally after positive or negative events. There are several sources of evidence to support this idea. Studies done on identical twins by psychologists David Lykken and Auke Tellegen reveal that Twin A's happiness correlates highly with Twin B's, both at the time the survey was originally administered and ten years later.[5] In other words, if you want to know how happy Twin B will be in ten years time, you can just ask Twin A how happy she is right now. This held true in Lykken and Tellegen's study even for twins who were separated at birth and reared separately throughout life. This is strong evidence for a genetic basis to happiness. Evolutionary psychologist Daniel Nettle also notes some strong reasons to believe there is a happiness set point: the information that most highly correlates with how happy you will be in the future is not what your job or age will be; it is not how much you will be earning or where you will be living or to whom you will be married. Instead, the single biggest predictor of how happy you will be in the distant future is how happy you are now.[6] Though it seems well established that

---

4   Nettle (2005: 102–03). See also Diener and Biswas-Diener (2008: 148–49).
5   Lykken and Tellegen (1996).
6   Nettle (2005: 110–11).

there is a happiness set point for each of us, there is also evidence that we can deliberately alter this within a certain range.[7]

On the view that happiness includes external conditions, many of these are not fully under our individual control. Our ability to reason, for instance, can be hampered by mental disability; enjoying political liberty can be curtailed by our society; in spite of healthy habits, our bodies break down; and even living authentically with others requires that they be genuine, and we are unable to control how others act towards us. It seems clear that we are not able to determine these conditions in our lives, at least not alone. So does this mean we can do nothing to control our happiness? Not necessarily. Some of these things might instead be under our *collective* control. If we organize our societies carefully enough, we might be able as a group to make available a number of these external conditions. For instance, strong social institutions that safeguard liberty and provide education can at least help to secure some of the central external elements of the happy life. Living under such social conditions would put each of us in a better position to pursue happiness. After society has dealt with the external conditions, the remainder of our happiness resides in setting our inner mental lives in order. This is one reason why many who emphasize external conditions for happiness also emphasize how important having the correct form of society is to individual happiness. It is also one major reason for thinking that happiness is not only an individual value, but a collective value – a *political* concern.

Still, even if through political arrangement we could collectively influence our levels of happiness, as individuals we have little say over which society we are born into and whether that society is able and willing to meet the external conditions of our happiness. Moreover, even if our society is arranged appropriately, we still need things to be provided to us by others, such as love from our parents or respect and honor in our community. Anytime our happiness depends on the actions of other people, it will not be completely up to us. How happy we are will still be largely a matter of luck: the natural lottery of life.

Think again about Truman. When still ignorant, was his happiness up to him? If his happiness requires authenticity or freedom, then he has little control over it. On the other hand, if his happiness depends on some mental state, such as feeling pleasure, or having a certain attitude, then he is able to have some measure of control over his happiness, even while not being

---

7   Diener and Biswas-Diener (2008: 158).

fully in control of his own life. The upshot of our conversations here is that, on every view, it seems that happiness is at least somewhat up to us. There are things we can do to improve our level of happiness. The question is how much control we are able to exercise.

In just a few short pages, we have already raised many questions with respect to happiness that require further exploration. But there are many more that we haven't even touched on yet. Perhaps what the case of Truman highlights is that there is a difference between a *happy life* and a *life that is going well*. In other words, maybe before Truman found out his life was fake, he was happy, but not living a good life. Furthermore, what is the relationship between being moral and being happy? Can a person be a happy immoralist? We will explore these and other questions in the chapters to come.

Chapter 3:   Happy Lives, Good Lives, and Moral Lives

ON JANUARY 24, 1989, at the age of 42, serial killer Ted Bundy was executed by electric chair. At the time of Bundy's final arrest eleven years earlier, Bundy had already raped, tortured, and killed at least 30 young women, though he was suspected in the murders of many more. It is unclear when exactly he killed his first victim, though some speculate it could have been as early as age 14. The brutality of his murders exemplified the work of an absolute monster, involving blunt trauma, strangulation, decapitation, rape, sodomy, and necrophilia. He often returned over the course of several days to repeatedly have sex with his victim's corpse. Bundy spoke of a "sickness" inside him that compelled him to cause sexual violence to women; he also spoke of needing to "possess" his victims. In fact, so strong was this need that he never divulged where he buried their remains, thus exerting one final act of control over them. Referring to his murders as his "life accomplishments," Bundy indicated that he felt no guilt for his actions, claiming that he was in the "enviable" position of not having to deal with such an emotion. In part, this was the result of his rejection of conventional morality, including the need to respect the rights of others. Bundy explicitly denied that there could be any objective moral principles and that there was any significant difference between killing a person and killing an animal. Yet, throughout his murderous rampage, Bundy lived a seemingly normal life. He had a degree in psychology and worked on many political campaigns, and he appeared to many as charming and charismatic. Despite being a psychopath, he was able to blend in enough to carry on a long-term relationship with his girlfriend.[1] Now, was Bundy happy?

If you are inclined to think that Bundy was happy, you are likely thinking about his experience of pleasure or satisfaction. Bundy did enjoy pleasurable experiences and probably had many feel-good moments in his life. He appeared to take much pleasure in killing and stalking his victims. Bundy also seemed to satisfy many of his desires, and he had a clear plan around which he organized his aims. He pursued the life of a serial killer rather than a career in politics or psychology. Thus, it appears that on both the hedonist and desire satisfaction views of happiness introduced previously, Bundy's life could be considered a happy one.

Of course, it is likely that hedonists and desire satisfactionists would acknowledge that while Bundy was happy, he certainly could have been happier if he had made different decisions. That is, if he had made different choices in life, these would have yielded more pleasures both in terms of quantity and quality, as well as a more healthy overall emotional life. Or if he had set different commitments and goals, he could have more effectively pursued them and so lived a more satisfying life. In fact, some hedonists and desire satisfactionists might even believe that Bundy was *un*happy. Although he experienced moments of pleasure and satisfaction, it might well be the case that these were punctuated by more frequent and more intense pains and dissatisfactions. It is hard to know without being able to ask Bundy himself. Though there is some ambiguity about the exact nature of Bundy's own mental states, provided he had enough pleasant experiences or took enough satisfaction in his life, it is plausible that he could have been happy. To be sure, this sort of happiness is not necessarily something to be admired – it is not the sort of thing that we ought to aim for in our own lives. However, to say that he is unhappy on the grounds that we do not *value* the pleasure and satisfaction he felt might simply be to disregard Bundy's own psychology.

On the other hand, you might think that Bundy's immorality prevents him from being happy because you think that happiness requires that a person be moral. If a monster like Bundy can be happy, then this seems to strip happiness of all interest and value for us. In other words, it might strike some as rather bizarre to believe that such a bad person could still enjoy the positive experience of being happy. After all, we might like to think that happiness, being a good thing, is available only to those who are

---

1   Michaud and Aynesworth (1983).

themselves good, at least in some minimal sense. So if it turns out that such vicious people can nevertheless be happy, then we might well ask whether happiness can really be all that valuable. In other words, any theory that counts a deeply immoral person as happy either makes happiness trivial or reveals itself as the wrong view of happiness. The third theory of happiness introduced previously, eudaimonism, agrees with the latter and argues that Bundy's immorality precludes his being happy. Yet eudaimonism also adds another reason that would explain his unhappiness: Bundy did not flourish as a human person. Flourishing involves more than just the ability to experience pleasures and satisfactions, and Bundy's life seems deficient in many domains.

Putting aside the question of Bundy's happiness for the moment, we might want to ask another question about him: Did his life go well? That is, did he live a life that was good for him? Asking this question is asking about whether Bundy achieved "well-being." In other words, did the features of Bundy's life make it advantageous or of benefit to him? It will strike many as obvious that there are plenty of respects in which Bundy's life could have been better, even for him. His life was just missing too many elements. Apart from the moral question, not only did he rob himself of a dignified life, but he also deprived himself of a lengthier life filled with future pleasures and satisfactions. Moreover, Bundy was quite mentally and emotionally unhealthy, suffering from a deep-seated psychological disorder that he would have been better off without. After all, anyone who derives pleasure from necrophilia must be psychologically disturbed and corrupted. Additionally, the natural reaction to killing someone is guilt, shame, and regret. Yet Bundy did not feel guilt for his crimes. When interviewed, Bundy remarked: "Guilt doesn't solve anything, really. It hurts you ... I guess I am in the enviable position of not having to deal with guilt."[2] Far from being positive, Bundy's absence of guilt reveals a diseased and distorted mind. He also admittedly struggled within himself, wishing at least sometimes to be different than he was. This indicates a fractured identity, something that certainly detracts from living a good life. Bundy also had to keep much of his life secret from others, even those closest to him, having always to hide his tracks and invent lies in order to avoid being found out. He was not authentic and sincere in his relationships. He was isolated and alone.

Additionally, Bundy was first captured and imprisoned at the age of 29, though he managed to escape twice before being recaptured a third and

---

2   Michaud and Aynesworth (1989: 288).

final time two years later. He explicitly expressed his desire to be alive and free, denying any involvement in the murders until confessing just moments before his death in an unsuccessful attempt to delay his execution. Bundy's life was prematurely ended at age 42 by electrocution, a gruesome, painful, and also shameful way to die. Therefore, it seems pretty clear that Bundy's life did not go well. Judged by nearly any standard, there are clearly many significant ways in which his life could have gone better for him.

But does Bundy's life not having gone well *require* us to then say that he was unhappy? Or is it possible that Bundy was happy, but that he did not have a good life? If so, then what it means for a life to go well is different from what it means to be happy. Indeed, on some versions of hedonism and desire satisfactionism, the elements missing from Bundy's life do not detract from his *happiness*; they detract only from his *well-being*. Then again, there are other views that maintain that happiness is deeply connected with a good life, such that the two cannot be separated. Bundy's life not going well *does* require us, then, to say that he was also unhappy. From the perspective of eudaimonism, for example, happiness cannot simply be reduced to the experience of positive mental states, because sometimes pleasures or satisfactions are bad for us. Sometimes, in fact, they can make our lives go worse. In such cases, pleasures and satisfactions, far from constituting our happiness, actually contribute to our *unhappiness*. Even if Bundy felt good most of the time, this does not automatically mean that he was happy. Instead, his thrill at killing actually points to his being unhappy, as it reflects a disharmonious psychology and a vicious nature.

What we see, then, is that in some cases it is possible to answer "yes" to the question of whether Bundy was happy, while also answering "no" to the question of whether his life went well. This then suggests that perhaps the good life is something different from happiness. That is, there are certain things important to the living of life beyond one's happiness, and it is this broader conception of a life well lived to which the concept of well-being refers. It is thus an open question how, if at all, these two concepts are related to each other. Is happiness an essential part of the good life? Is happiness not at all connected to a good life? And if happiness is just the experience of pleasures and satisfactions, even when these result from deeply immoral actions, how much value does happiness actually have? Are we then truly after happiness? Or should we aim for something else instead? Perhaps what we *really* want is a good life. Maybe what matters to life is not so much happiness but whether or not our lives go well. These are some of the questions we will explore in this chapter as we examine the relationships between the happy life and other valued pursuits such as the good life and the moral life. Let's turn first to a more thorough examination of what it means to say of a life that it is good.

Is What's Good for You Good for Me?

"Well-being" refers to what is *good for* a person, that is, how well a person's life is going. To achieve well-being is to live a "good life," to live a life worthwhile for the person who lives it. For our purposes, we will use the terms "well-being" and "good life" interchangeably. A good life is not an issue of what might be good absolutely without qualification, but instead is an issue of what is good *for someone*. A person living a good life is living a life that has value to that person. Living a good life is something we care about and aim at for ourselves, and also wish for others. It is also normative – it is action-guiding and reason-giving. Thinking about a good life helps us decide how to live. We want to know what it is so that we can plan and organize our lives in ways that will lead to it. We can judge that a life is a good life for someone according to whether the features of her life make it advantageous or desirable to her. Since a good life is concerned with what is in a person's interests or of benefit to a person, it is considered a *prudential* value. This is contrasted with other kinds of value, such as moral or aesthetic value.

Philosopher Valerie Tiberius makes clear that well-being is "what we have when our lives are going well for us, when we are living lives that are not necessarily morally good, but good *for us*."[3] Sure, we often use the word "good" in moral contexts, such as when we say of someone that they are a good person or when we say that being charitable is good. But we also use the word "good" in countless other, non-moral ways. For instance, we talk about good knives and good cars, good books and good movies, good tennis players and good artists, and even good liars and good thieves, among lots of other uses. Thus, it is important that we not confuse what it means for a life to be *good* with what it means for a life to be *moral*. The use of "good" in "good life" does not necessarily suggest that the life must be moral in some way, although it is certainly true that many accounts of the good life involve living morally. However, at least at the outset, this an open question. It is, therefore, possible that one could live an immoral life and yet, simultaneously, have a good life. Generally speaking, the good life refers to a life that is good for an individual in the broadest sense, where

---

3   Tiberius (2006: 493).

what is good for a person may or may not include morality, reputation – or even happiness, for that matter.

Evaluating lives as good or bad, better or worse, excellent or deficient, requires us to employ some standard or set of standards. The question is whether the standards we use to judge good lives are particular to each person, or whether they are more universal, perhaps based in what is in the overall interest of human persons. Because well-being is primarily a notion of what makes a life good for *each* particular person living it, it remains an open question whether what makes a life good for me is the same as, or shares things in common with, what makes a life good for you. In other words, while each of us might live good lives, there might not be such a thing as "*the* good life," or a singular way of living for all people that is better than any other. Then again, we might think that there are certain basic interests common to all of us that would make all of our lives go better. So does a person get to choose the standards for her life, or are there certain elements common to a good life, whether or not a person values these as her own?

To begin to address these concerns, consider the following analogy. Suppose your friend Evadene points out a passing car and says, "That's a great car!" She has thus appraised the car as being a good one. For a car to be good rather than bad, it will have to meet certain standards. We look at a car and see whether or not it meets these standards, and in so doing we sort good from bad cars. These standards might include fuel efficiency, power, durability, looks, and safety, among others. Good cars meet the standards to a high degree, and bad cars don't. Yet suppose what Evadene means when she says, "That's a great car," is only that it looks good. Here, the only standard she is using to formulate her judgment about the car is an aesthetic standard. If this is the case, then this seems to depend on her individual taste, and you might not agree with her. She may find a burnt-orange mid-80s Chevette a sharp-looking beast, while you think it is hideously ugly. In the case of aesthetic taste, the standards of evaluation appear particular to the individual. This explains the common expression "Beauty is in the eye of the beholder." On the other hand, if by "great car" she means that it performs well, then the standards will be more universal, such as fuel efficiency, power, and so on. Which of these is most important might well vary given the purpose to which we are putting the car, for example, whether it is being used in races or for a family road trip. Still, given a fixed purpose, the standards are universal: racecars are evaluated first and foremost according to power.

Now, to evaluate whether Evadene is living a good life will also require applying some set of standards. But will these standards be particular to the individual, like judgments of taste, or will they be universal, applying to all of us? One might think that evaluating lives requires employing a set of objective standards. If there were certain basic interests common to all of us, such as Maslow's hierarchy of needs, then these could form the basis of a set of objective standards used to judge good lives. Maslow's hierarchy includes things like basic physiological and safety needs, as well as belongingness, self-esteem, and self-actualization.[4] We might further specify the exercise of certain human abilities central to our nature, such as reason, health, autonomy, liberty, political engagement, emotional attachment, and moral virtue. We might also include the standards for psychological health and the absence of mental disorders, such as those in the *Diagnostic and Statistical Manual of Mental Disorders*. Surely there will be some debate about the exact standards we should adopt as relevant to judging a life as a good one; still, each standard will need to be connected to what is actually of value for a person as a human being. Objective standards are not justified according to a person's own private system of values, beliefs, and desires. Instead, they are justified according to how well they capture our practical and prudential interests as human persons. These interests are what they are, independent of whether you yourself value or even recognize them.

Conversely, if we evaluate a person's life according to her own particular wants and values – standards that she herself accepts – then a good life is evaluated according to subjective or particular standards. In such a case, we each set the standards for our own lives according to the values that we recognize and accept, and so our standards may differ in significant ways from each other. This means that we will not evaluate Bundy and Evadene according to the same set of standards. To evaluate Evadene's life, we will have to apply the values and norms accepted by her. For instance, Evadene might well think that her life would be miserable and not worth living if she were a murderous sociopath. On the other hand, to evaluate Bundy's life, we will need to apply the standards that he himself set on his life and see whether his life measured up to those standards. And it seems pretty clear that Bundy rejected morality as important to his life. In fact, he seemed to suggest that adhering to moral values, such as respecting the rights of others, would be "shackles" that stood in the way of his living happily.[5] The fact that *we* think his life would have been better with moral values tells us more about *our* standards for our own life. Of course, as noted earlier, even

---

4   Maslow (1943).
5   Pojman (2003: 171–72).

judged by *Bundy's own standards*, his life would have been better off if he had not been imprisoned and executed, since he clearly wanted to go free and remain alive. This then suggests that the reasons Bundy's life failed to be well lived might be based on the standards that Bundy himself placed on his life, and might have nothing to do with some universal set of standards applying to all of us.

To further assess this issue of whether the standards for a good life are objective or subjective, ask yourself, first, whether you would be willing to trade places with Bundy, and, second, what your reasons are for being willing or unwilling to do so. Part of the notion of a good life is that it is worthwhile and valuable for the person who lives it. Would *you* find Bundy's life worthwhile? If you would switch places with Bundy, then this suggests that you think he lived a good life and that you also value or endorse his particular standards for your own life. But if you would not switch places with him, why not? Is it because you have different standards for your own life, and so you think you would not be living a good life if you lived Bundy's life? In that case, the standards for evaluating a good life are subjective, and so Bundy did live a good life even though you admit that you wouldn't sanction his standards for your own life. Or is it because you do not actually think that Bundy lived a good life at all because you think the standards for a good life are more universal? In other words, because his life was missing certain crucial objective elements, Bundy did not live a good life, and *this* is the reason why you would not switch places with him. How you answer might indicate an initial position regarding whether you think the standards for well-being are universal or particular.

Having briefly discussed the concept of a good life, it is now time to explore what relation it holds, if any, to our concept of happiness. This, in turn, requires that we ask a more fundamental question about the nature of happiness: what kind of claim are we making when we say of someone that he is happy? Are we merely describing his psychology, or are we saying something good about him?

Happiness: Description or Evaluation?

To say of "happiness" that it is an evaluative term is to say that statements involving happiness include a value judgment. While they may also include descriptive content, evaluative terms make *evaluations*, such as of approval or disapproval. Evaluative statements can express aesthetic value, moral value, prudential value, scientific value, or economic value, among others.

Descriptive statements, on the other hand, aim *only* to factually describe something without placing any value upon the description. To illustrate the difference between descriptive and evaluative terms, consider the difference in meaning between "killing" and "murder." If we analyze the meaning of "murder," we realize that contained within it is an evaluation. To murder someone is more than just to kill him. There are other acts of killing that are not murder, such as killing in self-defense or accidental killings. Saying that a killing counts as a murder layers something more onto the killing. In particular, a murder is an *unjust* or *wrongful* act of killing. Built into the very meaning of the term is the evaluation that the killing is wrongful. When we describe something as a murder, we are automatically evaluating it as wrong, bad, or unjust. On the other hand, when we say only that a person was killed, we are leaving open the question of whether that killing was wrongful.

As another example, the word "renowned" includes the descriptive content of being well known, but it also includes the evaluative content of being excellent. To say of someone that she is renowned implies that she is well known, which is a factual matter, but it *also* implies a positive value judgment that she is excellent, which is a possible matter of disagreement, irresolvable by simply consulting a set of facts. The same would be true if we called her "notorious." Again, while being notorious includes the descriptive component of being well known, it also negatively evaluates the person.[6] In other words, it is *good* to be renowned, *bad* to be notorious, and we cannot tell merely from the fact of being well known whether this might be good, bad, or indifferent. This example illustrates that sometimes two terms ("renowned" and "notorious") might share the same descriptive content while having contrary evaluative contents. Here is yet another example: there is a difference between calling someone "driven" and calling him "obsessed." Here, both terms describe the character of a person who is determined and diligent in pursuit of some end. Yet "driven" seems to evaluate that behavior as positive, whereas to call someone "obsessed" is to make a negative evaluation.

What, then, should we say of "happiness"? Is it an evaluative term similar to "murder" and "renowned"? Or is it a purely factual description like "killing" and "well known"? When we describe someone as happy, are we saying something good about her or are we leaving open the question of whether being happy is a good thing? To judge a person happy in the evaluative sense is to appraise her life, to judge that her life is better off or

---

6   The examples of "renowned" and "notorious" come from Hughes and Lavery (2004: 64).

more desirable *on account of* her being happy. To call someone happy in this sense is to commit ourselves to thinking her life is the *better* for it. If we can derive value from the very nature of happiness itself, then it must be inherently evaluative; it must contain evaluative content and not just factual content. While there are some versions of hedonism and desire satisfaction-ism that treat happiness as inherently evaluative (as we will see in the coming chapters), *all* versions of eudaimonism straightforwardly treat happiness as such. According to eudaimonism, to be happy is to flourish as a person. Notice that "flourishing" is clearly an inherently evaluative term, signaling fulfilling one's potential in *positive* ways – a person cannot flourish in ways that are bad for her. Flourishing, therefore, indicates a positive evaluation of a life rather than something merely descriptive.

On the other hand, to think of happiness as a purely descriptive term is to merely describe one's psychology without directly saying anything about whether those mental states are valuable. Perhaps, for example, collecting and consuming an inordinate amount of Halloween candy causes a child to be happy; yet we might not automatically conclude that her life is the better for it. To describe such a child as happy, therefore, does not imply anything one way or the other about whether this is positive. Maybe being happy is a good thing, maybe not, but we cannot know this simply on account of happiness itself. Calling someone "happy" does not settle the case one way or the other. This would require further argument. Only hedonism and desire satisfactionism can allow for happiness to be purely descriptive, since they are the only theories that identify happiness with a psychological state. Nevertheless, we hasten to add that not all hedonists and desire satisfaction-ists treat happiness as descriptive; in fact, many are also quite comfortable claiming that happiness and well-being are one and the same.

How Might the Happy Life Be Connected to the Good Life?

Now that we have examined reasons for thinking of happiness as either evaluative or descriptive, we have the tools to inspect the possible connections between happiness and living a good life. Many contemporary psychologists and philosophers claim to be studying happiness from a purely descriptive point of view.[7] On this viewpoint, saying "she is happy" is merely a statement of fact, akin to saying "she is well known" or "she is tall." These ways

---

7   For example, Daniel Haybron, Daniel Kahneman, Daniel Nettle, Fred Feldman, and Sonja Lyubomirksy.

of describing a person are purely factual and descriptive in nature. There is no inherent value judgment in saying that she is happy or tall. As a purely descriptive term, happiness does not directly imply anything about value. It alone implies no lessons concerning how to build a life. Those who endorse this account of happiness want only to describe what the state is and what causes it, but they want to leave open questions of whether a person *should* pursue happiness — questions concerning the *value* of happiness.

One would need a further argument to describe happiness understood descriptively as having some value. Such an argument would have to appeal to things other than the nature of happiness in order to explain its value. As an analogy, there is nothing in the very nature of being tall that makes it good. However, if a person is an aspiring basketball player, then her being tall is valuable. Yet its value comes to it by way of the fact that the person has other interests, i.e., playing basketball. So while happiness would not be intrinsically valuable, it nonetheless may still have some *extrinsic* value to the good life. To say that something is extrinsically valuable means that it is not valuable for its own sake, but rather is valuable because it is related to some intrinsic good. Extrinsic value is, therefore, a derivative kind of value. If happiness is purely descriptive, then at best it must have only extrinsic value by way of its relationship to well-being. Perhaps, for example, we just find ourselves desiring happiness and so include it in our understanding of a good life. In such a case, the connection between happiness and the good life would be contingent, relying on the fact that we desire it. Intrinsically valuable ends, on the other hand, have their value independent of human desire.

To help illustrate another method for how we might add value onto the descriptive sense of happiness, let's suppose that happiness is the experience of pleasant emotionality. Though pleasant emotionality might not have any value in itself, it might well be correlated with what does have value, namely our well-being. In other words, it might well turn out that typically, though certainly not always, when our lives go well we experience pleasant affect as a result. Hence, we might take happiness to be a more or less reliable indicator of our lives being good. If so, then happiness may be considered extrinsically valuable insofar as it is a useful "proxy" for knowing that we are living a good life.[8] Of course, this would require additional argument,

---

8   This seems similar to what Haybron and Feldman suggest (see Chapter Eight of Feldman 2010; Chapter Nine of Haybron 2008), as well as to how some contemporary economists and psychologists talk about subjective well-being and its role in total well-being (see the OECD Better Life Index at http://www.oecdbetterlifeindex.org).

part of which would involve offering empirical evidence that pleasant affect does, in fact, correlate with the good life. Yet in order to make good on this claim, we would also need to specify a particular account of well-being. Indeed, for some people, such as ascetics or certain existentialists, pleasure would not be a reliable proxy for a good life because it is shallow and so is something to be avoided. Given an ascetic or existentialist account of well-being, then, far from signaling a good life, experiencing high degrees of pleasant affect indicates that you are not living as you should. In such a case, the happy life would have no value whatsoever, and it would also share no connection at all with a good life.

Indeed, some psychologists explicitly state that happiness has only a very limited value to the good life, and it can often be overridden by other important considerations. For instance, psychologist and hedonist Daniel Kahneman states, "happiness is not proposed as a comprehensive concept of human well-being.... Maximizing the time spent on the [pleasurable] side of the affect grid is not the most significant value in life, and adopting this criterion as a guide to life may be morally wrong."[9] After all, there may be other more important things in life, such as moral obligations or a concern for our own agency, that would make the pursuit of happiness deeply problematic. To call a person happy, then, is not to say her life is better, since a person may enjoy a happy experience even when her life is going horribly wrong in other ways. On the descriptive sense, happiness might figure into the good life, or it might not; whether happiness is part of well-being is up for debate.

Applying this reasoning to Ted Bundy, to call him happy in the purely descriptive sense implies nothing of value. It does not suggest to us that we should fashion our lives after his. Just because killing others appeared to make him happy, this does not mean that we should take up a murderous lifestyle, even if we would get pleasure out of it too. To say that he is happy is not to immediately say he is better off for being so, or that his life is going well, or that we should envy him for his happiness, or that we desire to live like him in order to get the happiness he has. In this way, being happy might be unrelated to well-being or even detrimental to it.

On the other hand, many philosophers *begin* with the idea that happiness is an essentially *evaluative* concept (like "renowned"), such that one cannot meaningfully talk about happiness without treating it as something one ought to pursue. On the view that happiness is an inherently evaluative

---

9   Kahneman (2000: 691).

concept, already at the outset happiness says something about value and well-being. Happiness is a *good* thing and we organize our lives around getting it. Saying "she is happy" is not a mere description, but rather an evaluation of the person, and all things being equal, her life is better *because she is happy*. Applied to Bundy, this would mean that if we *were* to call him happy, we would be claiming that his life is better off on account of his happiness. Even if Bundy's life was ultimately not a good one, he did have at least one good thing going for him: he was happy.

So we appear to have two different senses of happiness: descriptive (or merely psychological) and evaluative (or prudential). The fact that both senses of happiness are used, often without qualification, means that we need to be careful when reading texts on happiness. We need to disambiguate which of the two possible senses the author intends. After all, one of them assumes that there is a tight connection between the happy life and the good life, and the other does not. Philosopher Daniel Haybron explains the difference:

> The theorist of prudential happiness stipulates at the outset that happiness is valuable, a kind of well-being, and then asks whether this condition is merely a state of mind. The theories of psychological happiness, on the other hand, stipulate that happiness is just a state of mind and wonder what *sort* of psychological state it is. Having answered this question, we may then ask how valuable this state is. Perhaps it is not valuable at all.[10]

Therefore, Haybron suggests that we should agree to use two different terms to capture these different senses. He thinks that "happiness" should be reserved for the second sense – the purely descriptive, psychological sense of happiness – and "well-being" or the "good life" should be used to denote the evaluative, prudential sense of happiness.

In light of Haybron's proposed distinction, we might now want to revisit our earlier intuitions about happiness from the previous chapter. You will recall that in considering the case of Truman, we noticed that we have both of the following intuitions concerning the nature of happiness: first, happiness is simply experiencing life in a certain way; and second, happiness is *more* than just how we experience our lives. As we were considering these intuitions, we assumed they were both about happiness and so we

---

10 Haybron (2003: 305).

recognized a clear conflict between them. We determined that because they could not both be true, at least one of them must be given up. However, perhaps our assumption was mistaken. Is it possible that our two intuitions actually serve to reveal two distinct features of a life? If so, our conclusion that we must reject one in favor of the other might be too fast.

In light of our discussion about the good life, perhaps we should re-evaluate what we would say in the case of Truman. For instance, maybe we would be willing to say that he is happy but not living well. Because he enjoys pleasant mental states, Truman is happy. Yet his life did not go well because it was a sham, even though he was unaware of it. If so, then it seems that our first intuition properly concerns happiness while the second concerns the good life. Likewise, we might also be inclined to believe that Bundy was happy because he reported being satisfied with how his life had gone, and yet we might deny that he experienced well-being on the grounds already suggested. So, again, maybe our first intuition indicates that happiness is a way of experiencing life first-hand, whereas the second intuition reveals that there is more to the good life than what we experience. If the intuitions are not about the same thing in life, it is possible to accept both of them as true. So while happiness and well-being are frequently run together, it might be the case that in fact they pick out two distinct features of a life. These considerations offer some support for Haybron's proposal that we use two different terms to designate these separate concepts.

However, there are compelling reasons for thinking that we should *not* accept Haybron's recommendation. In fact, on the viewpoint that happiness must be inherently evaluative, his suggestion is very much misguided. To reduce the term "happiness" to a mere description of a psychological state without inherent value seems to miss something central to the idea of happiness. In other words, according to those that endorse an evaluative conception of happiness, any analysis of happiness that fails to include a discussion of its intrinsic value is not really an analysis of happiness. To think of happiness devoid of value implies that we don't really care about it; instead, what we really care about is well-being. But we *do* care about happiness. We care about it in much the same way as suggested by the concept of well-being. We think a happy life is, all things considered, a *good* life to have. Hence, contrary to descriptive psychological accounts, there is a more robust and important sense of happiness that captures and explains more satisfactorily why we plan our lives around achieving it, and why we think that the happy life is good for the person who lives it.

Consequently, philosopher Julia Annas argues that to use "happiness" only in a purely descriptive sense would be to artificially restrict its use to the most *trivial* contexts.[11] In fact, she argues, any reasonable theory of happiness must somehow explain both why humans like and want to be happy, and why we take happiness to be a *proper* end of action. Why do we all have such an overriding practical interest in being happy? Why do we organize our life pursuits around this ideal? And, more to the point, why do we think it is appropriate to do so? All of us have a strong desire for happiness, and we think being happy is desirable both for ourselves and for others. Happiness is enviable and admirable, and it seems to be the sort of thing we should aim for in our lives.

Annas thus claims that we should not so easily cede the term "happiness" to the purely subjective, psychological-state view. To do this would make it extremely difficult to interpret rather common ways in which we use the term. For instance, if happiness is merely a description of our psychological experience of life, then it certainly seems quite odd that we wish people happy new years, happy marriages, and happy lives. What do we mean when we wish people happy lives? We certainly don't mean Bundy-type lives. We don't wish for others to harm innocent people just so long as that makes them feel good. Or consider when we look into the crib at our newborn baby and wish for her a happy life. We are not simply wishing our child to have a life full of feel-good moments with many experiences of satisfaction. Yet on a purely descriptive reading of happiness, this can be all that we are wishing. If all that mattered was her experiences of pleasure and satisfaction, she could attain happiness by way of any countless number of life choices, including drug use, prostitution, theft, and robbery. Instead, we mean more than this; we mean something much less trivial. We care *how* those moments come about, and we care what kind of person she will end up becoming. We would not wish a life full of drug-fueled, ill-gotten pleasures upon our children. At the very least, this suggests that we often do use "happiness" in much the same way as we use "well-being."

Of course, if a happy life and a good life are the same, we must again grapple with which of the two intuitions to reject. We might reject that the happy and good life refers to experiencing life in a certain way, or we might reject that it refers to more than just how we experience our life. Still, accepting that happiness and well-being are the same does not on its own settle which of the two intuitions we ought to give up. For example, there are versions of hedonism and desire satisfactionism that operate on the

---

11 Annas (2004: 45).

premise that happiness is the same as well-being. And yet, because pleasure and satisfaction are ways in which we experience life, such views reject the second intuition. After all, one need not assume that well-being must always be sourced in something beyond one's experience of life. Jeremy Bentham, for example, argues that experiencing pleasure and avoiding pain are the essential characteristics of both a happy and good life. So too does John Stuart Mill, who argues that the happy life consists in the life of pleasure and avoidance of suffering; but he is quick to note that certain pleasures matter more to our happiness than others, because they are produced in a way that is good for us. Hence, Mill thinks that to call a person happy is to say that his life is going well, as he is experiencing pleasure in a way that is appropriate to his nature. The idea that happiness can be identical to well-being even while referring to psychological states will be further explored in later chapters. Here, we have offered only a quick prelude. Nevertheless, we can already see that these kinds of views reject the second intuition for both the concept of happiness and that of well-being.

To the contrary, eudaimonists, such as Plato and Aristotle, reject the first intuition. They assert that happiness is the same as to flourish as a human person, and so they naturally identify happiness with well-being. Yet, unlike Bentham and Mill, eudaimonists believe that happiness and well-being must consist in *more* than one's simple experience of life. Happiness cannot be reduced to a first-hand experience because it involves living an excellent life, fulfilling one's positive human potential. There are many more dimensions in life according to which one can excel than that of psychological experience. And even within the psychological domain, eudaimonists think it matters to happiness how one's pleasures or satisfactions are achieved. The focus is on living excellently, rather than on a person's psychology. And while flourishing is typically accompanied by pleasure and satisfaction, it need not always be so. So perhaps we were too quick to think that Bundy could be happy. On those accounts that identify happiness with the good life, Bundy is actually unhappy. He either did not experience pleasure and satisfaction appropriately, or he did not flourish as a person.

For now, whether or not happiness is evaluative remains an open question. But, if it is, then it seems clear that the happy life and the good life must share some close connection. But to what *degree* is happiness of value to a good life? Perhaps happiness is best understood as just one element of well-being among many others, but one that might be overridden by other values, such as our moral or familial obligations. Or maybe happiness is a *necessary* element of well-being, but there is still more to living a good life than simply being happy, such as possessing good health or having political freedoms. This kind of relationship is more like a part-whole relationship, where happiness is one essential component of the overall good life. We can find similarities with other concepts, such as "axle" and "car" or "ace of spades" and "deck of cards." Or it might be that happiness is *identical with* well-being, whether that means that "happiness" and "well-being" are synonymous or co-extensive.[12] If so, then to live a happy life *just is* to live a good life. Again, we find this kind of relationship among other concepts as well, such as "motor vehicle" and "automobile" or "water" and "H_2O." Whatever the case, so long as happiness has intrinsic value – a value on its own merits and in itself – then it must be included in (or exhaustive of) well-being.

Now, to say that happiness is *not* identical to the good life means that there are other things that matter to our well-being. Moreover, these other elements may be of greater value than happiness, such that our well-being might require our happiness to be set aside when it conflicts with them. This rings especially true if we think of happiness as the experience of pleasure or satisfaction. Consider the example of parenting. Many adults who choose to become parents do so knowing full well that they will be sacrificing much future pleasure. The late sleepless nights of caring for a crying newborn baby, as well as all the stress and worry that comes along with caring for children at any age, are offset by a greater sense of meaning and fulfillment. Many parents make the choice to have children because they believe that it will contribute to their well-being and make their lives better. Even so, we *also* think happiness is something valuable and worth pursuing, and that our lives would be *better* if they contained pleasures and satisfactions. In this way, happiness is an important part of a good life. So while parents are willing to sacrifice some of their happiness for parenthood, most would certainly judge a life that could accommodate both as the very best kind of life. That is, parenthood and pleasure would be a better kind of life than one with only parenthood but without pleasure.

---

12 Two terms are synonymous when they are semantically equivalent. This means that in any context we could exchange the one for the other and not affect the meaning of the proposition. "Water" and "H_2O" or "dislike" and "loathe" are examples of synonymous expressions. On the other hand, expressions are co-extensive when they pick out the same set or class of things without being semantically equivalent. For example, "creature with a heart" is co-extensive with "creature with kidneys," but they do not mean the same thing. Other examples include "equiangular triangle" and "equilateral triangle," or "Superman" and "Clark Kent." Whether happiness and well-being are synonymous or just co-extensive will not affect what is to be said about their connection in this book, and so we will stick to the admittedly more vague locution of "being the same" so as not to beg any questions.

Or reflect on the following scenario: say you are given a choice to live one of four kinds of lives: living as an unhappy slave, living as a happy slave, living as an unhappy free man, or living as a happy free man. Do you know which life you would choose? In fact, could you rank your choices among all four lives? It seems obvious that, if given the choice, we would choose to be a happy free man. Moreover, our last choice would be to live as an unhappy slave. But what of the other two possibilities? Which seems preferable to you? Some might believe that the unhappy free man's life is better, more full of well-being, than is the life of a happy slave. If so, this would seem to imply that personal freedom is a much more important value to the good life than is happiness. In such cases of conflict between happiness and some other value, we are sometimes willing to sacrifice some happiness for a better kind of life. Others, though, may decide differently. Some would rather forgo freedom in order to preserve a happy life.[13] This reminds us that even if we think happiness is important to the good life, we might not all assign it the same overall weight in our well-being. Thus the standards according to which you evaluate your life as going well might be different from the standards of others.

We have now considered reasons for and against thinking of happiness as inherently evaluative. We have also considered the possible connections happiness might have to a good life. So far, it remains undecided whether the happy life and the good life share any significant relationship. Moreover, if they do relate, the nature of that relationship is also still undecided. In later chapters, we will look in more detail at the sorts of arguments available to those who believe happiness and well-being are the same. Until then, it is important to keep these ideas in mind as we explore the main theories of happiness. It is also important to note here that thinking of happiness as evaluative, or as an important element of well-being, or even as identical with well-being, does not entail any particular view of happiness or well-being: happiness can be the experience of pleasure, a state of satisfaction, or even human flourishing. That is, hedonism, desire satisfactionism, and eudaimonism can each place an important value – and even an ultimate value – on the nature of happiness. Let us now explore the ways in which the moral life may or may not be connected to a happy life.

---

13 Then again, we might question whether the notion of a "happy slave" is confused, on the premise that happiness is identical with well-being and where the standards for a good life are objective. For example, on eudaimonism, a happy and good life consists in human flourishing. Liberty is a necessary constituent of flourishing, and so anyone who lacks freedom must necessarily fail to be happy.

The Happy Life and the Moral Life

If it is valuable at all, being happy is a self-directed value. We value happiness in our own lives; we want it for what it brings to us. Though we may also want it for others, it is because we think that *their* lives will be better for it, not *ours*. Hence the happy life seems primarily self-regarding. It is a prudential value concerned with what is in one's private interest. On the other hand, a moral life meets the obligations and duties we have to others. It is primarily other-regarding. In fact, one of the defining elements of the moral life is that it continually challenges us to forgo our own desires and interests to serve those of the wider community. This suggests that the happy life and the moral life might come into conflict. Can our other-regarding concerns and self-regarding concerns be brought into harmony with each other? And, if they cannot be harmonized, which should give way when they conflict?

Certainly, it is often taken for granted that the self-regarding prudential interests of an individual can at least sometimes conflict with other-regarding public interest. For example, a military draft might well serve to protect the interests of a community against foreign aggression, but for those who are drafted, such a policy does not serve their private good. In this case, one would not be able to directly conclude that a happy life results from a moral life, or vice versa. On the other hand, the ancient Greeks believed that one's private interest must include the interests of others. That is, once we accurately understand what is *truly* in our private interest, we will come to realize that there really can be no conflict between other-regarding and self-regarding interests. As an obvious example, parents often state that the well-being of their children is of the utmost concern for them; their primary interest, what would make them feel as though their lives were happy, would be for their children to grow up to be successful adults. Parents seem to appreciate what we sometimes overlook: there might be no possible conflict between what is good for (at least some) others and what is good for us. Perhaps an individual's happiness is not wholly self-interested but also requires other-regarding concerns.

Bishop Joseph Butler contends that the common opinion which holds that self-love and the love of thy neighbor are in competition with each other – so that if one pursues the public good one will not be working toward one's private interests – is actually wrong. According to Butler, furthering the interests of others contributes to our own interests and happiness. In fact, engaging in actions aimed to benefit others will likely make one happier than will those that are directly aimed at one's own benefit. This is so because our desire to help others is its own reward: the virtuous life is a reward unto itself. With respect to most of our other desires, our satisfaction or gratification comes when the desire is fulfilled. So, for instance, if our desire for a promotion is left wanting because it goes to a colleague, then we are left frustrated and our happiness suffers. But, as Butler notes, some pursuits contribute to happiness even when they do not succeed. Even if our pursuit of benevolence is frustrated, it will give us some degree of happiness. While of course we hope to achieve our benevolent ends, and we would be happier if we did achieve them, *trying* to promote the good of others can on its own increase our happiness. As Butler writes in his *Fifteen Sermons*,

> In case of success, surely the man of benevolence hath as great enjoyment as the man of ambition; they both equally having the end of their affections, in the same degree, tended to: but in case of disappointment, the benevolent man has clearly the advantage; since endeavoring to do good considered as a virtuous pursuit, is gratified by its own consciousness, i.e. is in a degree its own reward.[14]

The idea is that sincerely trying to do good by others gratifies us, even if we are not ultimately successful in our attempts. In this way, acting in other-regarding ways may well serve self-regarding ends. Hence, in addition to the fact that successful other-regarding actions have been shown to contribute to our happiness, it is also true that, even when unsuccessful, such actions can also elevate our happiness. Perhaps, then, true self-love involves love of one's neighbor. If so, then maybe our self-regarding and other-regarding values are more fully aligned than is commonly assumed. Based on these considerations, we might try to further argue that the happy life requires a concern for *all* others; the happy life just is the moral life.

Clarifying the potential relationships between the happy life and the moral life at the outset of our inquiry is important, because some of those who write on happiness take it as obvious that there is no connection, whereas others assume the opposite. There are many possible links between happiness and morality. Some of these connections are conceptual, others causal. With respect to the possible relationships between the *concept* of a happy life and the *concept* of a moral life, we will consider three broad

---

14 Butler (1726), Sermon 11, par. 13.

accounts. On the first view, the happy life just is the moral life. To be moral just is what it is to be happy, such that living the moral life entails living a happy life. Essentially, the moral life and the happy life pick out the very same kind of life; they are co-extensive and may perhaps even be synonymous expressions. On the second view, the moral life is an essential ingredient of the happy life. One cannot be happy unless one is living morally, though more may be required for the happy life than just being moral. Even so, acting morally will always increase a person's level of happiness. Like the first account, this view also holds that happiness arises only out of moral conduct, such that immorality automatically precludes one from being happy.

Finally, on the third account, there is no direct connection between the happy life and the moral life. They are independent and unrelated, though they may both be valued on their own. On this account, whether a person is moral does not entail whether she is happy, and vice versa. A happy person may be moral, or she may not. A moral person may be happy, or he may not. Interestingly, on this third view, it is possible that, although the two are conceptually independent, being moral may nonetheless *causally* contribute to our happiness. In other words, even though the moral life does not entail the happy life as a matter of definition, still we may want to act morally so as to make our happiness more likely. Indeed, maintaining our happiness seems more difficult when it requires acting against socially accepted values. When we do this, it is at our own peril. At the very least, we will face more scrutiny and likely suffer from more frustration than if we acted in accord with social norms. We further risk condemnation and alienation if our unacceptable behavior is discovered. In such cases, acting morally would have an instrumental prudential value to our happiness insofar as serving the interests of others might also serve our own interests. So while there may be many reasons to be moral, securing our own happiness might also be one of them. This might be what motivates the decision-makers of large corporations to fund charitable projects: charity furthers the corporation's communal reputation, which in turn greases the wheels of profit. The relationship between morality and private happiness might be similar to the relationship between acting charitably and securing corporate profit: the moral act is not valued on its own but only because it contributes to some self-interested end. On the other hand, maybe this is not the case and acting morally does nothing to further our happiness. In that case, we will need to figure out which should take priority in cases of conflict.

The Happy Life Requires the Moral Life

The most encompassing standpoint regarding the connection between the concepts of the happy life and the moral life is that they mean the same thing – they are synonymous expressions. Living the moral life means living the happy life, and vice versa. There are no additional ingredients needed to secure happiness other than living a morally just life. Those who are familiar with the philosophy of Plato will recognize that this is precisely his approach. In fact, one of the central projects of the *Republic* is to show that the life of the virtuous man is *always* happier than the life of the vicious man, even in a context wherein the virtuous man has a false reputation for being unjust and is therefore racked, scourged, and crucified. On the other hand, it seems very odd to claim that a man who is tortured will always remain happy so long as he remains moral. To say so seems to stretch our concept of happiness in odd ways. Plato tries to explain this away by arguing that it is a mistake to think of happiness as some kind of positive psychology. True happiness, he contends, consists in living in an excellent way, which means that happiness cannot merely be some kind of mental state.

In contrast, Plato's student Aristotle argues that, surely, the happiest and most excellent life would be one that is not only morally virtuous but *also* pleasant (among other things). This naturally suggests the view that while morality may be necessary for happiness, it is not the only element of happiness. Happiness requires moral virtue, but there are additional ingredients. Still, to lack moral virtue prevents one from being happy, and acting morally always and necessarily improves one's level of happiness; it simply is not enough on its own to guarantee that one will be living a happy life. Whether one thinks of morality as necessary for happiness or as the same as happiness, both views assert a tight connection between the moral life and the happy life. A large portion of Chapter Nine will be dedicated to working out the differences between Plato and Aristotle with respect to the relative role of moral virtue in the happy life.

Note the overt identification of the happy life with the good life in theories that make morality indispensible to happiness. This is no accident. Those views that think of the moral life as identical with the happy life, or even as a necessary element of happiness, are able to do so because they equate the happy life with the life well lived. In other words, endorsing such a tight connection between the moral life and the happy life relates to one of the central claims of eudaimonism: happiness cannot merely be a mental state, but instead is the same as flourishing. Any account of happiness that reduces it to the mere experience of a subjective mental state faces the problem of evil pleasures or satisfactions. What matters to a person's happiness according to eudaimonists is not merely that a person feels pleasure, but that she feels pleasure *as she should*. Thus the Greek eudaimonists Plato and Aristotle clearly think that being happy is always a good thing for the person who experiences it. Even further, they contend that the happy life and the good life are the same. They also take the standards of evaluation to be universal, applying to all of us in virtue of our shared human nature. In light of these considerations, it makes sense that they believe the moral life is essential to the good and happy life. After all, if the standards for appraising happiness are universal and based in flourishing, they will include the moral dimension, given our nature as moral beings. Nonetheless, one need not endorse the central claims of eudaimonism in order to connect happiness with morality. It may be the case that morality serves happiness in instrumental ways, even in cases where the standards for happiness are subjective, and even where the connection between the happy life and good life is less strident.

Morality Isn't Required for Happiness (But It Sure Helps)

Some, such as philosophers Steven Cahn and Robert Nozick, argue that a person can be both happy and immoral. On such theories, determining that a person is happy reveals nothing to us about her moral character. A person who is deeply happy and contented in her life may nevertheless be a thoroughly vicious person. Private happiness feels good from the inside, but feel-good experiences and satisfactions can be produced by both moral *and* immoral conduct. Nozick writes, "Precisely which of the many different possible positive evaluations does happiness make of a life as a whole? Not that the life is a moral one, for that needn't make one happy."[15] In other words, from the fact that a person is happy we are not entitled to draw any conclusions about his moral character. Conversely, whether a person is moral reveals nothing to us about his happiness level. We cannot automatically infer that because he is moral he must also be happier as a result. Moral conduct can produce painful experiences and dissatisfactions just as it can produce pleasant and satisfactory ones. The child who stands up to the bully in the schoolyard to protect his friend might well experience pain as a result, despite the fact that his action was virtuous. Likewise, adultery, though immoral, leads to pleasurable experiences.

We should think more about what this implies. If it is possible to live an immoral life and yet be happy, then it is possible that some moral saints

---

15 Nozick (1989: 113).

are emotionally in shambles, while some thoroughly vicious characters are feeling good, satisfied, and contented in life. The following transcript of a recorded conversation between Ted Bundy and one of his victims highlights this possibility:

> Then I learned that all moral judgments are "value judgments," that all value judgments are subjective, and that none can be proved to be either "right" or "wrong." ... Nor is there any "reason" to obey the law for anyone, like myself, who has the boldness and daring – the strength of character – to throw off its shackles.... I discovered that to become truly free, truly unfettered, I had to become truly uninhibited. And I quickly discovered that the greatest obstacle to my freedom, the greatest block and limitation to it, consists in the insupportable "value judgment" that I was bound to respect the rights of others. I asked myself, who were these "others"? Other human beings, with human rights? Why is it more wrong to kill a human animal than any other animal, a pig or a sheep or a steer? Is your life more to you than a hog's life to a hog? Why should I be willing to sacrifice my pleasure more for the one than for the other? Surely, you would not, in this age of scientific enlightenment, declare that God or nature has marked some pleasures as "moral" or "good" and others as "immoral" or "bad"? In any case, let me assure you, my dear young lady, that there is absolutely no comparison between the pleasure that I might take in eating ham and the pleasure I anticipate in raping and murdering you. That is the honest conclusion to which my education has led me – after the most conscientious examination of my spontaneous and uninhibited self.[16]

Notice that Bundy treats value judgments as matters of subjective taste, similar to taste in food. According to Bundy, only the self-regarding values of pleasure and happiness are motivating reasons for action. Moreover, he claims that the pleasures he will reap from killing and raping his victim are much superior to those of eating meat. Although nearly all of us have different tastes from Bundy, it does seem that what gives one pleasure, and to what degree, seems determined completely by the individual. Should the fact that Bundy's pleasures were the result of deeply vicious behavior automatically disqualify them as contributing to his happiness?

---

16 Pojman (2003: 171–72).

Cahn answers that although we can define "happiness" so that Bundy and others who pursue immoral ends cannot be happy, to do so is a "philosophical sleight-of-hand" that is unwarranted. In fact, Cahn thinks that the reason why some of us are uncomfortable calling Bundy happy is not that he is truly unhappy, but "rather, that *we* are unhappy with *him*."[17] In other words, our repugnance at the thought of Bundy being happy reveals more about our disgust with his actions than it does about whether Bundy himself was happy. As noted previously, to say that he is unhappy on the grounds that *we* do not value his pleasure or satisfaction is to disregard Bundy's own psychology.

Still, it does seem that, more typically, acting in moral ways causally contributes to our happiness. For example, it seems obvious that if Bundy had not been caught, imprisoned, and eventually executed for his crimes, he could have been happier. Acting according to his immoral desires opened him to serious external social sanctions. As a result, he likely experienced frequent frustration. Of course, this seems to suggest that Bundy's happiness could have been served in either of two ways: if society had changed its values to more closely align with his, then he would not have faced being ostracized, punished, or otherwise penalized for his behavior; or, if he had been able to somehow alter his natural inclinations and urges to more closely mirror what is socially acceptable, he could have been happier. But given his circumstances, it seems that he was not as happy as he otherwise could have been. Hence, someone like Bundy who lives outside of conventionally accepted morality, even if he himself does not accept these moral standards, will have a difficult time being happy if only because he will constantly be butting up against these norms as he navigates his environment and attempts to achieve his aims.

In addition to the social consequences one faces when acting immorally, one might also face internal impairments to happiness. Bundy continually worked to keep his behavior secret, making sure not to slip up and reveal his actions. This takes energy and effort, and likely caused stress and anxiety. His happiness was affected by his immoral conduct, if for no other reason than that he had to work to keep it private. Philosopher Philippa Foot explains:

Presumably the happy unjust man is supposed ... to be a very cunning liar and actor, combining complete injustice with the appearance

---

17 Cahn (2004: 1).

of justice: he is prepared to treat others ruthlessly, but pretends that nothing is further from his mind. Philosophers often speak as if a man could thus hide himself from those around him, but the supposition is doubtful, and in any case the price in vigilance would be colossal. If he lets even a few people see his true attitude he must guard himself against them; if he lets no one into the secret he must always be careful in case the least spontaneity betray him.[18]

When a person violates the moral, legal, and social norms of his society, he is no longer capable of genuinely relating to other human beings, having always to lie and cover up his true nature. The vigilance required to keep up a fake persona exacts a heavy psychological cost on one's happiness.

To be sure, Foot is speaking of a thoroughly immoral person, not unlike the example of Bundy. Still, the same lessons can apply to the rest of us in terms of smaller immoralities. For instance, if we steal from our friends, we might lie about it to avoid scorn or retaliation. Or if we fail at something, we might avoid revealing it so as not to disappoint our loved ones. Or if we decide to skip work, we might lie and call in sick so as to avoid losing our job. In all of these cases, we hide our true actions from those close to us, which places on us a burden, as we are likely to suffer the pangs of guilt and shame as a result, and we will need to be wary of accidently revealing our act of deception. To act in ways we feel are morally wrong, therefore, weighs on our psychology.

What's more, acting in morally virtuous ways seems to contribute positively to our happiness. On the basis of empirical studies they conducted, psychologists Elizabeth Dunn and Michael Norton argue that people become happier when they act in other-regarding, pro-social ways.[19] For example, in one study, they asked participants to rate their happiness level and then gave them an envelope containing cash. One group of subjects was told they should spend the money on themselves by some time that evening: paying off bills, covering some expense, or even just buying a little treat for themselves. Other participants were told that they must spend the money on someone else, either by giving it to charity, buying a gift for someone, or something of that sort. After both groups followed the instructions and spent the money on either themselves or others, they were again asked to rate how happy they were. The results are rather telling.

---

18 Foot (1958: 103).
19 Dunn and Norton (2013: 108–10).

Those who spent the money in self-regarding ways saw no change in their level of happiness. Yet those who were asked to spend it on others were measurably happier. This was true no matter how much money they were given – the increase in happiness was as strong whether they were spending only five dollars or twenty dollars on others. Dunn and Norton conclude that it does not matter much what amount you spend, only that you spend it on someone other than yourself. On the other hand, if we spend our money in purely self-regarding, antisocial ways, not only might it fail to contribute to our happiness, but it could in fact make us feel worse. The nice thing about this advice is that you can easily try it yourself. The next time you go through a drive-thru, try also buying something for the person behind you in line, and then pay attention to whether you experience a boost in your happiness.

For these reasons, it might be in our prudential interest to act morally: it might serve our happiness to be moral, even if only in an instrumental way. First, acting morally will help us to avoid social sanctions and punishments for immoral conduct. Second, acting immorally causes internal harm, as we experience the effects of guilt and shame and the stress of having to keep up appearances, which negatively weighs on our psychology. Third, acting morally can boost our happiness by making us feel good for helping others. Of course, these reasons for acting in accordance with morality imply nothing about whether we should act morally *for its own sake*. Instead, the argument is that living a moral life *usually* contributes to our goal of having a happy life, even if living morally is not something we are otherwise compelled to do.

Thus, on this understanding of the relationship between the moral life and the happy life, it is still possible to be happy and immoral. In fact, *being* moral is not necessarily as important as *seeming* moral if our primary goal is to evade punishment. Additionally, it is not clear that everyone would face internal sanctions due to immoral conduct. After all, Bundy claims to have not suffered guilt for his behavior, likely a result of believing he was doing nothing wrong. It also seems doubtful that he would have received much pleasure through helping others. Accordingly, provided that a person has the reputation for being just and moral, and provided that he suffers no feelings of guilt and shame for acting against morality, then it is quite possible that he could enjoy some measure of happiness in life.

This reveals that if morality and happiness share no conceptual connection, then they will likely come into conflict in certain situations. If so, again, of what value is happiness to life? Let's consider someone on the opposite end of the moral spectrum from Bundy. Consider, for example, the life of Dr. Martin Luther King, Jr. Both Bundy and King represent cases in which apparently happiness and morality come apart from each other. Namely, one can be moral and unhappy, or immoral and happy. King was on the right side of justice, and yet, because the civil-rights movement meant changing what were accepted norms, he endured severe stress. He was harassed and jailed, he and his family received multiple death threats, and eventually he was assassinated. Although King was living justly, the racist context within which he lived meant that his happiness suffered. King's life suggests that acting morally might at times make it very difficult to be happy; at least sometimes, being moral can actively work *against* happiness. After all, to fully dedicate oneself to the moral life means that sometimes we must sacrifice our self-regarding values in favor of our other-regarding commitments.

Bundy, on the other hand, seems to have thoroughly pursued his own selfish desire for happiness, even at the expense of others' lives. Bundy chose the happy life over the moral life, while King chose the moral life over the happy life. On the other hand, it also seems obvious that King's life approached the good life more fully than did Bundy's. King's was a life well lived, dedicated to a worthy cause; his life was *better* because it was more moral. Bundy's life, on the other hand, seems an utter failure. What these considerations might well reveal is that our moral values are far more important to well-being than is a positive psychology. So when our enjoyment of life conflicts with our moral obligations, it seems as though living morally takes priority. Of course, on the view that happiness and well-being are the same, we might be *less* inclined to believe that our moral obligations can ever truly interfere with our happiness, such as on the eudaimonist view that the happy and good life requires human flourishing.

As we have seen in this chapter, there is no single way in which the concepts of happiness, well-being, and morality relate to each other. There are a number of possibilities. For example, some might hold that they all refer to something different. One form such a position might take is to think of happiness as a description of the psychological state of pleasure; well-being is an evaluation that life is turning out the way one wants; and morality is living up to our other-regarding ethical duties. Yet one might also think that these concepts overlap completely. For instance, maybe happiness and well-being refer to the same thing, and what it is to be happy and live well requires the exercise of moral virtue. As you can probably imagine, there are other combinations as well. Additionally, within each of the major theories of happiness, there is also disagreement over how these three concepts relate to each other. For instance, there are hedonists such as Epicurus and Mill who argue that living happily and living well are the same and require moral virtue; and then there are hedonists such as Kahneman who assert that happiness has little, if anything, to do with well-being. Still other hedonists, Fred Feldman for example, argue that living a happy life is completely unrelated to the question of morality. Obviously, this has been only a precursory discussion. These positions are all controversial, but a more thorough examination will have to wait until the major theories of happiness and their different versions have been more fully developed.

Part II: Happiness as
Pleasure

Chapter 4:   The Feel-Good Feature of Happiness

HUGH HEFNER, BORN IN 1926, lives an impressive life. He has built a media empire as the publisher and founder of *Playboy* magazine. He is a *bon viveur*, living a life of overindulgent opulence. Hefner has traveled the world, making use of a private jet that is more luxurious than most American homes. It includes a galley, a living room, a disco, a wet bar, and sleeping quarters for 16 guests, not to mention a master suite for Hefner. When not making the rest of the world his oyster, Hefner lives in a large mansion in Los Angeles, surrounded by beautiful young women, often dating several at once. He is constantly surrounded by celebrities, throwing and attending the most lavish parties.[1] He is wealthy, sophisticated, and uninhibited. Certainly, Hefner's life does not lack for pleasure and enjoyment, but is it *happy*?

If you are inclined to answer that Hefner has a happy life, an instructive question to ask is, why? What is it about his life that leads you to make the judgment that he is happy? To be sure, Hefner has done a great many things in his life, including philanthropic pursuits. However, most likely, those who think of Hefner's life as happy are thinking more about the women, money, and parties. He is the signature icon for the *Playboy* lifestyle, living a life of extreme luxury. His life appears highly pleasurable. Perhaps, then, a natural place to start our exploration into the three main theories of happiness is with the view known as *hedonism*.

---

1   Details of Hefner's life are based on information from an online biography (http://www. biography.com/people/hugh-hefner-9333521#synopsis) and also on an interview with Hefner (http://jimshelley.com/celebrity/hugh-hefner/).

Varieties of Hedonism

With respect to happiness, hedonism is the view that to be happy is to experience pleasure and to avoid experiencing pain. This view has widespread appeal, endorsed by philosophers, psychologists, sociologists, and economists alike. Perhaps one reason is that it captures the intuitive notion that happiness feels good, and that is why we value and pursue it. Certainly, this captures an essential feature of Hefner's life: we imagine that such a life, if nothing else, includes a lot of feel-good moments. The central appeal of such a life would just be the amount of pleasure (in all of its varieties) it includes.

In order to more fully understand hedonism, it is helpful to include here a few brief remarks on pleasure. Many hedonists define pleasure broadly enough so as to include both bodily and mental pleasures, though the exact nature of pleasure may differ among views. On many common hedonist views, pleasure is identified by its "feel-good" quality. We desire and seek out pleasure at least in part for how it feels. Nonetheless, hedonists might disagree with one another over whether there is a single feeling common to all experiences of pleasure, or whether there are a variety of types of feelings among pleasures. Some hedonists, such as Jeremy Bentham, define pleasure as a singular sensation, where all pleasurable experiences share a sensation that is "pleasure itself." Other hedonists, such as John Stuart Mill, hold that pleasures vary in kind and that there is no feeling common to all pleasures, though they are all still sought out for how they feel. On the other hand, hedonists such as Fred Feldman claim that pleasure is more appropriately an attitude: a positive psychological stance toward some object, which may or may not be accompanied by any felt quality. On this view, pleasure is less about any particular feeling and more about liking or enjoyment. We will more carefully explore these differences in this chapter and the next.

One of the more widely known hedonists is British philosopher and empiricist Jeremy Bentham (1748–1832). As just mentioned, Bentham thinks of happiness as pleasurable felt experience. It has an associated phenomenology, a term best explained as *something it is like to be in it.* That is, happiness has a characteristic *feel.* This also means that happiness is a type of conscious subjective experience. In conceiving of it in this way, hedonism accords with intuitions that many people have about happiness. For example, we think happiness feels good from the inside. Moreover, we find it difficult to imagine how something of which we are unaware could have any real impact on our happiness. Hedonism, therefore, accepts the first intuition discussed in Chapter Two: happiness is simply a way that we experience our lives, and so what does not enter into the realm of subjective consciousness has no effect on our experience and therefore also has no effect on our happiness.

Bentham asserts that happiness is a centrally important value in the life of a human being. Moreover, to experience frequent pleasure and infrequent pain is also what we mean by a good life, or a life going well for a person, since it is in each person's private interest to experience pleasure and to avoid pain. Additionally, pleasure psychologically compels our behavior and determines our moral obligations. Bentham writes:

> Nature has placed mankind under the governance of two sovereign masters, *pain* and *pleasure*. It is for them alone to point out what we ought to do, as well as to determine what we shall do. On the one hand the standard of right and wrong, on the other the chain of causes and effects, are fastened to their throne. They govern us in all we do, in all we say, in all we think: every effort we can make to throw off our subjection, will serve but to demonstrate and confirm it. In words a man may pretend to abjure their empire: but in reality he will remain subject to it all the while.[2]

From this passage it seems clear that Bentham thinks of pleasure as the defining element of both an individual's happiness and her well-being. In other words, the happy life and the good life are both explainable in terms of the amount of pleasure one experiences. He also believes that pleasure provides the sole motivation for our actions. Moreover, Bentham argues that pleasure determines our moral obligations by way of the Principle of Utility, according to which an action is morally right if it maximizes pleasure or minimizes suffering for all those affected. In his words, "it is the greatest happiness of the greatest number that is the measure of right and wrong."[3]

We should note at the outset that "hedonism" is actually a broad term that could refer to several distinct theories in philosophy, depending on what the theory aims to describe. If our aim is to describe happiness, *happiness hedonism* holds that pleasure, or the avoidance of pain, is the only important element to a happy life. The happy life is the pleasant life, and

---

2 Bentham (1789), Chapter I, Section 1.
3 Bentham (1776: 393).

the more pleasure in one's life, the happier one is. If our aim is to describe what makes a life go well or what is good for us, then *welfare hedonism* holds that pleasure, or the avoidance of pain, is the only important element in our life going well. Pleasure makes people's lives go better for them, while pain makes people's lives worse off. *Psychological hedonism* (sometimes referred to as motivational hedonism) maintains that pleasure is the only thing that compels our actions. We only ever act from the motive of securing pleasures and avoiding pains. Finally, in the arena of ethics, *ethical hedonism* holds that pleasure is the end of moral life and the only thing of intrinsic moral worth. Our primary focus in this chapter is to discuss and evaluate happiness hedonism, and we will use "hedonism" to refer to this view, unless noted otherwise.

It is important to realize that one need not endorse all the roles that Bentham assigns to pleasure. For example, we might think that he is correct in asserting happiness hedonism but maintain that there is more to well-being than pleasure, and so we might deny welfare hedonism. That is, we could, as discussed in the last chapter, decide that the happy life and the good life refer to different things. So, for example, we might think that while the happy life is the pleasant life, the good life might involve something other than, or at least more than, the pleasant life, such as conscious deliberation or moral virtue. Or we might accept Bentham's first two claims but reject the claim that the pursuit of pleasure is the only thing that compels our actions. We might also reject the claim that pleasure is the end of the moral life. That is, not all of those who think of happiness in a hedonic sense would likewise think pleasure to be the sole end of moral action. In fact, many[4] would argue that acting for the sake of pleasure is the paradigmatic case of immorality. Whatever other hedonists claim, it is quite clear that Bentham directly endorses all four, arguing that pain and pleasure determine not only how we do in fact act, but also how we should. We are psychologically compelled to pursue pleasure and avoid pain, and to secure the one and avoid the other makes us happy and serves our prudential interests. Finally, it is also the goal of all moral and political reasoning to maximize happiness in the world.

---

4   For example, Immanuel Kant.

Can Happiness Be Measured? The Felicific Calculus

Consider a life other than Hefner's, one that is also abundant in hedonic delights: that of Emeril Lagasse. As an award-winning chef, restaurateur, television star, and cookbook author, Lagasse lives a life of wealth and prestige. He is able to travel all over the world, making and eating the most gourmet food and drinking the finest wines. We might now ask an interesting question: which of these two men is happier? Which of these two lives involves more pleasurable experience? In order to answer questions about whether one person is happier than another, such as in the case of Hef and the Chef, we must use some system of measurement – otherwise, how are we judging the one life happier than the other? But can happiness even be measured? And if so, how?

Answering this question is at the heart of *quantitative hedonism*. According to this view, happiness can be quantified and empirically measured. All momentary pleasures and pains can be reduced to a single scale and can be meaningfully compared to one another. We can then collect measurements of these momentary pleasures and pains for an individual person and sum them in order to determine the happiness contained throughout some period of time, such as a day, week, year, or even a life. Finally, we can use the measures of individual happiness to determine the aggregate happiness of an entire group. As a result, we can quantify both individual and general happiness for a moment or over any duration of time.

Developing a system for quantifying happiness was among one of Bentham's greatest insights. He devised a formula for calculating a person's total happiness: the so-called "felicific calculus." In essence, the felicific calculus describes the properties of pleasure that we can measure. These features are used to determine the overall value of a single experienced pleasure, or pleasure episode, resulting in a specific measurement called a *moment utility*. By extension, Bentham thought that the felicific calculus could also determine the overall value of a single experienced pain, or pain episode. While Bentham did not use such terminology, contemporary philosophers call the units of measurement for these pleasure episodes "hedons," and for pain episodes "dolors." The idea is that one dolor of pain would be opposite but equal in absolute magnitude to one hedon of pleasure. Thus, at any given time one could determine one's overall hedonic balance by calculating the value of one's experienced pleasure and pain, and then subtracting one's dolors from one's hedons.

Bentham imagines that at any time we can place our current experience on a single scale much like Figure 4.1. Where one is placed on the scale is determined according to the value of one's moment utility. Interestingly, Bentham believes that one can be at only one place on the scale at any given moment in time. So either one's experience is pleasant and one is on the positive side of the scale, or it is painful and one is on the negative side of the scale, or one could be neutral.

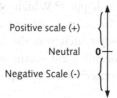

Positive scale (+)

Neutral   0

Negative Scale (-)

Figure 4.1: Bentham's Happiness Scale

In determining the value of a pleasure or pain, the most obvious features are *intensity* and *duration*. Intensity is a measure of the degree or strength of felt experience, similar to the measurement of the volume of sound in decibels. Intensity seems to be the principal property of pleasure that gives it its value, and sometimes the expression "hedon" is also used to pick out a pleasure's intensity. In thinking about a pleasure or pain's intensity, we can draw the analogy to when we are asked in our doctor's office to match the level of our pain to a smiley face chart or a numeric rating scale. Clearly, the intensity of a mosquito bite (the number of dolors it contains) is less than that of a broken arm. Or the intensity of eating a single piece of chocolate (the number of hedons it contains) is less than that of an orgasm. But, according to Bentham, we can also compare the intensity of the pain of the mosquito bite with the intensity of the pleasure of the chocolate, in order to determine which is greater.

Of course, intensity is not the only important aspect of a felt experience. Duration is how long the experience lasts, measured by an increment of time. Duration is also centrally important in terms of the value of a pleasure or pain. For example, a low-intensity but very long-lasting pleasure might be preferable to a high-intensity but short-lived pleasure. This might be illustrated by the following example. Suppose you are given a choice between going bungee jumping or spending the afternoon reading a mystery novel. While bungee jumping is very intense, it lasts only a matter of seconds before the experience is over. On the other hand, you can be immersed in a good book for hours. While the pleasure of reading a book is less intense than that of bungee jumping, you may nonetheless prefer the former experience for its duration (and not just because of a fear of heights!). Accordingly, while the intensity of a pleasure is important, so too is its duration.

To these two rather obvious features of pleasure and pain, Bentham also adds *certainty*. Certainty is the probability that one will experience the anticipated pleasure (or pain). So, for example, when we order a burger from our favorite fast-food chain restaurant – even if we order it while vacationing in another town – we can be fairly certain of the degree of pleasure it will yield. Provided we have tasted the burgers before, and given that the recipe stays the same, we can know in advance of our order what we are going to get with a high degree of reliability. Not all such ventures are this safe, however; some activities are far more risky in that we are uncertain how much pleasure it may contain, or even if it contains any pleasure at all. This would be like ordering a dish that we have never tried before at a foreign restaurant where we have never been. Whether such an experience will yield pleasure, and to what intensity, is highly uncertain. Bentham thinks that the fact that a pleasure is more certain is a mark in its favor, since we can count on it and, therefore, more assuredly plan our lives accordingly.

A fourth feature relevant to the measurement of pleasure and pain is its *propinquity*, or how far removed the pleasure is from us in time.[5] Some pleasures we expect to experience very far off into the future, whereas others are open to immediate gratification. To illustrate, imagine you are planning a surprise party for a friend. You know that the party will be exciting (at least if you plan it well!) and that you and your guests will experience lots of pleasure. Still, you have to wait six months to get the pleasures. So, though you must invest all the time, energy, and resources into planning the party now, you will not experience the pleasure for some time. Other pleasures are not like this. Instead, they are such that at the very moment we invest our energies into the process of securing them, we begin immediately to feel the expected pleasure, such as when we draw a warm bath.

---

5   The third and fourth features of experience according to which we measure the value of a given pleasure or pain episode (certainty and propinquity) seem different from intensity and duration. In particular, whereas intensity and duration are quite easily understood to be properties of the experience itself, treating our ability to predict when and with what probability an experience will occur might seem to confuse epistemological questions with the analysis of the nature and intensity of pleasure. Nevertheless, Bentham holds that in quantifying the value of a pleasure, it does matter to us if that pleasure is remote or highly uncertain, since it will reduce the value of the pleasure in our estimation.

It seems clear that an intense, long-lasting, certain, and temporally near pleasure is the best. Yet we might be willing to forgo immediate pleasures that are, even if intense, short-lived and uncertain in order to achieve a remote pleasure that is less intense, but far more certain and more enduring. For example, you may forgo attending a party hosted by a casual acquaintance this evening in order to use that time to study for a college exam tomorrow. It is possible that the party will be a raucous time, but you are not sure if there will actually be a good crowd; though if it happens to turn out to be a raging party, there will be plenty of loud music, dancing, and overflowing beer. On the other hand, you know that if you stay home to study for your exam, you have a very high chance of learning the material and receiving a good grade. Not only will this knowledge stay with you for a long time, but also, once you pass your philosophy course, you will be that much closer to receiving your college diploma.

The above four properties spell out the overall value of a moment utility: the pleasure episode or pain episode considered in itself. If we are trying to use the idea of happiness to help us plan our lives and determine how to act, then we need to figure out which *actions* tend to yield more pleasure and/or avoid more pain. To do this, however, we also have to consider two other features: *fecundity* and *purity*. These are not properties of pleasure or pain itself, but rather properties of the action that produces the pleasure or pain. Fecundity is the probability the experience has for leading to similar experiences: whether pleasure will lead to other pleasures, or pain will lead to other pains. Purity refers to the probability the experience has for *not* leading to opposite experiences: whether pleasure will not be followed by pain, or whether pain will not be followed by pleasure. Often, what has high fecundity has high purity and what has low fecundity has low purity. An example of an experience that is high in fecundity and high in purity might be reading poetry. Each line on the page can continue to inspire the imagination from the first to the last. Interestingly, what Bentham identifies as fecundity and purity seem to anticipate what contemporary economists call the "Law of Diminishing Marginal Utility." This is the idea that as one consumes more and more units of a specific good, the utility from the successive units continues to diminish, so that the additional benefit a person derives from successive consumptions will continue to decrease, perhaps even becoming negative. This is why eating that extra serving of turkey at a Thanksgiving feast is often not advisable. It seems clear that we would want to experience pleasures that are high in fecundity and high in purity, and if we must endure a pain, we hope it is low in both.

Nevertheless, there are many examples of actions that are high in fecundity but low in purity, or low in fecundity but high in purity. As an example of high fecundity but low purity, these are cases in which the activity leads to similar experiences, but unfortunately, it also yields experiences of the opposite kind. With respect to pleasure, an example might be something like drinking too much alcohol: it starts off great and exciting, and the chances of it leading to more excitement are very high (high fecundity); but it also has a very high chance of eventually leading to pain (low purity). Finally, there are actions that are low in fecundity but high in purity. Applied to pain, this would be a case in which a particular action produces an immediate pain but no future pains, and no future pleasures either. An example of this might be having a tooth pulled. While the act of having the tooth pulled is painful, the pain is no longer experienced after the tooth is removed (low fecundity); but neither does this action yield any experienced pleasure (high purity).

To these features, Bentham adds one more consideration with respect to pleasures and pains and the actions that produce them: *extent*. Extent refers to the number of people who are affected by our action. Extent is important when we are considering general utility as opposed to our own private utility. To sum up, if our concern is with our private happiness and how best to secure it, Bentham's felicific calculus would advise us ideally to pursue intense, long-lasting, highly certain, and immediate pleasures, and actions that will lead to more pleasures and few future pains. If our concern is with the general utility of the community at large, then we ought to consider those who are also affected by our actions, weighing in the values of their pleasures and pains as well.

"Hef and the Chef": A Summary of Quantitative Hedonism

So the picture that is emerging seems something like this: for a person to be happy at a given time, it must be the case that his hedonic balance is positive. The greater the degree of his hedonic balance, the happier he is. We can now see how quantitative hedonism would answer the question posed in the previous section with respect to whether Hefner or Lagasse is happier. In fact, quantitative hedonism tells us that this question has a clear answer. We can figure out which of these two lives contains more pleasurable experience by way of the felicific calculus. What we can do for both Hef and the Chef, at least in principle, is measure each of their happiness episodes, or moment utilities, and chart this out over an interval of time. If we want to know whether a person has had a happy month, then we can chart out, moment by moment, his hedonic balance, as shown in Figure 4.2. Then we can figure the shaded area on the positive side and on the negative side to determine the total pleasure and pain the person experienced over the course of the month, subtracting the pain from the pleasure to get an overall hedonic balance. If the balance is positive, then he is happy to that degree; if negative, then he is unhappy to that degree. We can also chart this out for a person's entire life to determine whether or not that person has had a happy life. Once we do this for both Hef and the Chef, we will have answered our question as to which of the two lives is happier.

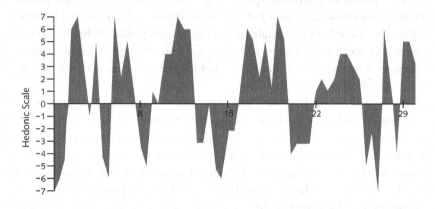

Figure 4.2: Daily Happiness

In conclusion, we can see many advantages in Bentham's view. First, it formulates a method for quantifying happiness and thereby developing a science of happiness. Second, it identifies the features of happiness that are important to its measurement and value. Third, the theory offers an account of what it means to be happy now (in a moment), to be happy for some time (happiness over a period), and what it means to live a happy life. Yet in order to use Bentham's view in the planning of our lives, we have to be good at calculating fecundity and purity. Are we, in fact, good at predicting the future pleasures and pains of our actions? In order to do so, we would need to verify that we have an accurate memory of our past felt experiences for us to be able to make future predictions based on them. Moreover, we would need to ensure that our predictions are made on the basis of that past evidence rather than on other extraneous factors. It turns out that in many cases we are bad at both of these tasks. For an explanation of our failure to accurately remember our past pleasures and pains, we now turn to psychologist Daniel Kahneman, who offers us a compelling revision of Bentham's project.

Remembering versus Experiencing Happy Events

Have you ever wondered whether it is less painful to rip a bandage off quickly as opposed to slowly peeling it off? To answer this question, one thing we might do is try to recall past experiences of ripping and peeling. Then we could compare the experiences in our memory to determine which of the two felt worse, and choose the option that would minimize our suffering. Unfortunately, things are not that easy. In a series of experiments, Kahneman brings to light the fact that human beings often do a poor job at accurately remembering the extent to which an experience pleased or pained them.

This has led Kahneman to suggest the metaphor of two selves: the *experiencing self* – the self that lives the experiences of life – and the *remembering self* – the self that stitches together a memory, a story, or a representation in terms of how life has gone for us.[6] Do the remembering self and the experiencing self tell us the same thing about our happiness? That is, do we remember our lives the same way as we experience them? The short answer is no. How we remember our life as having gone and how we experience it as it happens are different, and in many cases we do not remember our experiences accurately.

As evidence for this claim, consider the following experimental data. Kahneman and his colleagues asked individuals who were undergoing a colonoscopy to continuously rate their level of pain. The scientists then charted the reports of pain over the course of the procedure. Figure 4.3 shows the charts of two different patients. Which of these two patients had a worse time? Who experienced more pain? It seems clear that Patient B suffered more pain over the course of the experiment. After all, Patient B had similarly intense pain for the same duration of time as Patient A, but then had to endure additional time at a reduced level of pain. Therefore, the total quantity of pain experienced by Patient B is greater than that experienced by Patient A. But here is another question: How much pain would these subjects report having experienced after the fact? It turns out that if asked to recall the amount of pain, Patient A would consistently claim to have suffered a higher quantity of pain than Patient B. Moreover, if we

---

6   Kahneman (2011: 377–85).

subjected the same person to two different colonoscopies, say with two different surgeons, and then asked which of the two he would prefer to repeat, he would choose the second, longer and more painful procedure. Why?

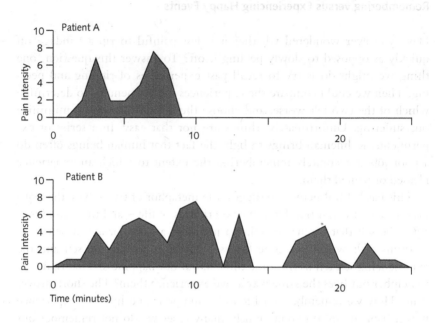

Figure 4.3: Pain Intensity Reported by Two Colonoscopy Patients[7]

Rather than actually recalling the event in vivid detail and being able to carefully sum the amount of pleasure and pain contained therein, it turns out that we take a shortcut. This shortcut, according to Kahneman, follows the "Peak-End rule."[8] Essentially, when asked to recall a past event and to evaluate the degree to which it caused us to experience pain and pleasure, we report a degree that is equivalent to the mean between the peak intensity of the experience (whether pleasurable or painful) and the intensity near the end. We neglect to take into account the duration of the event. When the remembering self tells us the story of our past, it fails to worry about duration and instead gives the ending most of the weight. That is, the remembering self subscribes to the idea that all good stories need to pay careful attention to the ending. This explains the colonoscopy case, because

7   Kahneman (2000: 674).
8   Ibid., 676.

for Patient A the average between the peak intensity and the end intensity were roughly the same: the pain was intense all the way through, so that the average pain felt was the same high number. For Patient B, however, the average intensity of the pain of the experience was lessened by the fact that he had additional time at less intense pain. So even though Patient B had to endure a longer duration of added pain, albeit at a lesser intensity, he remembers his experience as less painful than does Patient A.

The outcome of this is that many of us will choose to repeat an objectively more painful experience because we remember it to be less painful than it actually was (as if colonoscopies aren't already bad enough!). The key to understanding this counterintuitive choice is that remembered pleasure and experienced pleasure do not coincide. The story that the remembering self tells us about the experience when we recall it is not at all like the experience that the experiencing self endures. Kahneman uses the results of his experiments to argue that the experiencing self is the proper subject for the measurement of happiness.

Kahneman draws a distinction between memory-based approaches to happiness and experience-based or moment-based approaches. A moment-based approach utilizes real-time experiences of *moment utilities* (experienced pleasures and pains) to determine the total utility of a particular event. A memory-based approach, on the other hand, utilizes a person's retrospective assessment of a past event, which is called a *remembered utility*. Kahneman argues that calculations of utility are best captured in the moment-based method that tracks the pleasure or pain experienced by the subject in real time, since remembered utilities suffer from distortion and inaccuracy.

On Kahneman's view, then, happiness is determined by measuring the moment utilities of one's experience. To calculate a person's happiness over some duration of time, we need to measure a moment utility for each instant throughout the experience, rather than using the person's recollection. The proper method for measuring each moment utility will be the Experience Sampling Method. This method consists in providing subjects with a handheld device that beeps at random times throughout the day with questions that ask subjects to record their current activity and affective state. So, according to Kahneman, in order to answer the question of whether it is better to rip a bandage off quickly or peel it off slowly, we need to measure the pain in the experience while it is happening – in other words, if we want to know how something actually affects a person, we will need to ask him while he is experiencing it. Given the evidence from the colonoscopy study, it is reasonable to predict that if we were to calculate moment

73

utilities for both the ripping and peeling of bandages, we would find that the more intense but shorter-lived ripping would contain less overall pain. In the end, claims Kahneman, relying on the Experience Sampling Method to measure moment utilities offers the most accurate reflection of a person's happiness or unhappiness.

Like Bentham, Kahneman is a quantitative hedonist, arguing that what it means to be happy is that a person experiences more pleasure than pain. Kahneman differs from Bentham, however, in how to measure pleasure. Kahneman describes his particular view as *objective happiness* because his system of measurement is more reliable and less subject to the distortions plaguing remembered utilities. It is important to point out that his use of "objective" in this sense is different from other ways in which happiness is referred to as objective. For example, sometimes when happiness is called objective, we mean that there are certain features of happiness that are the same for everyone; the very *nature* of happiness is objective. This, however, is not what Kahneman means by the word. Instead, his use of it refers to the higher degree of accuracy obtained in measuring happiness according to moment utilities. According to Kahneman, the problem with most measures of happiness – including many of the features identified by Bentham – is that they rely on the remembering self to accurately retrieve and report data. But as we have seen, retrospective reports of the past can be influenced by a host of variables, such as the Peak-End rule, making these reports less reliable and thereby more "subjective" with respect to measurement.

Kahneman also refines and enhances Bentham's project by amending the latter's view of affective space. Kahneman notes that, we should not only take into account the intensity and the duration of a pleasure, but we should also consider whether the pleasure is an aroused state or one of serenity. Both types of pleasure exist, and so valence (from pleasant to painful) isn't the only concern; we need to factor in the dimension of arousal as well (from frenetic to lethargic). For example, there is a difference between the thrilling pleasure of being on a rollercoaster and the tranquil pleasure experienced while taking in the view atop Pike's Peak. Likewise, there is a crucial difference between the agitated distress of serious anxiety and the quiet pain of melancholy or apathy. To capture these differences, Kahneman offers us a new map of affective space, as shown in Figure 4.4. Kahneman thinks that this is the most accurate way to measure momentary happiness. We should therefore ask someone to make a mark on this sort of affect grid, which captures the two dimensions of valence and arousal, rather than on a single-lined sliding scale as in Figure 4.1. Consequently, if we posed the question to Kahneman as to whether Hef or the Chef is leading a happier life, he would not only advise us to consider the arousal dimension of pleasure, but require us to gather these measurements of their happiness in real time as well.

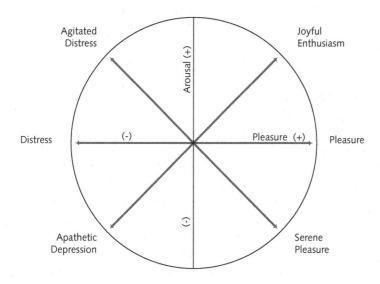

Figure 4.4: Map of Affective Space[9]

Using Kahneman's insights, then, there are a number of ways in which to choose our pleasant experiences more wisely. One is to use a variation of the Experience Sampling Method. This involves keeping a positive activities journal in which we record our experiences along with our perceived pleasure and pain levels as the experiences are happening. Much of the time, many of us aren't even aware of what we have done in a given day. We fail to pay attention to our experiences. Writing our activities down in a journal helps us to become more aware of what we are doing and why. It also helps to target specific areas to change. This is similar to a food diary, where people record what they eat on a daily basis either to lose weight or to diagnose health issues. Alternatively, instead of a positive activities journal, there are Experience Sampling Method apps available for

---

9   Ibid., 682.

smart phones.[10] There are a variety of such happiness-tracking apps; many of them beep at random intervals throughout the day, prompting you to describe what you are doing as well as how you are feeling at that moment. They then keep a real-time record of what things provided you with the most pleasant experiences and can issue a report regarding which activities, people, or times of day are best for your happiness. The information from either the positive activities journal or the smart-phone app could then be used in planning future activities. Rather than relying on a vague and inaccurate memory of what things you enjoy, you would have a record of what activities you actually like to do.

The Worry of Adaptation

Some pleasures behave in an odd way: the more of them we experience, the less they please us. This phenomenon is called "adaptation." Adaptation refers to the fact that we adjust to both positive and negative experiences, assimilating them into the background features of our life, returning to our baseline level of happiness. In other words, the initial pleasure (or pain) provided by a new experience begins to wear off over time as a person gets used to her new state, so that after some time she returns to a level of happiness similar to that prior to the experience. For example, in the days following the purchase of a new car we will experience a great deal of pleasure. After some time, however, maybe a few months, we will no longer experience the same degree of pleasure, if any at all. In a ground-breaking study, Brickman, Coates, and Janoff-Bulman explored this idea of adaptation.[11] The scientists studied people who had recently won major lottery prizes in order to see whether such a major life event had a lasting impact on happiness. In fact, what they discovered is that after a relatively short amount of time (just a few months) the lottery winners returned to a level of happiness similar to before the win. As another example, anyone who has lived on a college campus is familiar with this fact: eating the cafeteria food three times a day for an entire semester leads to a quickly diminishing appetite. Of course, when a friend or family member visits, they may be

---

10 Some of these apps include: *Track Your Happiness* (www.trackyourhappiness.org), *Expereal* (www.expereal.com), *My Mood Tracker* (www.mymoodtracker.com); and *Happiness* (from www.GoodtoHear.co.uk). There are other happiness-tracking apps that also include happiness-improving activities, such as *MoodKit* (www.moodkitapp.com), which includes cognitive behavioral therapy techniques.

11 Brickman, Coates, and Janoff-Bulman (1978).

baffled at why you are so unhappy with the cafeteria fare as it seems quite tasty to them, most likely because they have not had to eat the same food for three months in a row. In this case, adaptation has made what is ordinarily acceptable food taste terrible. Yet, as illustrated by your guest who, instead, enjoys this very same food, it is important to note that adaptation does not have as much of an effect when these experiences are spread out. In other words, given enough time in between eating at the same cafeteria or restaurant, we are able to retain our enjoyment of their fare. So, the lesson is that we should vary our experiences judiciously.

The fact of adaptation has also been used to explain another puzzle. Economist Richard Easterlin has documented what has since come to be called the "Easterlin Paradox."[12] The paradox can be summarized as follows: if happiness were the same as subjective pleasurable experience, then it would stand to reason that the levels of pleasure experienced in a life should correlate with the amount of wealth a person enjoys. After all, the more wealth a person has, the more she is able to purchase enjoyments. However, Easterlin notes that this prediction seems not to be supported by the evidence. In fact, people in countries as different in Gross National Product as the United States and Cuba (which at the time of the study had a per-capita income five times less than that of the US) report similar levels of happiness. This fact seems best explained by adaptation. As income rises for a person, she experiences an uptick in her happiness levels, but only for that time until she adapts back to her previous levels. As a result, increased wealth will not correlate with increased happiness in the long run, since the pleasures won by the new wealth are quickly assimilated into the background conditions of her life.

Sometimes adaptation is also discussed in connection with what is called the "hedonic treadmill."[13] As a result of our tendency to adapt to our new experiences, returning to our previous baseline level of happiness, we constantly seek out new experiences in order to bring us more happiness. In other words, as we adapt to an event, we no longer take the same amount of pleasure out of it (or even perhaps none at all); because of this, we are kept in a continual pursuit of more things that we think will bring us pleasure again. Yet each new pleasant experience is also subject to adaptation. As a result, we crave more and more pleasant experiences in order to attain the same level of happiness. In essence, we are constantly chasing after pleasures

---

12 Easterlin (1974: 105–06).

13 Brickman and Campbell (1971) first suggested the idea of a treadmill effect.

rather than remaining content in the moment. It is almost as if we are running harder and harder but getting nowhere. We can see then how the use of a treadmill analogy is apt here.

Easterlin also offers a nice illustration of the treadmill effect.[14] He asked a group of young Americans two questions. First, participants were given a list of major consumer goods (such as a house, car, television, second home, etc.) and asked to specify which of these items they thought were important to their happiness. Second, they were asked to check off all the items they currently owned from the list. Subjects reported desiring 4.4 items while owning 1.7 items. When the same two questions were asked of the same people sixteen years later, they reported desiring 5.6 items but owning 3.1 items. In other words, in spite of accumulating more goods, the participants remained roughly two items short of what they thought was important for the life they wanted.

Of course, we do not adapt to all events on the same timeline. Some take longer, some take hardly any time, and some things don't seem subject to adaptation at all. Adapting to marriage happens but it takes a few years;[15] adapting to winning the lottery takes only a few months;[16] and it seems that adapting to a noisy environment might not happen at all.[17] Still, we may well wonder whether adaptation and the treadmill effect should have us worried about hedonism as a view of happiness. For if we are constantly stuck on a treadmill pursuing pleasure after pleasure, is this really the best guide for planning our lives? Happiness is something we care about, and insofar as we are unable to reach reliable or lasting pleasure, in what sense is hedonism a good normative commitment to adopt, or a good theory to follow?

On the other hand, perhaps adaptation isn't so much an objection to quantitative hedonism as it is merely a fact to be accounted for. Even if we cannot control adaptation, we can slow it down and learn the rates of adaptation for certain things or events and then choose or not choose them accordingly. In this way, knowledge of adaptation can also help us to avoid those irrational highs and lows we sometimes experience. It is important for us to be mindful that sometimes when we place tremendous importance on attaining some object or goal, this importance might be overstated, for the pleasure provided by many of these things soon fades. This is also true with painful experiences: the initial pain caused by many misfortunes often subsides after

---

14 Easterlin (2003).
15 Diener and Biswas-Diener (2008: 154–55).
16 Nettle (2005: 75).
17 Ibid., 83–84.

a short period of time.[18] Our lives will not end without the latest version of the iPhone or the newest television. Nor will our lives be utterly horrible if that girl or guy we ask out on a date turns us down or a colleague we work with takes credit for something we have done. Knowing that this occurs, we would then be less likely to chase after those immediate highs, and more likely to have a suitably mitigated reaction to many negative events.

Therefore, perhaps one of the lessons we can take from Kahneman is that if we utilize the Experience Sampling Method to build our knowledge of the adaptation rates of specific kinds of experiences, then we can choose those experiences that we adapt to more slowly and that are longer in duration. We would thereby be able to increase our levels of pleasure in a more informed way and in a way that would make our happiness more stable than it would be if we blindly pursued pleasures to which we quickly adapt. For example, because we do not appear to adapt to loud noise, this suggests that when looking for a place to live, we should place avoidance of noise high on our list of priorities. We would be much better off avoiding neighborhoods near airports or train tracks than we would be focusing on other things such as the size of the house. We quite quickly become accustomed to our house size,[19] so it is best not to prioritize it, since we end up wanting an even bigger house after some time, no longer taking as much pleasure as we initially did. In other words, the size of our house is subject to the treadmill effect discussed earlier.

Still, Kahneman questions whether all such cases of adaptation are truly due to a *hedonic* treadmill. While some adaptations do clearly involve a hedonic treadmill in which we take less pleasure over time in the same experience or thing, he notes that other adaptations are due to rising aspiration levels or expectations. That is, what might explain why we find less happiness in some experiences, such as our possession of material goods, is that we are also on a *satisfaction* treadmill.[20] We continue to derive the same amount of pleasure from the experience, but we are no longer satisfied by it.

Even if adaptation is not itself a significant worry for hedonism, there may be other serious concerns. For example, Bentham's and Kahneman's quantitative hedonism values pleasure in quantitative terms only. Second, it disregards the many diverse *kinds* of pleasure being measured, assuming that all pleasures and pains are commensurable. So we might question whether

---

18 See, for example, Brickman, Coates, and Janoff-Bulman (1978).
19 See Lyubomirksy (2007), and Dunn and Norton (2013).
20 Kahneman (2000: 687–88).

this quantitative model put forward by Bentham and Kahneman appropriately captures what we mean when we ask whether one's life is happy.

We Love Happy Endings

Philosopher Robert Nozick (1938–2002) argues that, contrary to quantitative hedonism, when it comes to pleasure we are concerned not only with its total amount. In fact, we also worry about how our pleasure is distributed throughout our lives.[21] He asks us to imagine that we have graphed two different lifetimes in the way the hedonist would, in order to determine

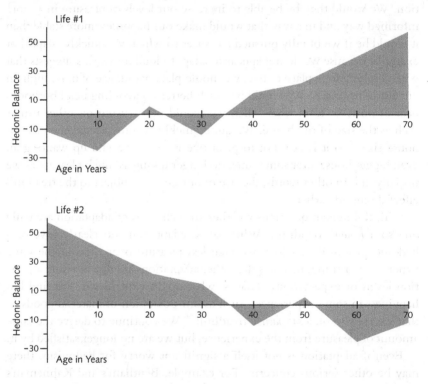

Figure 4.5: Happiness Levels of Two Lifetimes

the amount of pleasure contained in each. So, for example, we might get the two graphs shown in Figure 4.5. Life #1 starts out relatively unhappy, but as the life progresses, the person feels more and more happiness. Life #2

---

21 Nozick (1989: 100).

is the mirror image: the life is immensely enjoyable at the beginning, but as it progresses, the person's happiness level decreases. Supposing that the lives really were mirror images of each other such that they each contained the same amount of overall happiness, then according to quantitative hedonism, we would have no reason to prefer the one life to the other. But is that true? Do you think that if given a choice between these two lives you could identify a clear preference? Nozick thinks you would prefer the first life, and he thinks he knows exactly why.

Nozick argues that the reason most would prefer the first life is that the distribution of happiness throughout a lifetime matters to us. That is, in addition to the overall amount of pleasure contained in our life, we also care about what he calls "narrative direction": the upward or downward trajectory of the pleasure spread throughout our life. Intuitively, we place more weight on how our lives end than on how they begin, and we would prefer a life that contains an upward rather than downward trend of pleasures. For example, we would much rather start out our lives with some pains and frustration in order to reap the pleasures and benefits of our hard work and effort later on in life. Indeed, this characterizes many people's everyday lives, where early on we undertake rigorous years of schooling that are accompanied with stress-filled late nights of diligent effort so that we may obtain the career choice of our dreams, which provides us with opportunity for success, travel, leisure, and an enjoyable retirement. This life seems clearly preferable to one that starts off well, with lots of pleasures in youth, but filled by middle age with constant daily pain resulting from a debilitating illness. Assuming an overall equal amount of happiness in each life, we want the life that ends well. In fact, Nozick bets that we would even be willing to give up some amount of happiness in order to secure an upward trend in our life. However, quantitative hedonism cannot explain this intuition, since on that view, what matters to a happy life is only the total amount of happiness experienced throughout it.

Is There Just One Type of Pleasure Feeling?

A second worry with quantitative hedonism is that it assumes that all pleasures and pains are commensurable. Recall that Bentham believes there is a unique feeling of pleasure that attends all pleasurable experiences. All pleasant experiences have something in common: they induce in the mind of the person having the experience a particular feeling identified as pleasure. Pleasure has its own characteristic feel and is the same each time we experience it, whether it be caused by a taste sensation or an auditory sensation. But is this right? Is there really only one type of feeling that we describe under the heading "pleasure" for all pleasant experiences?

Imagine you were given a choice between receiving one hedon of gustatory pleasure or one hedon of auditory pleasure. For example, maybe you get one hedon from eating a morsel of tasty food and one hedon from listening to the melody of a songbird for fifteen seconds – could you decide which option to take? If Bentham is correct, each instance of pleasure feels the same, and since they come in equal amounts, you should be indifferent with regard to which you receive. As he puts it, "the [children's] game of push-pin is of equal value with ... poetry. If the game of push-pin furnish more pleasure, it is more valuable."[22] To explain why, recall that Bentham and Kahneman both assert that the only way to make such choices is according to the quantity of pleasure contained in each. Because we are always compelled to pursue pleasure and avoid pain, we always choose the option that has more pleasure. Yet in this case, that is not at all helpful. You cannot decide between the two experiences based on which gives you *more* pleasure since they offer equal quantities. In fact, according to Bentham, this choice really amounts to a choice between one hedon of pleasure or one hedon of pleasure, since pleasure feels the same no matter what causes it. Hence, perhaps the only way to make a choice in this case would be to flip a coin.

Still, intuitively it seems that many of us would prefer one option to the other, even when they come in equal amounts. We might even imagine that we could reliably predict what others would choose. For example, Emeril Lagasse, given his fondness for food, would likely choose the one hedon of gustatory pleasure, while the composer Philip Glass would perhaps opt for the one hedon of auditory pleasure. Notice, then, that in making such a choice we recognize that others might choose differently from us. What can explain this? It cannot be the amount of pleasure, since Lagasse and Glass each receive equal amounts. Maybe what explains this is that pleasure is not a singular sensation. It makes sense that we can compare the pleasures of taste with the pleasures of sound (or other sensations) without thinking of quantity. Perhaps what this means, then, is that these are different types of pleasure with their own distinct intrinsic feels. Instead of there being only one kind of pleasure, there are many varied pleasures. For example, the feeling of warmth in the shower is one type of pleasure and the feeling of taking in a beautiful natural scene another, each feeling different from

---

22 Bentham (1825), Chapter III, Section 1.

the other. If this were the case, then we could explain why we prefer the one hedon of gustatory pleasure over the one hedon of auditory pleasure according to the fact that we desire the pleasures of taste more than those of sound (in this instance). Of course, this requires us to reject Bentham's claim that pleasure always feels the same no matter what causes it. It also requires us to offer an explanation for why all these distinct feelings, none feeling the same as any other, are all categorized together as pleasures. If not for a similarity in feeling, what makes something a pleasure?

Perhaps an easy answer is just to say that they both feel good. But this will not get us too far. After all, what is it in virtue of which we count some feelings as good and some as bad? One answer is that a feeling is a good feeling if we desire it. What we mean when we say something feels good is that we desire to have that feeling, and what we mean when we say something feels bad is that we desire to avoid that feeling. Perhaps, then, this is the test of a pleasure. Something is a pleasure if we desire it for how it feels, whether those feels be the same as other pleasures or not. This is exactly how philosopher John Stuart Mill defines pleasure:

> Desiring a thing and finding it pleasant, aversion to it and thinking of it as painful, are phenomena entirely inseparable, or rather two parts of the same phenomenon; in strictness of language, two different modes of naming the same psychological fact: that to think of an object as desirable ... and to think of it as pleasant are one and the same thing; and to desire anything, except in proportion as the idea of it is pleasant, is a physical and metaphysical impossibility.[23]

Of course, if this is the correct account of pleasure, then we can desire some pleasures more than others, and moreover, this stronger desire might have little to do with quantity. This, however, opens a new avenue of evaluation with regard to pleasures – something beyond intensity and duration must be taken into account.

Mill (1806–73) argues that the quantitative hedonism of Bentham (and, by implication, of Kahneman as well) needs to be augmented, since it seems to miss a central feature of happiness: some pleasures matter more to us than others, not because they are more intense or longer lasting, but because they are more *desirable*. Mill therefore thinks that Bentham's phenomenology of pleasure is wrong: there is no common feeling shared by all pleasurable

---

23 Mill (1861), Chapter IV, Paragraph 10.

experiences. If we consult our own experiences, and ask whether there is some single distinct feeling called pleasure that is present each time we enjoy an experience, the answer seems a resounding no. The pleasant experience of taking in the view atop Pike's Peak feels qualitatively different (has different intrinsic feels) from the pleasant experience of eating savory food or getting a massage or hearing a melodious songbird. And if there really are different kinds of pleasures, then it makes sense to ask which of these pleasures we prefer. Which ones contribute more to our happiness, and why?

In large part, the theory of *qualitative hedonism* developed by Mill can be seen as a correction to hedonism in light of two concerns. The first, discussed above, is that pleasure does not come in only one variety, but instead there are various pleasures, all with their own distinct intrinsic feels. The second concern is that hedonism counts trivial and arbitrary pleasures as important to happiness, which, according to the critics, makes hedonism a "doctrine worthy only of swine."[24] However, Mill believes that such criticisms are applicable only to crude forms of hedonism. After all, unlike quantitative hedonism, Mill's qualitative hedonism de-emphasizes the amount of felt pleasure and focuses more on whether the pleasures we experience are those of higher quality. According to Mill, a smaller amount of a higher-quality pleasure does more to contribute to our happiness than does a larger amount of a lower-quality pleasure.

The fact that qualitative discriminations are important to happiness seems rather obvious to Mill. He notices that we account for both quality and quantity in all other decisions, and so it would be absurd to believe that in the case of pleasure, only quantity matters. For example, if we have a budget of $20 and are choosing a wine for dinner, we do not simply ask how much we can get for our money. We are also concerned with the quality of the wine, passing on the jug wine for something more refined. The same holds in evaluating diamonds: carat weight is not the only important consideration. We also grade its quality in terms of cut, clarity, and color. Often we find a smaller diamond more valuable precisely because of its higher quality. Since we evaluate wines and diamonds with regard to both quantity and quality, it would be odd if, in the domain of pleasures, only quantity were of importance. Furthermore, if quality matters in our estimation of the value of a pleasure, then contrary to quantitative hedonism, it is possible for a person to be happy despite enduring a preponderance of painful experiences, provided that the few pleasures she does enjoy are

---

24 Ibid., Chapter II, Paragraph 3.

the right ones: those sufficiently high in quality. Hence the amount of felt pleasure is no longer the determinate measure of a person's happiness. What would ground these qualitative judgments between pleasures? Why might we think, to return to Bentham's example, that the pleasures of poetry are higher in quality than those of the game of push-pin?

What Makes a Pleasure Higher or Lower in Quality?

So far, the picture Mill is developing is that there are different types of pleasures (pleasure is not a simple and singular sensation), and because of this, it makes sense to ask if some are better than others. Moreover, to say that one pleasure is better than another would mean that we desire its felt qualities more than we desire the felt qualities of some other pleasure. Notice that judgments about the quality of a pleasure, then, are always relative judgments; that is, they are always judgments of preference between two pleasures. But why do we desire some pleasures over others? Mill offers two independent explanations for why certain pleasures are more desirable. The first explanation is one that even quantitative hedonists could accept: "utilitarian writers in general have placed the superiority of [higher quality over lower quality] pleasures chiefly in the greater permanency, safety, uncostliness, etc., of the former – that is, in their circumstantial advantages rather than in their intrinsic nature."[25] According to Mill, in the long run, higher-quality pleasures yield more hedons of pleasure than do lower-quality pleasures, and so we want them more. While the higher-quality pleasures are often less intense than the lower-quality ones, they tend to have a longer duration, and are more certain, fecund, and pure. Thus they serve our happiness better over the course of our lives. Because this argument relies solely on the quantities of felt pleasure, it is consistent with the claims of both Bentham and Kahneman. However, Mill actually believes that there is another, stronger explanation, which relies on the fact that some pleasures are more desirable because of their intrinsic feels, and not only because they yield more pleasure. We just desire some feelings more than others.

To begin, we should take note of an obvious point: in order to competently judge which of two pleasures we desire more, at the very minimum we must have experienced both. We would be utterly unqualified to determine whether enjoying an hour-long professional massage is preferable to a twenty-minute hike in the woods, if we had never had a massage or had never been hiking in the woods. Provided we have experienced both of the

---

25 Ibid., Chapter II, Paragraph 4.

pleasures, what explains their difference in quality is our preference for one pleasure over the other:

> If I am asked, what I mean by difference of quality in pleasures, or what makes one pleasure more valuable than another, merely as a pleasure, except its being greater in amount, there is but one possible answer. Of two pleasures, if there be one to which all or almost all who have experience of both give a decided preference ... that is the more desirable pleasure. If one of the two is, by those who are competently acquainted with both, placed so far above the other that they prefer it, even though knowing it to be attended with a greater amount of discontent, and would not resign it for any quantity of the other pleasure which their nature is capable of, we are justified in as-cribing to the preferred enjoyment a superiority in quality so far out-weighing quantity as to render it, in comparison, of small account.[26]

So a higher-quality pleasure is one that is so desirable for its intrinsic felt qualities that we would be willing to forgo any amount of a lower-quality pleasure in order to secure it. This shows that at least sometimes the amount of pleasure gained is irrelevant to our choice of which pleasure to pursue, thus further undermining Bentham's idea that sheer quantity is the only value according to which we evaluate pleasures.

In particular, Mill identifies pleasures that employ our "higher faculties" as just those types of pleasures for which we would sacrifice great quantities of lower pleasures. Higher-quality pleasures are those that are more central to human happiness and that employ our higher faculties, whereas lower-quality pleasures are peripheral and trivial. But just what are these supposed higher faculties that are the source of higher pleasures? As an animal we seem to have the capacity to experience physical sensations. Of course, we share this with other sentient beings, and it is the source of lower pleasures. However, we have other abilities too. Mill identifies our higher human capacities as moral judgment, aesthetic appreciation, political engagement, and rational contemplation. It would make sense, then, that those activities that stimulate these central capacities of our nature would excite us more than would mere pleasures of the body. If this is correct, it makes sense that the pleasures of poetry would be preferable to the pleasures of push-pin since the former excites our aesthetic sensibilities.

---

26 Ibid., Chapter II, Paragraph 5.

According to Mill, the conception of happiness with which we must work is one that is intimately connected to our nature: it must attend to the fact that we are sentient, moral, aesthetic, political, and rational beings. Because of this, a life that does not make use of these faculties cannot meet the conditions of what it means to be happy. This is why "it is better to be a human being dissatisfied than a pig satisfied; better to be Socrates dissatisfied than a fool satisfied."[27] It is not for the fact that Socrates will enjoy a greater amount of pleasure in his life that we prefer his to the life of the satiated pig. Instead, we judge his life to be more intrinsically valuable precisely because it is a *human* life. Provided that whatever small amount of pleasure Socrates does enjoy is a result of the exercise of his humanity, it will be of such high quality as to outweigh all the other frustrations.

In fact, we would choose Socrates' life over the pig's just for the *chance* to experience these higher-quality pleasures, even where there is no guarantee that we will be successful. After all, a person "can never really wish to sink into what he feels to be a lower grade of existence."[28] We cannot honestly choose for ourselves the life of a pig, as a pig is not actively and consciously involved in the living of its own life, but appears to be a largely passive responder to its environment. Yet part of what it means to be happy is that we are involved in the circumstances that lead to our pleasures. In other words, it seems that pleasures are happiness-constituting only when they come to us as a result of our own deliberative life choices. We are made happy by a life that is shaped by our choices and character, and though this opens us to acute suffering and the possibility of failure, we still would rather be authors of our own experience than passive consumers of a world untouched by our influence.

Moreover, once we realize that to choose the life of the pig is to give up centrally important features of our life as a human, we cannot take the choice seriously. Consider, for example, whether you would trade places with your dog. While our dog Zeeah can feel pain and pleasure and other sorts of positive and negative emotions, she cannot engage in moral reflection. She does not contemplate the truths of mathematics or appreciate the beauty of the cosmos. Neither does Zeeah sit around contemplating God's existence or the fact of her own mortality. No, only humans suffer existential crises. To desire to be our dog, then, would mean that we desire to commit a form of suicide, as these sorts of mental activities are deeply intertwined with our sense of who we are as a being. Again, it is true that

---

27 Ibid., Chapter II, Paragraph 6.
28 Ibid.

our ability to ponder such questions and evaluate life according to moral and aesthetic qualities opens us to more acute sufferings; however, these sorts of abilities – moral, aesthetic, and rational – are peculiarly human. It would make sense, then, that those activities that stimulate these central capacities of our nature would excite us more than would mere pleasures of the body, and would yield a felt experience that we desire more than mere pleasures of sensation. As such, the very idea of a "happy" pig or dog makes no sense, since such a life cannot possibly satisfy the human notion of happiness. This more ably explains the normative authority of happiness: not only why we are drawn to it but also why we think that its pursuit is an *appropriate* goal in life. It explains why we value it for ourselves and others and why we think it is a good thing to be happy. In other words, Mill's qualitative hedonism is more than just a theory of happiness; it is also a theory of human well-being.

Given that the quantity of pleasures has little to do with happiness, we have to wonder how to determine what it would mean to live a *happy life*, overall. For Bentham and Kahneman the idea is quite simple, at least in principle: we chart out the moment utilities over the course of a person's life; then we figure the quantity of pleasure that is contained in the life, subtract the quantity of pain, and if the balance is positive, the person's life is happy to that degree, but if the balance is negative, then the person's life is unhappy to that degree. For Mill, such a calculation will not work, since, after all, the pig's life would be extremely happy on this model, while Socrates would be a miserable wretch. But this just doesn't fit our intuitions. The pig's life is missing something essential. Though it has huge quantities of pleasures, none are of the superior sort. On the other hand, though Socrates might experience more pain than pleasure in his lifetime, he might still be considered happy if the pleasures he does experience are higher in quality.

Therefore, to the question posed earlier in the chapter as to whether Hef or the Chef is leading a happier life, there may not be any obviously clear answer. First, to some it doesn't seem clear that Hugh Hefner and Emeril Lagasse are happy at all. After all, aren't the pleasures of sex and food of lower quality? Then again, the mere fact that a pleasure comes from the body is not enough to determine that it is of lower quality. For example, Mill states that the pleasures of health are of higher quality, yet health seems to be concerned only with the body. What matters is whether Hefner and Lagasse engage their higher faculties in the living of their lives. If Lagasse, for instance, is creating culinary art and is fully engaging his aesthetic sensibilities in the crafting of excellent cuisine, he might actually reap higher-quality pleasures from the cooking and consuming of food. Someone might make a similar point with regard to Hefner, arguing that he, too, may be engaging his aesthetic sensibilities in a way that yields for him higher-quality pleasures.

Once we introduce qualitative distinctions among pleasures, however, the issue of comparison and measurement becomes much more difficult. First, what sort of instrument can we use to calculate moment utilities? If there are many distinct kinds of pleasures, we would need a measure for each. We would not be able to simply ask a subject, "How much pleasure are you experiencing at this moment?", since there is no single pleasure scale. Instead, we would need a separate scale for every kind of pleasure: one for gustatory pleasure, one for auditory pleasure, one for aesthetic pleasure, and so on. Determining how to convert all of these different scales into a single pleasure score is far more complicated on the theory of qualitative hedonism. Moreover, even if we could somehow figure out a way to measure each individual type of pleasure and combine them into a single pleasure score, there is another problem in determining which life is happier.

Even if both Hef and the Chef have lives that contain a relatively equal quantity of pleasures and also include a sufficient number of higher-quality pleasures, each of us desires some pleasures more than others. And which higher-quality pleasures you find most desirable will almost assuredly be different than what your neighbor desires most. On Mill's account, pleasures differ in quality according to which ones those who are competent to judge find more desirable. In this way, the kinds of pleasures under consideration matter. What we find desirable is a matter of our own subjective preference, and each of us has different preferences. Some would prefer a life of culinary delights to that of the playboy regardless of the quantities of pleasure contained in each. This might well depend on which of these lives best fits your character, for example. Some of us might find the pleasures of the playboy lifestyle ill-suited to our nature, so we would not actually receive much pleasure from these experiences. Therefore, to be happy is not a simple function of how much pleasure we enjoy, but also whether those pleasures we experience are the ones we desire most. According to qualitative hedonism, quantity of pleasure is not nearly as important to our happiness as is the quality of the experiences we enjoy. In this way, many consider qualitative hedonism to be an improvement on earlier versions of hedonism in that it accords more with our commonsense intuitions about happiness. Nonetheless, there is still a worry with the project of sourcing our happiness and well-being in pleasurable feelings: we sometimes desire things for reasons other than how they feel.

Desiring Things Other Than for How They Feel

Hedonists, as we have seen, argue that all that matters to happiness is pleasure, but Nozick believes that this is not an accurate account of the nature of happiness. He highlights activities that we find enjoyable and that contribute to our happiness, yet we would not describe them as pleasurable. Before stating his objection, we should clarify how Nozick understands pleasure. After all, we have seen that Bentham and Mill have a disagreement over the nature of pleasure. Bentham argues that it is a unique sensation that comes along with every pleasurable experience, while Mill argues for a variety of pleasures with distinct phenomenal feels. Nozick defines pleasure as follows:

> By pleasure or a pleasurable feeling I mean a feeling that is desired (partly) because of its own felt qualities.…. I do not claim there is just one felt quality that always is present whenever pleasure occurs. Being pleasurable, as I use this term, is a function of being wanted partly for its own felt qualities, whatever those qualities may be.[29]

Thus Nozick agrees with Mill that if we desire a particular experience because of how it feels, then we find it pleasurable.

However, contrary to Mill, Nozick argues that sometimes we desire things that are not pleasurable, wanting these things for reasons other than their felt qualities. Surely, we like certain experiences not because of how they feel but for some other reason. Here, then, we see a departure from Mill's claim that desire is always tied to pleasure. Nozick offers us an example of "tennis played very forcefully; lunging for shots, scraping knees and elbows on the ground, you enjoy playing, but it is not exactly – not precisely – pleasurable."[30] Think of how sore and exhausted you might be, suffering from dry mouth, side stitches, and sweat in your eyes. And yet you are enjoying yourself: you are competing at your best, and your opponent is playing hard. Clearly, the felt qualities of this experience are not the driving motivation behind your choosing to engage in this activity. You are doing

29 Nozick (1989: 103).
30 Ibid., 104.

it for some reason other than the pursuit of pleasure. Yet, despite the fact that you are not in it for the pleasure, you think that after the match you are happier as a result (well, unless you end up losing!). This suggests that things other than pleasure are important to one's happiness.

Or consider another example offered by Nozick. He notes that a person who wants to write a poem usually wants it for reasons other than the felt qualities of writing. In fact, usually it is written without regard even to the felt qualities of being known to have written the poem. More typically, a person who writes a poem does so because "he thinks *it* is valuable, or the activity of doing so is, with no special focus upon any felt qualities."[31] According to Nozick, cases like playing tennis or writing a poem reveal that although felt pleasures are desirable, they are not the only things we want out of life and they are not the only things that contribute to our happiness. We may value activities for reasons other than how they feel and, when we do, engaging in them can make us happy.

So, does this spell the end for hedonism? Certainly Nozick believes that happiness cannot be simply reduced to the experience of pleasure. However, it might be too quick to think that these examples undermine the claims of hedonists. After all, though playing a grueling tennis match might be attended by the physical pains listed above, it often also comes with positive emotions like the excitement at hitting a great winner or the exhilaration of rallying from behind to win a match. These emotional responses to playing a hard-fought tennis match are types of pleasurable feelings themselves, and so they may well be the reason why we enjoy playing tennis. If so, then maybe we enjoy tennis and writing, just as the hedonist claims, for the reason that we find such activities pleasurable.

A second response available to the hedonist rests on thinking that pleasure itself might be more like an attitude than a feeling. We often say things like "I take great pleasure in the success of my students." This seems like a rather natural way of speaking, and yet when we say such things do we mean that we are experiencing felt pleasures? Probably not. More likely, when we take pleasure in some fact or other, we mean to suggest not so much that it made us feel good, but rather that we look upon it positively. In this way, we could make sense of someone reporting that she took pleasure in spending the afternoon in her study writing poetry. She does not mean to imply that the process of writing felt good, or that she anticipates the joyous accolades to be bestowed upon her once she publishes her latest

---

31 Ibid.

work. In fact, she might have no intention of ever sharing the poetry she created, yet it still strikes many as intuitive to believe that she could take pleasure in her writing activities. Thinking of pleasure in this way – as more of an attitude directed at different facets of our life rather than as a feeling – would overcome Nozick's objections to hedonism. However, it would also require rejecting the claims of Bentham, Kahneman, and Mill that the essential and defining feature of pleasure (and so happiness) is its feel-good quality. Whether making this trade-off is worth the cost is a topic we will discuss in greater detail in the next chapter.

Chapter 5: Taking Pleasure in Things and Feeling Joy

Imagine a woman who is just about to give birth. Imagine she has been wanting to have a baby for a long time, and was thrilled when she found that she was pregnant.... Suppose she is now in the hospital in the final stages of labor. She has decided to try to have the baby without being completely knocked out with drugs. So she is in pain. The doctors and nurses are encouraging her to push. Sweat is running down her face; she is groaning and breathing hard. Then, with a scream of pain, she gives one last push and the baby emerges. The baby takes its first breath. And is declared fine. The mother then collapses in tears of joy and relief. Suppose afterward her husband asks her to describe her emotional state at the very moment when the baby was born. The new mother then says, "I think the pain was the worst I have ever felt.... But at the same time I think that was one of the happiest moments of my life."[1]

DOES THIS RESPONSE STRIKE you as plausible? Could this woman reasonably assert that, although she was in some of the most intense pain she had ever experienced, it was still one of the happiest moments of her life? It does seem a rather familiar description of the process of childbirth: painful but happy. Yet, if this is the case, then it seems rather clear that happiness hedonism is false.

---

1   Feldman (2010: 34–35).

Philosopher Fred Feldman offers two further illustrations of this same point. The first is Wendell: a man who purchases a device that is supposed to greatly enhance the pleasure of his future orgasms. Upon receiving the product and trying it for the first time, Wendell is deeply disappointed. Though he does get some pleasure (12 hedons worth, according to Feldman), he was expecting much more (somewhere in the range of 400 hedons). So, despite the fact that Wendell's hedonic balance is positive, he is still unhappy. But this should not be the case according to the feeling-based varieties of hedonism we have discussed so far. In fact, Feldman notices that such versions of hedonism get it wrong in the opposite direction too. He imagines a woman, Dolores, who has been suffering from serious chronic pain for some time. When she begins taking a new pain-management drug, her pain is reduced greatly. Although she still feels pain, she is happy about this reduction. Again, this seems difficult to square with many varieties of hedonism. After all, so long as Dolores is feeling pain she should be unhappy on the hedonist model. It is true that after taking the drug she may be less unhappy, but nevertheless she would not be described as happy. Commonsense intuitions about such cases remind us that a person can be unhappy at a time when he is feeling more pleasure than pain; and that a person can be happy at a time when she is feeling more pain than pleasure. Thus, hedonism seems not to accord well with our evaluation of such cases.

These cases form the basis of a formidable objection to the versions of hedonism we have so far considered: namely, the fact that we can experience both unhappy pleasures and happy pains. Feldman argues that there are many such cases where people are unhappy that they experienced less pleasure than anticipated (though they got some), or where they are happy while experiencing pain (though less pain than before). However, if happiness is understood wholly in terms of felt pleasure, hedonism seems unable to deal with such cases. After all, on these views, you are happy just so long as you are feeling pleasure. Certainly, feeling less pleasure than you imagined you would suggests that you are not as happy as you thought you would be, but you are happy nonetheless. But if Feldman is correct that we can actually be *unhappy* when we experience felt pleasure, then this raises serious issues with defining happiness in terms of the experience of pleasurable feelings.

One can imagine a potential response from a qualitative hedonist. Mill, for example, might point out that Feldman's objection fails to be sensitive to the higher-/lower-quality pleasure distinction. After all, the examples of Wendell and Dolores seem based on the experience of only lower-quality pleasures and pains. Perhaps higher-quality pleasures are not subject to this sort of odd fact. Maybe, so long as one is experiencing a higher-quality pleasure one is always at least somewhat happy. This, for example, might well explain the response of the mother who just gave birth. Her emotional response to the healthy birth of her child would be a clear case of higher-quality pleasure. So, while she does experience a large quantity of physical pain, her happiness is increased due to the superior quality of the emotional pleasures associated with having children. Even so, it is possible to imagine situations in which people experience higher-quality pleasures but do not reap as much pleasure as anticipated, and where we are inclined to believe they are unhappy as a result. For example, going to the symphony might turn out to be a disappointment. Perhaps it was okay, but not great, lacking a sufficiently poetic and dramatic end. It seems reasonable that the concertgoer could sincerely judge herself unhappy despite feeling some small measure of higher-quality pleasure because she was disappointed with the performance. Maybe this merely furthers Mill's point that judgments about the quality of pleasures are always relative. Hence, given what the concertgoer expected, the experience did not measure up, and so the overall experience was not pleasant.

Yet to support his argument Feldman can also point to other expressions that we commonly use. We often say things like, "I was happy with the result," where we seem to imply that it met or exceeded our expectations. For example, if I need you to set a broken bone while we are out hiking and you don't know anything about doing that sort of thing, I might indicate that I was pretty happy with the result (all things considered), even though it was, in another sense, a pretty bad job of setting the bone.[2] If it makes sense that one could be happy at the poor setting of a bone, then it seems as if Feldman's question remains: Is happiness really to be identified with the experience of feeling pleasure? As noted above, these concerns apply equally to quantitative and qualitative hedonism. As a result, Feldman thinks that the classical forms of hedonism discussed in the previous chapter are wrong, but that there is an alternative account of pleasure according to which hedonism gets these cases right.

---

2   Thanks to Richard Fumerton for the example.

Pleasure Is an Attitude, Not a Feeling

Feldman wishes to defend hedonism as the correct theory of happiness, but he thinks that so far, Bentham, Kahneman, and Mill are all wrong with respect to the nature of pleasure. By offering us a different account of pleasure, Feldman believes that his form of hedonism – *attitudinal hedonism* – captures certain insights about happiness while also being able to handle the challenging cases mentioned previously. How can this be done? In what other ways are we to think of pleasure? All the views discussed so far have the following feature in common: pleasure is felt subjective experience. In other words, pleasure is a feeling (or some set of feelings). Feldman rejects this shared claim. Instead, he argues there is a type of pleasure that is not a feeling at all, but an attitude – he names this sort of pleasure *attitudinal pleasure*. Moreover, Feldman argues, attitudinal pleasure is more central to the concept of happiness than is felt pleasure.

According to Feldman, we attribute an attitudinal pleasure to someone when we state that he is "pleased by" or "takes pleasure in" something. In this way, attitudinal pleasures are always *intentional* – the attitude is always about some *object*, such as an event, thing, or state of affairs. To draw an analogy, consider another common attitude: wishing. One cannot just wish – one must always wish *for something*. A wish without an object is no wish at all. It is the same with other common attitudes including desiring, preferring, believing, hoping, taking pride in, or being satisfied with. An attitude, then, is always directed at some object and is a mental stance you take in relation to that object. While some pleasures and pains are also intentional, they are not always. Some feelings involve basic physical sensations of pleasure and pain, such as an itch: an itch is not about any object; it is just an itch. More importantly, according to Feldman, attitudinal pleasure has no characteristic *feel*. For example, Rick might be pleased that his old high school won the state baseball championship. The object of Rick's pleasure is the fact of his old team winning the championship. Though Rick is happy at the success of his former team, he doesn't *feel* pleasure. Still, he does take pleasure in some particular object. Rick's pleasure is thus best understood as an attitude and not a feeling.

Additionally, contrary to Mill's claim, Feldman argues that desiring something and finding it pleasant are not the same. Though they are both pro-attitudes, Feldman argues that it is quite possible to desire something, believe you are getting it, and yet not be pleased by it. For example, imagine Mindy going to visit her friend recovering from surgery in the hospital.

Mindy may want to visit her friend, believe she is successfully on her way to doing it, and yet not take pleasure in it. For any number of reasons, visiting a recovering friend in a hospital may not please her, not least of which is the fact that her friend had to go through a painful surgery in the first place. So, according to Feldman, desire and pleasure are not as intimately related as Mill imagined.

Feldman believes that there is another reason to prefer his account of pleasure to the feeling-based account. In particular, he argues that feeling-based pleasures depend on prior attitudes; that is, attitudes influence feelings. Imagine eating a really spicy Thai curry for dinner. For some people who like hot and spicy foods, the mention of this meal already has their mouth watering. Eating such fiery fare is enjoyable and adds to their overall pleasure. Still, similar-tasting food eaten by another who has no tolerance for spice might lead to suffering and pain. For this person, a burning tongue and lips do not make for pleasurable experiences. In fact, this is a very interesting point that is worth highlighting: *similar feelings can be experienced as either painful or pleasurable, depending on the attitude of the person experiencing it.*

That qualitatively similar feelings can be experienced either as pleasures or pains leads Feldman to argue that Bentham and Mill have the relationship between a feeling and an attitude backwards. They seem to argue that we desire something because when we experience it, we feel good. This makes the feeling the primary cause of our attitudes – we desire, or want, or like, or wish for something because it feels good to us. For Bentham and Mill, first we have an experience, which then leads to the formation of an attitude concerning the experience. The attitude is positive if the experience feels good, and negative if it feels bad. Feldman rejects this experience-to-attitude account. Instead, he argues that the attitude is the primary cause of our feelings of pleasure and pain. That is, we do not experience the raw sensation or feeling as a pleasure or a pain until we attend to it (whether consciously or not) with the relevant positive or negative attitude. Hence, he endorses an attitude-to-experience account. We experience the feeling as a good feeling if we take attitudinal pleasure in it, and we experience it as a bad feeling if we are displeased by it. It is, however, important to note that the formation of the relevant attitude need not be a conscious process or the result of rational deliberation. The upshot of Feldman's point is that there is no raw sensation or feeling that is by its very nature a pleasure or a pain. Rather, it is at least possible that every feeling we are capable of experiencing could be pleasurable or painful depending on whether or not the person experiencing it is attitudinally pleased or pained by it.

Although things feel good as a result of our taking the appropriate attitudes toward them, Feldman points out that we can take attitudinal pleasure in more than feel-good sensations. In other words, we can be attitudinally pleased by things that feel no way at all. In this way, his account of pleasure is more expansive than those accounts that are feeling-based, because our attitudinal pleasures need not even involve feelings. We can be attitudinally pleased that our beer tastes so refreshing, but we can also be attitudinally pleased about things other than our own sensations, such as a rise in the stock market, or the fact that our old high school won the state championships, or any other state of affairs in the world. We can take pleasure in another's success, or in the decrease in world poverty, or in knowing that our online order has been successfully processed and shipped. There seems no limit to what is potentially pleasing to us. So, although Feldman believes that feelings are made by attitudes, he argues that attitudes can be about far more than feelings. Thus, because Feldman's attitudinal hedonism expands the category of pleasure, it also broadens the realm of things that can influence our happiness, since now more than feelings can have an impact on it.

Despite their differences, attitudinal pleasures also share much in common with felt pleasures. One similarity is that in order to be pleased or pained by something, a person must be aware of it. Even attitudinal hedonism endorses the intuition that happiness is about how we experience our lives. Just as one cannot have a pleasurable feeling or a painful feeling without being conscious of that experience, one cannot experience attitudinal pleasure or displeasure directed at objects of which one is unaware or about things that one cannot grasp. On this point all varieties of hedonism agree: only states of which we are consciously aware can have an influence on our happiness. Building off this point, we can experience pleasure, both in the attitudinal and feeling sense, even when our experiences are illusory. Or as Feldman puts it: false pleasure is possible.

Furthermore, Feldman believes that units of attitudinal pleasure and displeasure can be measured, at least in principle, according to intensity and duration. One can also simultaneously experience multiple attitudinal pleasures with varying degrees of intensity. For example, Pete could take pleasure in both the eating of an epic burrito and his drumming performance of Metallica's "For Whom The Bell Tolls," but be more pleased about eating his burrito. In other words, we can make meaningful comparisons between different episodes of attitudinal pleasure and displeasure by way of their degree of intensity. This can then be captured in numerical form in much the same way as the moment utilities of quantitative hedonism. Thus, while

Feldman disagrees with Bentham and Kahneman on the nature of pleasure, attitudinal hedonism nevertheless shares important similarities to quantitative hedonism with respect to the issue of measurement and over how to determine whether a person is happy for a moment, a period, or for a life. That is, we can measure each attitudinal pleasure as a moment utility, so that the more units of attitudinal pleasure one has, the happier one is, and we can do this for any duration of time.

In summary, we can now see how attitudinal hedonism has an easy time dealing with the sorts of cases that trouble the feeling-based models of hedonism. Wendell's disappointment and Dolores's delight are both attitudes directed at their situation. In the case of Dolores, she experiences attitudinal pleasure at the reduction in her felt pain and is thus happy. Likewise, in the case of Wendell, he experiences attitudinal displeasure at the fact of his paltry orgasm and is thus unhappy. To determine Wendell's or Dolores's happiness level, then, we would sum up all of the units of attitudinal pleasure (or displeasure) that Wendell or Dolores is experiencing at the moment. In the case of Dolores, this would include being pleased that she is experiencing less physical pain recently, being pleased about the high likelihood that she will no longer feel such intense pain in the future, being pleased about the fact that there is cause for hope for complete pain elimination, while also being displeased that she continues to experience some pain. After calculating the intensity of these different levels of pleasure and displeasure, we will likely arrive at a positive hedonic balance, according to which it is appropriate to consider Dolores happy. Hence, while feeling-based versions of pleasure have trouble making sense of cases like this, attitudinal hedonism seems to accord with our commonsense convictions.

Where's the Fun in Happiness?

One central complaint with attitudinal hedonism is that it takes all of the fun out of pleasure. What is interesting to note is that there are many pro-attitudes we regularly experience but which are of no delight or joy to us. For example, a person can approve of the use of military force to stop some perceived terrorist threat, where approval is a pro-attitude, and yet there is no positive feeling associated with that attitude. Yet if pleasure is an attitude lacking any associated feeling, as Feldman suggests, then it seems as if the pursuit of happiness loses some of its appeal. After all, part of our motivation to seek out happiness is the rather common idea that being happy feels good. Accordingly, one of the more compelling reasons for thinking that hedonism is true is that it would easily explain our intuitions. In fact, it seems obvious that the hallmark feature of pleasure – its most centrally defining element – is its feel-good quality. As such, defining pleasure as an attitude seems to stretch the concept in odd ways and makes it more difficult to understand why we should believe happiness and pleasure are at all related. So, while Feldman's attitudinal hedonism is able to overcome worries with feeling-based accounts of pleasure, brought to the fore by cases like Wendell, Dolores, and the pregnant mother, it does so at the cost of sacrificing this characteristic feel-good feature of pleasure.

For these reasons, perhaps pleasure is best thought of as a feeling and not an attitude, and if so, strictly speaking attitudinal hedonism is not a version of hedonism after all, since "attitudinal pleasure" is not *really* pleasure. In fact, we may wonder whether being pleased about something is really any different from simply being satisfied with or having a fulfilled preference for something. By way of his emphasis on attitudes, it seems that Feldman shares more in common with the view of desire satisfactionism to be discussed in the next couple of chapters. Nonetheless, on any account of pleasure, if hedonism is true, then a happy life will be a life full of pleasure. To be happy we should actively seek out those things that bring us pleasure. Do we do this? Or is there reason to think that we do a poor job at desiring what feels good? And, if the latter, what does this imply about the connection between pleasure and happiness?

Do We Actually Want Those Things That Bring Us Pleasure?

If hedonism is going to be put to practical use, then it is important that we plan carefully. We must develop a strategy to secure either large quantities of pleasure or many higher-quality pleasures. It is important for us to want the right things: those things that bring us pleasure. Yet to do this requires that we align our desires with what we like. It seems that wanting and liking are intimately connected in such a way that what we want (desire) is simply a matter of what we like (find pleasing). So here is the question: are we good at this? Do we do a good job at desiring only those things that please us? Or is it the case that we often want what we do not like?

There is some evidence for believing that, at least sometimes, we want what we do not like. That these two can sometimes come apart has a biological basis: the brain processes that control our desires are separate from those that control enjoyment, and so you can desire something and yet not like it once you have it. What explains this fact about us is that the chemical and physical interactions in the brain that are associated with the two systems are different, as are their purposes.[3] The liking system involves opioids and its operation is short term. When our brain is flooded with opioids it ignores competing demands and other activities in order to focus on the current event. Essentially, the purpose of opioids is to focus our attention on the task at hand. On the other hand, the wanting system involves dopamine. Dopamine engages our desire and motivates us to pursue things. Its function is to shape long-term behavior. While many things that stimulate the dopamine circuits also stimulate the release of opioids in our brain, this is not always the case.

An experimental example reveals this distinction between wanting and liking. In one study of heroin addicts, the subjects were able to receive an injection by pressing a lever 3,000 times in 45 minutes (about once every second). In some cases, the injection included a moderate level of morphine, and in others it contained only saline. After receiving the injection, the participants were then asked to rate the quality of the injection and whether they would like to repeat pressing the lever to receive another injection. As expected, those who received a dose of morphine rated the injection as pleasurable and wanted to repeat the process to get more. However, those who received an injection of saline reported that it did not give them any pleasure and that they did not want to repeat the process. In these two cases, then, the wanting and the liking systems were working together: liking the effects of the injection led to wanting it again, and not liking the injection led to not wanting it again.[4] However, the researchers created a third condition. This group, upon pushing the lever, was given an injection with very low levels of morphine – so low that when asked to rate it the participants stated that they received no pleasure from the injection. Yet oddly, when asked if they would like to repeat the experiment to get another hit, they said yes! Their wanting system was activated by the low dose of morphine even though it was not high enough of a dose to activate the liking system. It seems that in this third condition the subjects ended up wanting what they themselves knew they would not like.[5]

Of course, heroin addicts are atypical cases. They are, after all, paradigm cases of addiction. What about the rest of us? Do we often· want what we

---

3   Nettle (2005: 127–28).
4   It is interesting to note that this experiment might help to support Mill's account of the relationship between attitudes and feelings as against Feldman, since it seems clear that in this case the feeling was driving the formation of the subsequent attitude and not the other way around.
5   Lamb et al. (1991).

do not like? Do we fare any better than addicts at aligning our desires with what brings us happiness? According to psychologists Daniel Gilbert and Timothy Wilson, it turns out that, unfortunately, we are not that much better at accurately wanting. In fact, the two speculate that much of the explanation for our unhappiness at any given time can be explained by the fact that we want what we do not like and we fail to want what we do like; they call this *miswanting*.

Gilbert and Wilson explain that at least three problems impede our attempts to want well. The first is that we often imagine the wrong effect. We predict that the experience we are about to have will be of a certain nature, and yet when it arrives, it is completely different. This echoes the difference first introduced to us by Kahneman between the experiencing self and the remembering self; but here, Gilbert and Wilson draw a difference between the experiencing self and the *desiring self*. The remembering self is directed toward the past, the experiencing self is directed toward the present, and the desiring self is directed toward the future. Kahneman's experiments demonstrate that we are often bad at remembering the actual amount of pleasure or pain we have experienced in our past, which then has an effect on the choices we make with respect to planning for our happiness. However, as Gilbert and Wilson's studies show, we also make mistakes when it comes to accurately imagining the happiness we will enjoy as a result of future events. So, for example, we imagine that being a celebrity would be great, but we forget to include in our fantasy of fame the loss of privacy, the public scrutiny, the paparazzi, the frightening stalkers, and the loss of personal liberty that comes along with such a life.

A second explanation of miswanting is that we often use the wrong theory about future liking. Gilbert and Wilson describe an experiment that illustrates this nicely. The subjects in this study were told that for the next three weeks they would return to the lab on Monday and be given a snack to eat. They were then asked to decide which snack they wanted to have for each of the next three Mondays. Most of the test subjects decided not to order their favorite snack for each of the three weeks. They opted instead to mix it up and throw in some variety, perhaps choosing their second-favorite snack for one of the weeks. After the subjects ate their snacks and were asked to evaluate how much they enjoyed eating what they had wanted, it turned out that they were disappointed on those days when they did not get to eat their favorite snack.[6] Though it seems predictable that the subjects

---

6 Gilbert and Wilson (2000: 181).

would not enjoy their second-favorite snack as much as their favorite, what puzzled Gilbert and Wilson was why the subjects wanted something that they knew perfectly well they did not like as much. What explains this? Presumably, when the subjects were planning their menu, they were thinking that eating the same snack too many times in a row would not lead to the most pleasure. After all, variety is the spice of life, right? But in applying this general idea to this particular case, they forgot to account for the fact that the snacks were spread over three weeks. As a result of planning their future under a faulty assumption, the subjects served only to undermine their own future enjoyments.

Third, our miswanting is also sometimes explained by that fact that we routinely misinterpret our own feelings. It turns out that our current moods have an influence not only on how we rate our overall happiness, but also on how we rate expected future experiences as well as past ones. In other words, Matt might think that he will really love hiking at Minnehaha Park next weekend because while contemplating the prospect of doing so he experiences excitement. But what he might fail to realize is that it is not the prospect of hiking that is actually responsible for his excitement and positive mood, but rather the news he just received about the Minnesota Twins winning the World Series. When he goes hiking next weekend and finds himself disappointed, he might wonder why he ever thought he would have so much fun – especially given that he usually finds hiking rather pedestrian!

Because we are victims of miswanting, we sometimes end up choosing to engage in activities that actually prevent us from achieving happiness. For example, many think that having more options open to us would lead to an increase in our happiness. Gilbert and his colleague Jane Jenkins conducted a study that challenged this assumption.[7] Subjects in the study were first taught how to take and develop black-and-white photographs. After developing their two favorite photographs, they were asked to donate one to the experimenter's "photography project" and were allowed to keep the other. Subjects in one group were told that once they made their choice they could not change their minds, whereas subjects in a second group were given five days during which they could change their mind and switch which photo they donated. After the end of the study, the subjects were interviewed with regard to how happy they were with the photographs they decided to keep. Surprisingly, those whose decisions were irreversible

---

7   Ibid., 192–93.

reported higher levels of happiness with their chosen photos. On the other hand, those who were given the option to swap out their photos, even if they chose not to, were less happy. Apparently, even having a small window of opportunity to change their minds led to not being as happy with their choice as those whose initial decisions were final. Contrary to popular opinion, then, the freedom to choose in certain cases might not actually lead to our happiness. Notice, too, that this is not due simply to our choosing poorly, but instead is due to the mere fact of having a choice at all. Of course, this is utterly counterintuitive, but it might explain why we all continue to make the same predictable mistakes when planning for our future happiness.

So if we combine Gilbert's evidence for miswanting with Kahneman's evidence for misremembering, we arrive at the following fact: not only are we bad at remembering what made us happy in the past, but we are also bad at predicting what will make us happy in the future. So what should we do if we want to be happy? If happiness just is experiencing certain pleasurable states, as the hedonist says it is, but we cannot accurately align our wantings with our likings, then what advice can we give ourselves about how to be happy?

As Gilbert notes, one way to improve our predictive power is to ask people who are currently engaged in the activity how much pleasure they are experiencing, especially if it is something we have not tried before.[8] Again, this is because those who are currently experiencing an event are the most reliable judges of what it is like to be in that state. This can be especially helpful when one is planning for a distant future self whose interests might now be unknown. If we think about our current desires, we can easily see how different they are from what we used to find pleasurable. The desires you enjoyed as a high-school student most likely seem utterly childish to you now. So why would you think that the pleasures you enjoy in your 20s or 30s will still strike your fancy in your 60s? For example, many young professionals begin to plan for retirement early. Of course, knowing how much one needs to retire comfortably depends to a great extent on the sort of life one envisions in retirement. If one wants to be able to travel the world and live adventurously, one will need far more than if one plans on settling down in a quiet Midwestern town to enjoy one's garden and family. But how can you know now which future will bring you the most pleasure? How can you know what your future self will be like? Relying on people who are already

8   Gilbert (2006), Chapter 11.

retired can help you more accurately predict what you will enjoy once you reach that age, though naturally, not everyone is the same, and so you will want to ask those who have a similar temperament and taste as you.

Even so, in the end, maybe what this information indicates is that we should not think of happiness as pleasurable experience. Maybe the fact that we do not always accurately remember and do not always reliably predict our pleasure shows that it cannot be all that important to our happiness. Yet the fact that the majority of people in the world report themselves as being happy begs for explanation. If what Kahneman and Gilbert say is true, then there might be two different explanations as to why we seem to be happy in spite of our frequent mistakes with regard to our pleasure. First, it might be that pleasure is not as important to our happiness as we might have thought, so thinking of happiness as pleasure is misguided. Or second, perhaps we all just get incredibly lucky, stumbling into pleasant situations even though we are bad at predicting and remembering what sorts of things actually bring us pleasure. But this would, in turn, seem to suggest that whether we are happy or not is simply a matter of luck and has little to do with what we can control. Then again, that happiness might depend in part on luck is not that far-fetched, since as previously mentioned, the root word of "happiness" – "hap" – means "fortune" or "luck."

Yet both of these explanations might be too quick, for the following reasons. First, the studies mentioned by Gilbert and Wilson show only that we are sometimes bad at wanting our likings, but not that we *never* want what we like. In fact, they do not even show that we miswant more frequently than we want well. We may well be quite good at wanting what we like, and to conclude otherwise based on a handful of artificial cases seems a bit like a hasty generalization. In fact, the studies clearly reveal that wanting and liking seem to be intimately connected, as the subjects want things that they *believe* they will like. Thus, while the experiments may question how accurate we are at wanting what we *actually* like, the studies do not demonstrate that we want what we *know* we will *not* like. In this way, Mill's earlier claim may still hold true: "that to *think* of an object as desirable ... and to *think* of it as pleasant are one and the same thing."[9] Second, even if one is convinced by Gilbert and Wilson's studies that wanting and liking do come apart in significant ways, this would not refute hedonism as a theory of the nature of happiness. At best, it casts doubt on our ability to practically deploy hedonism in our daily lives. That is, it may cause some concern with

---

9   Mill (1861), Chapter IV, Paragraph 10; emphasis added.

regard to our ability to effectively pursue happiness, if hedonism is true. Of course, that a theory has substantial barriers to its practical application should give us pause, especially when the subject matter in question is our own happiness, which has tremendous value to us. Thus, insofar as we are unable to reliably predict and attain future pleasure, in what sense is hedonism a good theory to follow? Can it offer us any guidance on how to plan a life so as to increase our happiness, or is it just a matter of luck?

Happiness Is Deep, Man

As hedonists have described it, happiness is determined by our momentary experiences. As such, happiness is episodic, meaning it occurs in discrete instants. Each instant has its own measure on the happiness scale, and these measures are referred to as moment utilities. This also implies that any event having an impact on our felt level of pleasure or pain, no matter how small in degree, has an effect on our overall happiness rating. But is that actually the case? Do we really think that our happiness is affected by a mosquito bite? It is true that we experience minor irritation as a result, but does that experience really have the momentum to affect our happiness? Philosopher Daniel Haybron thinks not. He offers the example of eating a cracker. Surely, provided Emeril likes the taste of crackers and this is a good cracker, he will get some pleasure out of eating it. Moreover, insofar as he gets some pleasure out of it, then, according to hedonism, this would have an impact on his momentary happiness level. It might even tip the scales in favor of happiness. For example, in the event that he is ever so mildly unhappy (or neutral), the eating of a cracker could in fact be the very thing responsible for making him happy. Yet, it seems a bit absurd to suppose that something so trifling, shallow, and fleeting as the eating of a single cracker could actually make someone *happier*. According to Haybron, our happiness is not affected by such passing pleasures; it is not so fickle.

One could imagine Bentham responding that the reason the eating of a cracker doesn't move one's happiness level is because the pleasure experienced in that moment is so lacking in intensity as to be almost wholly unnoticeable. Then again, it is not just the lack of intensity that prevents the eating of a cracker from contributing to my happiness, according to Haybron. Rather, it is the trivial and fleeting nature of the experience. It seems that even an intense experience such as a thrilling ride on a roller coaster or a painful shot in the doctor's office might fail to move our happiness levels.

If the reason trivial pleasures do not affect our happiness has little to do with their lack of intensity, then perhaps the problem is that they just do not last long enough. Eating crackers and getting shots are, after all, short-lived experiences, and so maybe the reason they do not affect our happiness is that they are fleeting. For example, though a five-second shoulder rub does little to elevate our mood, if it lasts an hour it might very well lift our spirits significantly. However, it is also true that some lengthy experiences can fail to impact our happiness. For example, one can today suffer a persistent but dull muscle ache due to a strenuous workout yesterday, and yet not be less happy as a result. In other words, it is not the duration, either, of an experienced pleasure or pain that determines whether or not it matters to our happiness. In fact, according to Haybron, "the trouble seems to be that such pleasures don't reach 'deeply' enough, so to speak. They just don't *get* to us; they flit through consciousness and that's the end of it."[10]

According to Haybron, the root of the hedonist's mistake is that she thinks of happiness as made up of pleasurable episodes. However, happiness is a more enduring and stable psychological state. While a person can suffer a minor pain or enjoy a minor pleasure, neither will reach far enough into her psyche to affect her overall emotional state. In other words, happiness is at the core of our psychological life, whereas transitory experiences of pleasure and pain are peripheral.

Given the problems with hedonism, Haybron offers a different account of happiness that rests on deeper feelings such as our emotions and moods. In so doing, he is able to capture the intuition that being happy feels good, while at the same time avoiding some of the pitfalls commonly associated with explaining that idea in terms of pleasure. Haybron's *emotional state theory* takes happiness to be a description of our entire emotional state. To be happy, on this view, is to exhibit a sufficiently favorable balance of positive over negative moods and emotions. Happiness is thus a feature of one's entire emotional state, and so to be happy is to experience a sort of *psychic flourishing*. We should be careful to note, however, that Haybron's description of happiness as a form of psychic flourishing might lead to a bit of confusion. He does not intend to suggest that happiness is therefore evaluative. In fact, he explicitly states that he is interested only in the descriptive sense of happiness, not in the prudential or evaluative sense. His use of "flourishing" therefore seems a bit misplaced, since as we have already pointed out, it is an evaluative term.

---

10 Haybron (2001: 506).

On Haybron's account, not all feelings are central enough to figure in our emotional lives in a way relevant to happiness. Haybron argues that there is an important difference between *central* and *peripheral affects*. Central affects are deep, profound, and pervasive. Common central affects include emotions and moods like joy, grief, exhilaration, shame, contentment, stress, feeling confident, or despondent. On the other hand, peripheral affective states are shallow, superficial, or trivial. These include amusement, minor annoyance, and physical pain or pleasure, among others. Peripheral states are at the surface of our emotional lives. In failing to recognize the difference between central and peripheral affective states, the hedonist mistakenly believes that peripheral states have an impact on our happiness, as in the earlier case of eating a cracker. However, according to Haybron, only central affective states alter our overall emotional condition, and thereby our happiness.

Haybron thinks that we typically recognize the distinction between central and peripheral affects even in ordinary conversation. We frequently talk about the deeper states in terms of being "soul crushing" or "gut wrenching," or about events that just "get to us," or "move us deeply." Similarly, on the side of peripheral affect, we frequently talk about something that "bounced right off her." According to Haybron:

> This sort of language is not careless metaphor; it signifies a genuine, and important, distinction in our emotional lives. It also hints at a link between happiness and the self that does not obtain in the case of (peripheral) pleasure. There appears to be an inner citadel of the self – the soul? – that many affects fail to penetrate. Central affective states seem to constitute changes in us, and are not merely things that happen to us....[11]

Notice the relationship between such central affective states and what we are. For example, we often say that we *are* depressed or that we *are* serene. Unlike central affective states, pleasurable and painful experiences seem not to penetrate deeply enough to alter our sense of self. Moreover, happiness seems more aligned with these central affective states than with mere surface-level pains and pleasures.

According to Haybron, central affects have five characteristic features. First, they are *dispositional* in that they dispose a person to experience certain

---

11 Haybron (2005: 300).

affects rather than others. Second, and closely related, they are also *pervasive* in that they permeate a person's entire experience. For example, a person suffering from depression often lacks motivation and so will frequently forgo experiences that could be enjoyable and raise one's mood. More to the point, such a state also colors the whole of one's experience. For example, the depressed person will find it very difficult to experience pleasure in things – even things that typically one enjoys. Hobbies and other activities that used to provide joy now leave one utterly uninspired. The converse is true of being cheerful. When in a cheerful mood, we tend to take more joy in our projects and we experience less intense pain. What might otherwise bother us seems to be quickly forgotten. In other words, central affective states not only affect our willingness and desire to do things, but they also affect how we experience those events as they occur. This seems different from the peripheral annoyance of dropping your pencil, or the pleasant experience of driving by a pretty house. These experiences do not seem to dispose us toward any sort of future experience – they don't seem to have any lasting effect on our moods and emotions.

The third feature of central affective states is that they are *productive*, meaning they have many different sorts of effects on us. According to Haybron, they cause physiological changes in the body such as increased heart rate and changes in energy level; they generate other affective states; and they can even bias our thinking and behavior in certain ways, as when we suffer anxiety and thereby anticipate the worst in every situation. Central affects are also *persistent* in that they tend to last a while when they occur. For instance, the experience of contentment is not transitory: it is durable; it lasts. Contrast that with an itch. Upon scratching it there seems to be no residue of the event left over in our psyche. It is gone and therefore cannot have an effect on our happiness.

Finally, according to Haybron, central affects are *profound*. Even when mild, they are experienced as states *of* us, rather than things happening *to* us. They seem to reside or well up from the inside rather than affect us from without. They get to us. Again, this implies that central affects alter the very person that we are (or at least, we experience them in such a way). However, pleasure and pain just do not have this effect. Pleasures seem largely to happen to us. We are passive consumers of our pleasures; they come to us from the outside. Yet happiness seems to be something that we *are*. It is more closely associated with our sense of self; it permeates our identity. It is as though happiness comes from within us, and it seems to change the conscious experiences we have: heightening enjoyment and diminishing pain. In fact, given the above considerations of central affects, and contrary to the claims of hedonism, it appears more likely that our level of happiness affects our experience of pleasure and pain and not the other way around.

According to emotional state theory, to be happy is for our emotional condition to exhibit a sufficiently favorable balance of positive over negative central affects. Still, we might wonder how positive our emotional state must be in order to be considered happy. According to Haybron, it cannot be the case that to be happy is merely to experience slightly more positive than negative affect. We would not call a person happy who is miserable nearly half the time. In fact, even a person who enjoys positive emotions a large majority of the time might yet be unhappy, if prone to bouts of intense sadness. The person who suffers from anxiety attacks illustrates this point. Though she might not have had an attack for a day or two, we would not consider her happy since she might suffer from an attack any time. The propensity to suffer outweighs the current experiences of positive emotion, precisely because it points to the unstable nature of the individual's emotional state. Or consider someone who is cheerful all day but who cries himself to sleep every night. Is he happy? Most would agree that a person in such a condition is not happy, though he experiences many positive emotions throughout the day. His nightly sobbing betrays a fragile emotional condition. As a result, determining how much positive emotionality a person must experience in order to count as happy is a complicated question, one that cannot be answered according to the aggregate balance of positive over negative affect.

Furthermore, one of the chief benefits of being happy, argues Haybron, is that happy people have a sort of emotional resilience that allows them to endure negative events, yet not suffer from a bad mood as a result. On the other hand, the unhappy person suffers, at least sometimes, from a sort of emotional fragility that is contrary to the emotional resilience characteristic of happy people. This reveals an important aspect of happiness: it is not merely a collection of positive emotions and moods, but it is a *propensity* to experience these emotions and moods. This is why we like to visit happy friends. When we know a person to be a happy person, we can trust that usually when we are around them they will be experiencing mostly positive moods (they won't be glum or blue). Of course, this makes for a better time for all involved!

Emotional state theory still has at least one thing in common with hedonism: happiness feels good. Although happiness is far too nuanced to be simply reduced to the aggregate balance of pleasure over pain as the hedonist would have it, argues Haybron, it is also the case that being happy is deeply connected with positive affective states. In this way, Haybron thinks that his emotional state theory can óvercome the problems of simple hedonism while also retaining its greatest insight into happiness: it feels good to be happy. And yet it is just this common commitment to the feel-good feature of happiness that is the source of an important objection to his view.

The Problem with Feelings

Haybron articulates a view according to which one is happy to the degree that she experiences psychological or emotional flourishing. To flourish emotionally just means that she has a sufficiently favorable balance of positive to negative emotionality. Leaving aside the thorny question of what counts as a "sufficiently favorable balance," there is another issue we must tackle: what makes an emotion "positive" or "negative"? How is Haybron sorting positive from negative affect?

Haybron himself seems to leave the question unanswered, stating, "The account remains confessedly vague.... For example, we have yet to see what exactly is meant by 'positive' and 'negative' affect."[12] It appears, then, that we must do the work to fill in the details ourselves. The most natural response might be to suggest that a central affect is positive, and therefore happiness-constituting, if it feels good to experience it. That is, what makes an affective state positive is that it *feels good*, and what makes an affective state negative is that it *feels bad*. Yet to divide positive from negative emotions according to how they feel is just to talk about happiness in terms of experiencing pleasant states and avoiding painful ones. To be sure, as Haybron points out, his view counts only certain *centrally important* emotional pleasures and pains as affecting happiness; yet, even so, it would still understand happiness fundamentally in terms of pleasurable mental states. Hence, if this is how Haybron draws the distinction, then emotional state theory seems to be a thinly veiled version of hedonism, albeit a sophisticated one.

Otherwise, Haybron will have to provide some other non-hedonistic explanation for how to distinguish a positive from a negative emotion. One possible way to do so is according to whether the emotion functions properly. In other words, one common view of emotions, held by Aristotle and

---

12 Ibid., 309.

Nussbaum, among many others, is that they are evaluations of our environment that serve to compel behavior. When emotions function properly, they cause us to respond appropriately to the situation, aiding in the living of our lives. They are good for us, or "positive." When they go haywire and interfere with living well, they are bad for us, or "negative." For example, both fear and anger serve particular purposes in certain situations. Anger sometimes serves the purpose of alerting us to serious damage that has been willfully inflicted upon us and motivates us to rectify this harm. Likewise, fear serves the purpose of alerting us to dangers that we are not fully able to protect ourselves against. When such emotions function properly, they aid in our happiness and overall well-being. On the other hand, feeling anger at something trivial such as a person forgetting your name, or feeling fear at seeing a small mouse scurry across the floor, would be inappropriate.[13] Such poorly functioning emotions fail to contribute to a happy and good life.

As another example, consider grieving at the death of a loved one. If someone did not feel grief in this situation, we would think that his emotional connection to his family is stunted and he is the worse for it. There would be something psychologically unhealthy about a person who feels no grief when someone he cares for has died. Yet how can a person who suffers from poor psychological health be thought happy? All of these considerations imply that emotions like anger, fear, and grief sometimes contribute to our happiness insofar as they signal positive psychological health. The same holds true in reverse for good-feeling emotional states: emotions like joy, elation, or contentment under certain conditions (like when they are felt after killing someone) are symptoms of poor psychological health, and therefore sources of unhappiness.

Still, understanding positive emotionality in terms of proper function involves specifying some normative conception of the human good; an account of what sorts of things contribute to our well-being. After all, for a thing to function properly, it has to perform well in light of some purpose or end. Even evolutionary biology distinguishes properly functioning from improperly functioning emotionality, according to whether or not the emotion in question serves our biological good: evolutionary fitness. And so what makes an emotion positive is that it serves our biological ends. Hence, if we are not sorting good from bad emotions according to whether they are pleasant or painful, then we will have to introduce some other standard of evaluation in order to explain why *these* emotions contribute to

---

13 In Aristotle's *Rhetoric*, Book II, Sections 2–3. Taken from Nussbaum (2012: 345).

our happiness and why *those* detract from it. Yet to make such a move seems to require that happiness be an evaluative (and not merely a descriptive) concept. Whatever this additional evaluative standard is, it will require some normative assumptions about what sorts of things are good for us. Thus, if Haybron's "psychological flourishing" is understood as something like proper functioning, while he might be able to avoid understanding positive emotionality along the lines of hedonism, he does so by treating happiness as an evaluative rather than a descriptive concept.

What is more, if Haybron chooses to remain descriptive about happiness, then he faces a strong objection implied by Nussbaum's account of emotions as proper functioning. More specifically, drawing the positive/negative emotion distinction according to whether they feel pleasurable or painful obscures the ways in which bad-feeling emotions can serve our happiness and total well-being (such as justified anger), and how good-feeling emotions can at least sometimes lead us away from the good and happy life (such as in the case of false hope or the experience of *Schadenfreude*). Therefore, according to Nussbaum, distinguishing positive from negative emotions according to how they feel to us is misguided.[14]

In conclusion, if Nussbaum is correct to think that we should not draw the distinction between positive and negative emotionality along the lines of how they feel, then it seems clear that all versions of hedonism (save maybe for purely attitudinal varieties) are in trouble. This applies to any theory that reduces happiness to feel-good affects only, whether we mean a singular sensation of pleasure itself (like Bentham), or the experience of a variety of higher-quality pleasures (like Mill), or even the experience of centrally important affects (like Haybron). If pleasant feelings can be bad for us and painful ones good for us, then it seems that either happiness does not amount to merely the experience of pleasure and avoidance of pain, or else happiness is sometimes bad for us, in which case it would lose most (if not all) of its value.

---

14 Nussbaum (2012).

Part III: Happiness as Satisfaction

Chapter 6:   Satisfied with What?

PHYSICIST STEPHEN HAWKING WAS first diagnosed with ALS (Lou Gehrig's disease) at the age of 21 while pursuing his studies in cosmology at Cambridge University. The disease affects the nerve cells in the brain and spinal column, resulting in a loss of motor function. It often leads to painful muscle contracture, spasms, and cramping. Hawking has endured the effects of ALS for over 50 years. Confined to a wheelchair, his ability to speak has deteriorated so that he has to rely on a speech device controlled by his cheek muscles, limiting his ease of communication. Despite the debilitating disease, Hawking has earned world acclaim as a top-rate scientist, penning both original contributions in the study of black holes and space-time, as well as popular books aimed at bringing science to the masses. He has earned many awards and accolades, including the Presidential Medal of Freedom, the Wolf Prize in Physics, the Albert Einstein Medal, and the Gold Medal of the Royal Astronomical Society. Hawking has achieved more than just academic acclaim; he is a household name. He is such a part of popular culture that he has even made guest appearances on television series such as *Star Trek: The Next Generation*, *The Simpsons*, and *The Big Bang Theory*. Outside of his life as a scientist and popular icon, Hawking is also married with three children.[1] Is it possible that Stephen Hawking is happy even while living with ALS? If so, then what in his life could account for his being happy?

---

1   This and the other information regarding Stephen Hawking was found at his personal webpage (http://www.hawking.org.uk).

It seems rather plausible to think that Hawking's could be a happy life. After all, he has earned prestige as a scientist and has accomplished more in his life than most. Perhaps these elements of life are enough to outweigh the physical and emotional toll that ALS exacts from its victims. Still, although he has likely experienced many episodes of pleasure, Hawking's life has included a great deal of pain by way of suffering the debilitating effects of ALS for over 50 years. As a result, quantitative hedonism appears to have a difficult time making sense of the idea that Hawking could be happy. Qualitative hedonism, on the other hand, could more easily account for this intuition. The reason it makes sense to consider Hawking happy according to this view is that those pleasures he has experienced are of higher quality: they are pleasures of the intellect, whereas the pains he suffers are, at least predominantly, physical in nature. Hence the qualitative hedonist might claim that although Hawking might have been happier had he not been made to suffer the effects of ALS, it is still plausible to believe that he has a happy life, on the grounds that he experiences higher-quality pleasures throughout it. In fact, one might even think that because Hawking contemplates deep questions of physics and cosmology on a daily basis, he might even have a higher *quantity* of (intellectual) pleasures than (physical) pains.

There is another more natural response, however. Perhaps, contrary to hedonism, happiness is not a feeling; happiness has less to do with a felt experience, and more to do with how we assess our lives. Some of those who reject hedonism insist that happiness consists in the satisfaction of desires or preferences. Happiness is more about whether our desires are satisfied rather than involving some feel-good emotion. Still, it is important to clarify that when we judge our desires to be satisfied, this can sometimes be attended by an affective response. In other words, satisfaction is not incompatible with the experience of pleasure. Still, just as the essential hallmark feature of pleasure is its felt quality, the essential defining characteristic of satisfaction is a cognitive judgment that does not necessarily involve a feeling. In light of this, it is possible that Hawking, in looking at his life, might quite easily judge that most, if not all, of his important desires have been satisfied and that therefore his life is a stunning success and he is thereby made happy. The view that happiness amounts to being satisfied is called *desire satisfactionism* (sometimes called preference satisfactionism).

Desire satisfactionism has some intuitive appeal, as is clear in the example of the Amish. It seems that the Amish are quite content and satisfied with their lives. Yet their lives lack many hedonic delights and border on asceticism. Insofar as we find it natural or at least plausible to think that at least some Amish people count as happy, we might be inclined to reject the hedonic theory of happiness in favor of a satisfaction account, since this seems to more easily explain our intuitions.

We should begin by distinguishing two different views of desire satisfactionism, determined according to the object of our desire. Recall that desires are attitudes, which are mental stances one takes in relation to some object or state of affairs. This object could be specific, such as a desire to climb Mount Everest, to listen to a favorite song, or to attend a party. Or the object of one's desire could be general, for example, that one's life as a whole goes well. When the focus is on satisfying our many specific desires, the view is called *local desire satisfactionism*. When the object of our desire is our life generally going the way we want it to, the view is called *whole life satisfactionism*.

Local Desire Satisfactionism

Local desire satisfactionism holds that happiness amounts to having as many satisfied desires and as few unsatisfied desires as possible. The higher the number of satisfied desires and the lower the number of unsatisfied desires, the happier a person is. This shares one aspect with both quantitative and attitudinal hedonism in that happiness is a matter of the *quantity* of satisfactions compared to dissatisfactions. Yet local desire satisfactionism has a broader view of what influences happiness beyond the mere experience of pleasure and pain. To be sure, many of us desire to experience pleasure and avoid pain, and insofar as these desires are satisfied, then on local desire satisfactionism this will contribute to our happiness. But we also desire other things. We desire a loving spouse and adoring children. We desire good weather and relaxing vacations. We even desire such abstract things as learning quantum mechanics. Indeed, what we are capable of desiring seems boundless.

As an added note, recall that – just like taking pleasure in something – desiring something and being satisfied with something are attitudes. Likewise, all of these attitudes are *pro*-attitudes, meaning that the stance one takes is positive. On local desire satisfactionism, we experience satisfaction when what we desire comes to be, and the more desires we have fulfilled, the more satisfactions we experience. Of course, we might question whether being pleased about something is really that different from simply being satisfied with something, which is another reason why we might think there is little to distinguish Feldman's attitudinal hedonism from local desire satisfactionism.

What it means to be happy at any given *moment* is that I have more satisfied than unsatisfied desires, and the more desires that I have satisfied, the happier I am. But what does it mean to live a happy *life*? On local desire satisfactionism, the answer appears rather straightforward: to live a happy life is to live a life with a high quantity of satisfied desires. Of the desires that we have, we should seek to satisfy as many as we can. Philosopher Derek Parfit describes how this process might work:

> We assign some positive number to each desire that is fulfilled, and some negative number to each desire that is not fulfilled. How great these numbers are depends on the intensity of the desires in question.... The total net sum of desire-fulfillment is the sum of the positive numbers minus the negative numbers. Provided that we can compare the relative strength of different desires, this calculation could in theory be performed.[2]

Thus the greater the sum of satisfied desires, the happier the life. This again is similar to what quantitative and attitudinal hedonism state about happy lives.

One other point is important to note here. In the initial definition of local desire satisfactionism given above, the emphasis was placed on having a sufficient number of satisfied to unsatisfied desires among one's collection of various specific desires. Thus it seems at least possible that as long as one's desires are satisfied, one is thereby made happy, even if one does not yet (or ever) become aware of this fact. This would be the case when a person does not *experience* his desires as satisfied even though they are. But this should strike some as odd. Imagine someone with a very strong desire to be a prestigious author. In fact, he has few other strong desires and holds this particular desire to be the most important in his life. Moreover, this man is, in fact, admired around the world for his work, and yet he considers himself a tremendous failure, convinced that those who read his work find it stale and unoriginal. Is it really the case that we should judge him happy simply on the basis that his most intense desire is actually satisfied? As we mentioned in Chapter Two, there is a strong intuition that only those things that enter the realm of subjective consciousness can have an influence on our happiness. Or conversely, our happiness is not affected by things of

---

2 Parfit (1984: 496).

which we are unaware. This is sometimes referred to as the "experience requirement."[3] Insofar as we think happiness consists in some sort of mental state, we will want to add the experience requirement to our definition of the view. Any view of happiness that takes subjectively experienced mental states to be the core of happiness adheres to the experience requirement, no matter whether the mental states that matter to happiness are feelings, satisfactions, or some combination of both.

Nonetheless, there are some desire satisfaction views that deny the experience requirement. These theories "reject the experience requirement and allow that a person's life can be made better and worse not only by changes in that person's state of consciousness but also by changes elsewhere in the world which fulfill that person's preferences."[4] Yet notice the use of "better" and "worse" here. This is no accident. Usually, desire satisfaction views that deny the experience requirement are more properly views of well-being, though they could also be views of happiness provided that happiness and well-being mean the same thing. We will use the term "local desire satisfactionism" to refer to the view that happiness consists in *experiencing* one's desires as satisfied, and the more of one's desires that are experienced as satisfied, the happier one is.

Local desire satisfactionism raises some serious concerns, however. For example, does each and every one of our desires matter equally to our happiness? This sort of worry is analogous to the worry expressed against Jeremy Bentham's quantitative hedonism that it is a "pig's philosophy." Recall that for Bentham, the pleasures of playing push-pin are equal to those of reading poetry as long as they are equal in intensity and duration. But some, like John Stuart Mill, object that this fails to recognize that the pleasures of poetry are superior in quality. We can raise a similar concern with local desire satisfactionism: are all of our desires equally important? We have many desires, and some of these desires are better for us than others; likewise, some of our desires are better for the world. Yet it seems at least possible on this view that someone can be made happy by satisfying as many of his desires as he can, *whatever those desires may be.* But what if he desires heroin above all else? His desire for heroin is certainly intense and could be fulfilled daily. In this way, it would receive a high numeric value on his happiness scale. Yet we seem to think there is something deeply wrong with holding that his happiness is best served by continuing to shoot heroin on a daily basis. Perhaps this is because we think that his desire for heroin, as an addiction,

---

3   Griffin (1986: 13).
4   Scanlon (1993: 186).

precludes him from having other important desires. Even so, these other desires are likely to be much less intense than his desire for heroin.

This is related in part to another concern we might have with the quantitative aspect of local desire satisfactionism. Is it really the sum *total* of desires satisfied that determines how happy I am? The view seems to suggest that the more desires I have fulfilled, the better off I am. But then, because local desire satisfactionism suggests that a life with more satisfied desires is preferable to a life with fewer satisfied desires, this would mean that a longer life would always be happier than a shorter life simply by virtue of containing more satisfied desires. Yet this just does not seem to fit our intuitions. As Parfit notes, it seems that a shorter life filled with highly valued satisfied desires, such as the desire for a loving family, great friends, a successful career, and ample recreation, would be preferable to a very long life in which only one's insignificant desires are fulfilled, such as, for example, making it to appointments on time, feeding oneself adequately, and getting sleep.

Related to this concern, what if a person desires very little in life? Consider for example a Buddhist monk. Here is the case of someone who perhaps has only one desire: enlightenment. In Buddhism, desiring is a source of suffering, since most desires ultimately breed unhappiness because they create craving and longing for things that are ultimately out of your control. As the Dalai Lama notes, the most reliable way to achieve contentment is not to obtain everything that you want, but to want and appreciate what you already have. So the aim is to reduce the number of your desires, since the fewer desires you have, the fewer desires that remain unfulfilled. Assuming the monk is able to become enlightened, would we not judge him happy? And yet he has only one satisfied desire.

Perhaps, then, a better way to formulate local desire satisfactionism would be to hold that it is the *ratio* of satisfied to unsatisfied desires, rather than the sheer number of satisfied minus unsatisfied desires. On this formulation of the view, one could be made happy by cutting back on the number of desires one has, in the hopes that one will increase the odds of being able to satisfy a majority of them. Yet this will only prove effective if the desires you keep are those that you are likely (or even able) to satisfy. It would be foolhardy to include among your desires a longing for fame or immortality: while obviously immortality is impossible, achieving fame is mostly beyond your control. In that way, you would tie your happiness to fortune or luck, since no matter how hard and diligently you work, others can fail to esteem you. This is similar to the advice of the Stoic philosopher Epictetus, who argues that one way to increase your happiness is to limit the number of your desires, retaining only those over which you can exercise unimpeded control. These considerations seem to show that we should prioritize our desires in terms of their importance to us. Fortunately, many of these concerns appear resolvable by the global version of desire satisfactionism: whole life satisfactionism.

Whole Life Satisfactionism

On whole life satisfactionism, the focus is on one general desire: that life as a whole go as one wants. In other words, the object of happiness is "one's life as a whole" and not the sum total of satisfied specific desires. In fact, a person might well be happy even if she has fewer satisfied than unsatisfied desires, provided that the desires that are satisfied are her important ones. The desire that life as a whole be going as one wants is a general desire, and to call this desire "general" indicates that we have different levels of desire. To help explain this notion, philosopher John Kekes distinguishes between first-order and second-order desires.[5] First-order desires are typical wantings – for instance, wanting to take a nap, eat a cheeseburger, have sex, listen to Huey Lewis and the News, have a family, or be charitable. On the other hand, we also have desires that take these first-order desires as their object: desires about desires. For example, we might find ourselves desiring that second piece of cheesecake (a first-order desire) and yet, because we are on a diet, we also desire not to desire it (a second-order desire). Similarly, many who smoke will often say that they wish they did not crave cigarettes so much, expressing a desire not to desire nicotine. Happiness amounts to the satisfaction of a very specific second-order desire, namely that our important first-order desires have been satisfied. This requires one to have considered which of one's desires are more primary. Happiness understood this way integrates one's entire system of desires into a general judgment about one's whole life.

At any given moment a person can be more or less satisfied with her life as a whole. She may think that at this moment she is satisfied with how her life has been going and think that her prospects point to a positive trajectory for her future. This appears to be the view assumed by those like psychologist Ed Diener, who claim that when we ask a subject to answer a question about life satisfaction, she integrates the whole of her life into a single response, usually on a sliding numerical scale. Often, for example,

---

5   Kekes (1982: 360).

subjects are asked to indicate their agreement with the statement "I am satisfied with my life" by marking a number on a sliding scale. For example, on a scale of zero through ten, a rating of ten indicates strong agreement, zero is strong disagreement, and five would be a neutral rating. Happiness in a *moment* is being satisfied with one's life as a whole at that time, and it can be represented numerically. The greater the intensity of one's satisfaction with life at that moment, the happier one is in that moment.

But to return to a recurring question, what does it mean to live a happy *life*? One answer is that we can combine a person's momentary general judgments about her life that she makes over the course of her life, charting these momentary satisfactions over time with a line graph like the one shown in Figure 6.1. After this, we can calculate an average life satisfaction

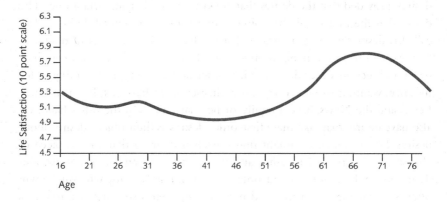

Figure 6.1: Life Satisfaction over a Lifetime

rating throughout the course of the life. Any average above "5" indicates a happy life, and the higher the score the happier the life. On the other hand, any average falling below the neutral point is an unhappy life, and the lower the score the unhappier the life. For the life charted in Figure 6.1, the average score over the course of the life is 5.38, so the person had a mildly happy life. Notice, then, that it is at least possible on whole life satisfactionism to understand happiness according to the *average* level of life satisfaction one experiences throughout life, rather than a sum total. Hence a shorter life might well be happier, provided that the average score of life satisfaction was sufficiently high. This reveals nicely how life satisfaction theories of happiness can overcome the worries with local desire satisfactionism expressed earlier. In particular, longer lives are not always happier than shorter lives, and the satisfaction of trivial desires will do little to change the mean score of overall life satisfaction.

Yet it is unclear when and how such life satisfaction judgments are to be made. Can this sort of general judgment be made midstream in one's life? That is, we might be skeptical that a person could *reliably* make this kind of global judgment in the middle of her life, since how can a person know what her future holds? This reservation is captured by the famous words of the sixth-century BCE Athenian statesman Solon: "Call no man happy until he is dead." For example, while things may have gone very well for a person up to the present time, and although he believes his future looks bright, he may suffer some devastating event the following year that ruins the rest of his life, which would lead him to reevaluate it and judge that his life is unsatisfactory on the whole. It makes sense to think that the judgment he makes later in life, after knowing all the things that will happen to him, is the more authoritative. So perhaps we cannot make a determination of whether we have lived a happy life until we have lived it all, which then suggests that this judgment can only be made on our deathbed, so to speak. What it means to have a happy life, then, might be that after surveying the whole of our life and how it turned out, we would judge it as satisfactory overall. The more strongly we assent to this judgment, the happier is our life. This view of happiness seems to lend some credence to Ludwig Wittgenstein's near-death claim, cited in a previous chapter, that he had lived a wonderful life in spite of experiencing a great amount of negative emotionality. On the other hand, much of life is often forgotten by old age, which might make us question whether our deathbed moment is really the most authoritative perspective from which to judge our lives as wholes.

When we make a judgment as to whether we are satisfied with our lives, it is not a simple matter of summing together the various events in our lives. Instead, we must construct a global judgment that generalizes whether our lives are going well overall, on the basis of all of the particular facts in our lives taken together as a whole. This process requires judgment and reflection, and how we do this differs from person to person – and it even differs for a single person over time. While we make judgments about our satisfaction with our lives quite often, it turns out that how we construct our judgment varies according to many arbitrary features of context. We then find ourselves with a number of different judgments of life satisfaction that we make at various points in our lives, many of which conflict with each other.

The above concern highlights an interesting question: are all of our life satisfaction judgments equally authoritative, or will some hold more weight than

others? Maybe, as suggested above, only *one* of these judgments is the definitive judgment as to whether one's life is happy. Consider how our judgments
of our lives change over time. Many of us have had the experience of perceiving our lives while in youth one way, only to later in life realize that these
beliefs were unfounded and that our high-school years, for example, were not
that bad. This suggests that judgments about our life as a whole are revisable,
especially in light of further life experience. Of course, this then raises the
question of whether *all* such judgments are equally revisable. Perhaps, for
instance, the life satisfaction judgment you make at this point in your life will,
in the future, be reevaluated by you as somehow misguided, just as you revised
your judgment about how satisfactory your life was in high school. It may be
the case that our golden years offer a new perspective on our life that was not
yet recognized in middle age. So we might want to view our current judgments of life satisfaction with a healthy amount of skepticism. We may want
to be cautious, especially if we intend to use such judgments to assess how
well our lives are going and to plan for the future. This relates to the advice
offered by Daniel Gilbert in the previous chapter with respect to soliciting
advice from others when planning for the future.

We might also want to clarify what exactly "one's life *as a whole*" refers to. It could refer to *scope*: namely, every aspect of one's life in all its
domains, such as work, family, wealth, health, recreation and leisure, etc.
On the other hand, it could refer to *completeness*: namely, the time period
of one's life from birth to death. Perhaps it is even a combination of both,
where happiness with one's life as a whole is finding it by and large satisfactory in most respects and generally throughout the entirety of one's life. On
this view, to be happy one must be satisfied with one's life overall, taking
into account one's past, present, and future. How, though, can we do this?
Philosopher Władysław Tatarkiewicz (1886–1980) goes a long way toward
answering this question.

That Which Is, Was, and Will Be

According to whole life satisfactionism, to be happy in a moment a person must be satisfied with his whole life: his past, present, and future.
Tatarkiewicz explores the distinct ways in which the past, present, and future all impact our present judgments of happiness:

> Satisfaction with life as a whole must be a satisfaction not only with
> that which is, but also with that which was and that which will be:

not only with the present, but also with the past, and the future. Therefore the feeling of happiness includes not only an agreeable present state, but also a favorable assessment of the past, and good prospects for the future. This plurality of satisfaction is essential to happiness.... Not only things which exist in present time and directly affect the individual, but also those which are no longer, or not yet in existence, have a bearing upon his happiness. Happiness is, by the nature of things, both retrospective and prospective in character.[6]

Here we can see that for Tatarkiewicz, aside from present conscious experiences, memories and predictions of the future also influence our judgments of overall life satisfaction and therefore have an impact on our happiness. He further notes that the past, present, and future are not three separate and isolated components, but are interrelated in their influence on our happiness.

Nevertheless, although the past, present, and future all influence our present happiness, they do not do so to the same degree. In fact, although many think that present experience is all that matters, it actually plays a very small role in our happiness. Tatarkiewicz explains: "The satisfaction we feel is an actual and real one, but actual and real satisfaction need not necessarily be derived from things existing in present reality."[7] That is, the object of our satisfaction may not be present experience, but instead might well be something in the past or the future. This claim by Tatarkiewicz seems to challenge the very idea on which Kahneman's objective happiness rests: if we want a true account of happiness we should focus solely on the experiencing self – the present self.

Consider the following question: How much of what you experienced this week do you think you will be able to vividly recall a year from now? For most, the answer is very little, if anything at all. Given this, we might think that the events of this particular week have little impact on our happiness. And yet right now, as our experiencing self lives the events of this week, we treat them as centrally important, as though they are the entirety of our happiness. On the one hand, living happily in the moment seems to be the insight behind such mottos as *carpe diem*, as well as the driving force behind many of our daily decisions. Yet, on the other hand, how we remember our life as having gone can be a source of great satisfaction or regret as well. And, as described in Chapter Four, how we experience life as it happens is often different from how we remember it.

---

6   Tatarkiewicz (1966: 1).
7   Ibid., 2.

Kahneman and Tatarkiewicz disagree regarding the true source of happiness. Does happiness rest solely on the experiencing self, or might the remembering self play a bigger role? Resolving this question seems rather critical, since how we plan our lives will depend on whether the experiencing self or the remembering self takes priority. Recall that Kahneman asserts that happiness is the same as the measure of pleasure over pain in the present moment. Even though it is true that after the experience is over, many of us no longer recollect how the original experience actually felt while going through it, our happiness still depends on these original feelings of pain and pleasure. According to Kahneman, happiness is constituted entirely by present experience.

However, Tatarkiewicz rejects this claim, arguing that, in fact, present experience plays a relatively insignificant role as an object of our satisfaction. Certainly, common experience seems to reveal that we direct more of our attention toward the past or the future rather than on the present moment. Indeed, one could argue that remembered experiences are more fundamental on the basis that we can continue to consume the memories of our present experiences long after they are over, even perhaps longer than the duration of the initial experience itself. For example, we often replay the episodes from our wedding in our minds for years on end. Or we find ourselves repeatedly recalling that moment when we scored the winning goal for our team's championship. We continue to savor these past events, giving them center stage in our consciousness, often holding on to these recollections for the rest of our lives.

Still, what about the fact that we misremember the past so frequently, as Kahneman points out? Is our happiness based on a fiction? Tatarkiewicz argues that what matters to our happiness has little to do with the actual past and the actual future, and more to do with the imagined past and the imagined future. That is, happiness depends on our memories and imaginings, regardless of whether or not they are accurate. He remarks:

> The real past, the real present, and the real future, even when combined, do not yet determine happiness and unhappiness. Acting simultaneously with them there is the past which never existed (but which we see in the vista of time) as well as the present which does not exist, and the future which will never exist. For in happiness and unhappiness alike, it is not a matter of what was, is, and will be in reality, but also that which we imagine and feel.... And thus happiness is also determined by things which never were and never will be.

It is determined not only by real things and events experienced at first hand, but also by the unreal.[8]

In other words, contrary to Kahneman, Tatarkiewicz argues that what matters to our happiness is not what we actually experience in each moment, but rather what we *remember* ourselves to have experienced, or what we *predict* we will experience. Even when our recollections of past events do not reflect the reality of what happened, they still have an impact on our happiness – it is these memories and imaginings that determine whether we judge our life to be satisfactory as a whole. Luckily, memory is often the ally of happiness, distorting our recollections in the service of our happiness. Tatarkiewicz calls this the "optimistic tendency of memory."

Tatarkiewicz offers several reasons to explain why the present plays a comparatively minor role in our happiness. One is that the present is fleeting. As the ancient Roman Stoic philosopher Seneca writes: "It has passed, even before it has arrived."[9] Though vivid in consciousness, the present moment is paltry when compared to our storehouse of memories and our anticipated future. The impact that the present can have on our happiness must be rather small, as a fleeting momentary episode rarely shifts the momentum of a lifetime. An analogy to an hourglass might help to illustrate his point. Imagine that the sand in the top bulb represents the "future," the sand in the bottom bulb the "past," and the sand passing through the neck the "present." There is almost always far more sand in the past, and hopefully more remaining in the future, than in the present. The present is but a single grain of sand passing quickly, and the weight of the past and future upon our happiness is always heavier. The present moment is but a miniscule fraction of what has yet to come and what has already past.

A second reason the present plays a small role in our happiness is that it often surrenders to the past or future. Anxiety about tomorrow can overshadow the present even when I am engaged in something I typically find enjoyable. For example, thinking about my upcoming surgery tomorrow brings to mind an uncertain future, which might color my present experience so that even when I am engaged in my favorite hobby, I cannot seem to enjoy the activity. Also, the present is often conditioned by the past so that, although we think the enjoyment we currently experience is due wholly to what is taking place before us at the moment, the source of our pleasure or pain really resides in the past. Tatarkiewicz writes: "Even when the object

---

8   Ibid., 8.
9   Quoted in ibid., 3.

of one's emotions belongs to the present, the source of those emotions may lie in the past. A voice or fragrance which delights us today often does so because it conjures up an experience of long ago."[10] For instance, we both grew up in the Midwest. Ever since moving to the Northeast, we have been more or less homesick. This has had an understandable effect: anytime we encounter something that reminds us of the Midwest, we experience positive emotions, so much so that even the smell of cow manure, because of its association with home, is a relatively pleasant experience.

Likewise, the present can be conditioned upon the future: the present can be full of toil and trouble, but it can seem pleasant nonetheless because of the expected future results. This may be illustrated by intellectual work, which is often challenging and arduous in the present, but also satisfying because of the anticipated wisdom it will bring both for the person engaged in it and for others with whom the fruits of the labor are shared. At the same time, Tatarkiewicz is not arguing that the present plays *no* role in our happiness; his point is rather that its importance is far less than commonly assumed.

The past, on the other hand, clearly and without question plays a large role in a person's happiness. It does so in a variety of ways. As mentioned earlier, our memories of our past can be recalled in the present. As we consume the memories of our past, they affect our present satisfactions. Additionally, the events of the past can shape our psychic dispositions, causing us to become trusting or mistrusting, for instance. As an example, imagine a person who has been shaped by her past to be paranoid. For whatever reason, she has been conditioned to interpret every event as a potential threat. What most would interpret as a compliment, she might think of as an attack. Hence, Tatarkiewicz explains, "The contribution of the past to happiness and unhappiness lies not only in the fact that it is the object of satisfaction or dissatisfaction, but also partly in the fact that it is the cause of satisfaction or dissatisfaction with the present."[11]

Still, it is interesting to note that being satisfied with the past is not always required for happiness. That is, a person could experience overall life satisfaction even if he endured a miserable past. In fact, insofar as he has overcome a disagreeable past, he might experience a more intense enjoyment of the present. Often, notes Tatarkiewicz, dissatisfaction with the past intensifies satisfaction with the present as well as with life as a whole. This is a rather common intuition about how we experience happiness. Many

---

10 Ibid., 3.
11 Ibid., 4.

times people say things like "past suffering makes a person value or appreciate the present enjoyments more," or "a rough past makes for a sweeter present." These sayings draw attention to a common psychological phenomenon referred to as a "contrast effect." When presently formulating a judgment about your life, you compare it to your past as a point of contrast. When your past is pleasant, your present satisfaction with life, even when things are going well, will not be as intense as when you have escaped an unpleasant past.

For example, psychologists Amos Tversky and Dale Griffin designed a laboratory experiment to illustrate contrast effects.[12] Subjects were told that they would be making investments in a stock exchange and that their cash payouts would reflect how successful they were in choosing the right investments. In fact, the investments they entered into the computer-simulated stock machine were fake, and their cash payouts actually depended on which pre-selected group they were placed into. The subjects made two rounds of investments. In the first round, one group of subjects won $2 and the other won $6. They were then asked to rate their satisfaction on a ten-point scale. As expected, those who won the bigger prize were more satisfied (8.7 to 6.4). In the second round, however, both groups received a payout of $4 and were asked again to rate their satisfaction. Those who had originally won $6 saw the second lesser payout as a disappointment, and so were less satisfied than before (7.5). However, those who had won $2 in the first round were delighted that their earnings improved, and so their satisfaction increased (7.3). This shows the contrast effect at work: those who earned more in the first round were, by contrast, disappointed with their second-round efforts, and the reverse was true for those who increased their winnings in the second round. These results imply that, through contrast effects, the past has an impact on our present judgments of life satisfaction.

Beyond contrast effects, Tatarkiewicz notes that the effects of the past on our happiness are more certain than the present or future. The present is full of uncertainty, often making it difficult to know whether it will or will not be a happy moment. For instance, recall what it is like to go on a first date. Many people will readily admit that while on the date it is hard to judge how well it is going. This uncertainty makes it possible that at the same time one is experiencing exhilaration, excitement, and enjoyment, one could also be riddled with anxiety, nerves, and embarrassment.

---

12 Tversky and Griffin (1991: 108).

Likewise, the future can be full of fear and anxiety. After the first date has ended and you are at home alone, it is likely that you will now worry about what your future will hold. By contrast, the past does not have these elements of uncertainty and anxiety. We cannot fear what has already happened, and we can know with a relative degree of confidence that what happened was either positive or negative. The effect of the past on our consciousness is more certain and less fickle than the present or the future. Thus happiness is, in large part, determined by our past.

Even so, Tatarkiewicz suggests that the future often carries the *most* weight in our judgments of life satisfaction, and therefore in our happiness. He states:

> The past? An old adage goes: "What was and is no longer, does not enter into account." ... The present? It is, after all, but a moment – and I can endure even the most dreadful moment, provided I know that things will be better soon. Many people feel this way. Consciously or otherwise, they link their happiness exclusively with the future, they measure it up to something which has not yet come, and perhaps never will come.... The past and the present have less significance in this respect than prospects for the future. Possession signifies less than hope.[13]

Many people, whether or not they are aware of it, evaluate how well their life seems to be going according to their prospects for the future. We can endure a painful present and overcome past turmoil provided that the future looks bright. This mirrors Robert Nozick's claim, discussed in Chapter Four, that the narrative direction of life matters, and in particular that we put more weight on happy endings than happy beginnings.

Perhaps Bernie Madoff could serve as a good example of this point. Madoff famously embezzled billions of dollars from thousands of unsuspecting investors over many years as part of a massive Ponzi scheme, committing the largest financial scam in US history.[14] He fraudulently amassed a great fortune, living a highly luxurious lifestyle for many, many years. Now imagine that Madoff has just learned that a warrant has been issued for his arrest and that tomorrow police will raid his home and office, confiscate his personal assets, and arrest him for financial fraud. Yesterday, his

---

13 Tatarkiewicz (1966: 6–7).
14 Yang (2014).

prospects for the future seemed great; now today, they are bleak. At this moment, it is very likely that he is unhappy. And no amount of reminding him how great things have gone until now – how great his past has been – could cheer him up. Moreover, even if he is able to spend his millions on one last hedonic binge before he is dragged off to jail, this would not change the fact that his happiness is ruined. Once Madoff is aware of how dark his future looks, neither reminiscing on a pleasant past nor throwing himself into an overly indulgent present could serve to alter his happiness for the better. In fact, Tatarkiewicz points out that the fear of pain is often more oppressive than the pain itself, and likewise with the anticipation of pleasure, as the actual experience can be a letdown. Hence the expectation of happiness or unhappiness has greater influence on our present judgments of life satisfaction than do the memories of the past or our present experiences, which are but fleeting.

Not Happy? Just Lower Your Standards

Tatarkiewicz argues that what matters to happiness is not so much what actually happened in the past or what will truly happen in the future; instead, what affects our happiness is how we *perceive* our past to have gone and how we *imagine* our future will go. It matters little whether our memory of the past or imagining of the future is distorted and false. In fact, he suggests that the optimistic tendency of memory tends to distort our recollection of the past so as to aid our happiness. If we attend to our past in the right way, we can ensure that we see our lives as improving by contrast. Likewise, if we only recall fond memories, we can feel as though our lives have been blessed. Thus the trick of happiness might merely be setting our sights so that we are always satisfied with how our lives are turning out.

Perhaps one lesson we can take from this is that we can alter our happiness by way of which standard we choose to compare our lives to. For example, winners of Olympic silver medals report being less happy than those who won bronze medals.[15] Presumably this is due to the fact that silver medalists are looking up at the gold medal winners thinking that they were so close to winning it all, whereas bronze medalists look at the field of competitors who did not medal and count themselves fortunate. Therefore, whether we make upward or downward comparisons alters our judgments of satisfaction. We can actually use this information to improve

---

15 Schwarz and Strack (1999: 67).

our happiness: we can decide always to make downward comparisons, only ever comparing ourselves to someone who is worse off than us.

This insight seems incredibly obvious, and yet many of us fail to consider this aspect when judging our lives overall. Historically, it might have been advantageous for our ancestors to make upward comparisons. They could take stock of how they were doing relative to those around them and in what ways their lives needed improvement. However, in contrast to earlier times when our only comparisons were among a very tight-knit community, in today's technological age we are now exposed to a global population of seven billion people. That's a lot of people we can compare ourselves to! Indeed, the mass media mercilessly marches images and stories of celebrities in front of us, which inevitably compels us to compare our lives to those who have much more. Not only that, but with such freedom of mobility, it is much easier for us to travel to any number of places to pursue any number of interests. Thus it also becomes much easier to think that the grass is greener somewhere else. It seems that our evolutionary programming has not kept up with the pace of development in the modern world; it no longer functions properly when we are comparing ourselves to the best of seven billion people, as this raises our expectations to an unrealistic standard: there will always be someone doing better than us. On the other hand, as noted, we can choose instead to compare ourselves with those who are doing worse off, which helps to foster gratitude and therefore satisfaction with what we already have. And we can do this, appreciating what we have, even while seeking to improve ourselves and our situations. It seems that learning the habit of making such downward comparisons would positively aid our happiness.

In a similar vein, Nozick suggests we can vary the benchmarks against which we evaluate our lives. Moving them up or down will help us to maintain our happiness. He writes:

> If there is any "secret of happiness," it resides in regularly choosing some baseline or benchmark or other against which features of the current situation can be evaluated as good or improving. The background it stands out from — hence, the evaluation we actually make — is constituted by our own expectations, levels of aspiration, standards, and demands. And these things are up to us, open to our control.... A person intent upon feeling happy will learn to choose suitable evaluation benchmarks varying them from situation to situation.... Happiness can be served, then, by fiddling with our standards

of evaluation – which ones we invoke and which benchmarks these utilize – and with the direction of our attention – which facts end up getting evaluated.[16]

Whether we choose to see a glass as half-full or half-empty, whether we choose to view a particular situation as a challenge or an opportunity, or whether we construe placing as runner-up at Wimbledon to be an achievement or a disappointment does seem to be a matter over which we have some measure of control. Yet, though Nozick agrees we *can* do this, he isn't so sure we *should*.

While Nozick admits that "no particular benchmark or baseline is written in the world,"[17] he nonetheless does not believe that this allows us to ignore certain crucial or salient aspects of our reality when evaluating our lives. That would be like choosing only to focus on the one smiling person standing in front of an angry mob – there are some features of our situation that we just should not ignore or cannot omit when making judgments. Nozick argues that if we adopted whatever standard best serves our momentary happiness, our evaluations would become arbitrary. Insofar as we think that happiness is a relatively stable and enduring state, it should not be made too easy to come by. He explains:

> Yet just this fact, that happiness depends upon how we look upon things ... may make us wonder how important happiness itself can be, if it is that arbitrary.... [T]o willfully and constantly shift baselines to suit various situations in order to feel happy in each seems flighty and arbitrary too. Perhaps, although the baselines are not fixed by anything external, we expect a person to show a certain congruence or consistency in these, with only smooth and gradual changes over time. Even so, a person could increase his happiness by setting his uniform sights accordingly.[18]

In particular, Nozick has two worries: first, he is concerned that shifting our sights so capriciously leads to inconsistency; second, even if we are consistent, we might well set the bar for happiness so low that it loses its value.

There is nothing immediately worrisome with the idea that happiness is in some important way up to us; instead, the concern arises when our

16 Nozick (1989: 114–15).
17 Ibid., 115.
18 Ibid.

happiness is the result of crudely adopting whatever point of view happens to be required at any given moment. The problem is especially acute when we toggle between inconsistent perspectives in order to maintain our happy disposition. In such cases, though we may be happy, our happiness seems to have lost some of its value. As another analogy, it would be like a student who yesterday deflected a professor's criticism of her paper by claiming that he is incompetent, today accepting that same professor's praise, remarking that he is particularly adroit at recognizing insightful ideas. Though these choices of viewpoint might serve her happiness yesterday and today, they are clearly incompatible. This lack in consistency might make us wonder whether she is undermining her own happiness in the future, setting herself up for future misery. But then again, she need only adopt a different outlook at that time!

Additionally, even maintaining consistent standards of evaluation might not be enough for happiness. After all, it does seem rather disingenuous to maintain a set of standards so low that waking, breathing, eating, and sleeping are all that it takes to have a happy life. We think we should have to work harder for happiness than that, and if not, then happiness seems quite worthless. We cannot significantly evaluate our lives when the standards of evaluation are so minimal.

Daniel Haybron expresses an even stronger concern. Even when we have not set the standards too low, there are still many different perspectives we can adopt in any situation. Further, there seems to be no clear answer as to *which* of our perspectives, if any, is the *authoritative* stance with respect to our life satisfaction. To Haybron, this seems quite troubling, as it suggests that, ultimately, our life satisfaction judgments are to a large extent arbitrary. He provides the following illustration of this worry:

> Whether you are satisfied with your life depends on how you look at it. Consider a woman of sixty-four who, a few months ago, lost her husband of many years. How ought she – from her point of view – to evaluate her life? Should she be satisfied or dissatisfied? She may well find herself vacillating between *both* attitudes: one day she thinks about her life in relation to those she regards as truly unfortunate, counts her blessings (of which she has many), and wholeheartedly considers herself lucky – she is genuinely satisfied with her life, and takes pleasure in her good fortune. But the next day she thinks more of her loss and the gaping hole in her life, and finds herself envying her married friends and wondering how she can go on. She is, at such

times, deeply dissatisfied, indeed bitterly angry. And when she steps back to reflect on these oscillations, she can't honestly say that either judgment is closer to the truth – both are perfectly sensible responses to her life, and both represent *her* outlook, her priorities. The problem is not that she is emotionally volatile. It is, rather, that she can think about her life from more than one perspective, none of which is pre-eminently authentic or authoritative.[19]

Haybron concludes that whether or not we are satisfied with our life fundamentally depends on which perspective we decide to choose, which is arbitrary, making whether or not we are satisfied equally arbitrary. Therefore, how satisfied we are with our life is simply a matter of how we choose to look at it; and, we can choose many different ways of looking at our life.

Even more, according to Haybron, each of these life satisfaction judgments could be reasonable and even authentic, yet there is still no decisive way to choose among them. In his words, "life satisfaction judgments are substantially *arbitrary*, in the sense that we can *reasonably* and *authentically* assess our lives in a wide range of ways, with no grounds – at least, no decisive grounds – for choosing among them."[20] For instance, we could choose to adopt a perspective of gratitude, where we compare ourselves to those less fortunate and focus on how great it is to have the lives we do. On the other hand, we could adopt a more Stoic perspective, according to which we compare ourselves to those we most admire, wondering whether we are making the best of our lives. Both perspectives could be equally reasonable and authentic, yet which perspective we adopt will radically alter how we evaluate our satisfaction with our lives. Further, Haybron admits that our choice of perspective will not *seem* arbitrary to us, since we typically adopt perspectives naturally and without much thought. Even so, he argues, these judgments are arbitrary nonetheless.

On the basis of these considerations, Haybron argues that life satisfaction judgments cannot play the practical role that is required of a theory of happiness: "Indeed, there is a voluntariness to life satisfaction that makes it hard to see how it could be a major life goal, as most take happiness to be: it's too easy to come by."[21] Without doubt, both Haybron and Nozick illustrate the fundamental insight that happiness just does not seem to be the sort of thing

---

19 Haybron (2005: 294).
20 Ibid.; emphasis added.
21 Ibid., 296.

that we can so easily manipulate. We ought, therefore, to seriously question the role of life satisfaction judgments in an account of happiness.

Additionally, psychologists have undertaken numerous studies that seem to confirm Nozick's and Haybron's worry over the fickle nature of life satisfaction judgments. These studies suggest that there might be even greater cause for concern. It is not just that we can adopt multiple, though equally authoritative, perspectives from which to issue judgments of life satisfaction. Instead, there is reason to doubt that *any* life satisfaction judgment is *ever* authoritative.

Mistakes Come Easy:
The Contextual, Arbitrary, and Fickle Nature of Life Satisfaction

Contemporary psychologists have collected empirical data about the sorts of circumstances that are correlated with our life satisfaction. Much of the information is gathered from people's self-reported answers to survey questions. Hundreds of thousands of survey respondents have been asked questions such as "Taking all things together, how satisfied are you with *your life as a whole* these days? Are you very satisfied, satisfied, not very satisfied, not at all satisfied?"[22] Or, alternatively, subjects are asked to indicate their agreement with the statement "I am satisfied with my life," by marking a number one through seven (where a rating of seven indicates strong agreement, one is strong disagreement, and four is a neutral rating).

The use of these measures is based on a few assumptions. The first is that people can integrate the whole of their life – all of the many different facets of their experience – into a single general judgment about overall life satisfaction. Second, it is assumed that people report their levels of life satisfaction sincerely and accurately. And third, when a researcher asks a subject a question about whole life satisfaction, the reported answer is assumed to reflect something of importance, namely, the mental state of *being satisfied with life as a whole*. These assumptions, however, have been met with increasing skepticism by both philosophers and psychologists.

Ideally, when people are asked how satisfied they are with their life overall, we would hope they would utilize a wide variety of information about their life and then integrate that into some sort of representation of their life as a whole. Yet psychologists Norbert Schwarz and Fritz Strack have extensively surveyed the scientific findings on life satisfaction and have found that

---

22 Kahneman and Krueger (2006: 7); emphasis in original.

this is not typically the way people actually answer the question.[23] Instead, they search the contents of their mind until they think they have enough information to make a judgment. This means, then, that one's judgment is going to rest on what is most accessible to one's mind at the time the question is asked. Presumably, what is accessible to one's mind might change on different days or in different circumstances, so the information one uses to answer the question today may not be the same as it is tomorrow. In fact, much of how a subject responds to a life satisfaction survey question is a function either of that person's judgment process, which is highly context-dependent, or of some feature of the survey instrument itself. Interestingly, what does *not* play much of a role is one's "careful assessment of one's objective conditions in light of one's aspirations."[24]

In order to judge how life as a whole is going "these days," we need to be able to compare how our life was in the past to how it is now. This in turn requires that we supply content to the phrase "these days." This involves specifying a *target* of our judgment: does the phrase refer to this past week, the past couple of months, or one or more years? We also have to formulate a *standard* to which we will compare the target in order to evaluate it positively or negatively. That is, according to what benchmark is our life happy or unhappy? It turns out, as discussed above, that we make our judgment based on what is most accessible and relevant to us at the moment. Also, context determines how this information is used, and whether it is *assimilated* as part of the target or used as a point of *contrast* changes the judgment we make. For example, if I am asked to evaluate whether I am satisfied with my life overall and what comes to mind is a recent negative event, such as losing my dog last month, and if I assimilate that negative event as part of how my life is going now, I am likely to be less satisfied with my life. On the other hand, if that negative event is used as a contrast to how my life is going now, then I may be more satisfied with my life since I judge it to have gone more favorably since losing my dog. As noted earlier, my life satisfaction judgments can also vary depending on who I compare my life to when making the judgment. For instance, if when judging my satisfaction with life I am comparing myself to those who are less well off, perhaps because I just watched a documentary on people in developing countries, then I am more likely to be satisfied with my life than if I compared myself to my neighbor who just put on an addition to his home. In all of these cases, my

---

23 Refer to Schwarz and Strack (1999) for an extended discussion of all of these findings.
24 Ibid., 62.

life remains the same; yet the judgments I might make about whether I am satisfied with my life can differ markedly.

Moreover, judgments of life satisfaction are influenced not only by what we think about ourselves or how we compare ourselves to others, but also by how we *feel* at the time we are asked the question. Finding a dime on a copy machine, spending time in a pleasant rather than an unpleasant room, having one's favorite sports team win rather than lose, enjoying good rather than bad weather – all of these have been shown to increase a subject's report of overall life satisfaction. Schwarz and Strack offer two possible explanations for this. First, it might be that when we are in a particularly good (or bad) mood and we are asked about our entire life, we tend to recall *mood congruent* events. That is, when in a good mood, we recollect mostly fond memories of our past and report greater satisfaction. Contrarily, when in a foul mood, we call to mind negative past events and report lower satisfaction.[25] On the other hand, another more direct explanation is that we might just assume that our current mood is as good an indicator as any for how our life is going overall. Thinking that our present mood is all we need to appraise our life as a whole, we then neglect to search our memories for further information about our life, ignoring potential evidence that might be relevant to our appraisal. Indeed, when respondents are asked why they answered a life satisfaction question as they did, current mood is the leading answer.[26] If this is accurate, then it seems that psychologists are mostly generating data about how people feel in the moment, and not about how life is going overall.

Yet how one feels in the moment is not supposed to be the same as life satisfaction. Although the question is asked a different way, and although life satisfaction is supposed to be something different from hedonic mental states, perhaps, in the end, life satisfaction surveys just measure the same thing as hedonic surveys. Interestingly, due to these concerns, many researchers, including Kahneman, have instead returned to Bentham's notion of happiness as the balance of pleasure over pain.[27] Additionally, many are careful to utilize the Experience Sampling Method, since it appears to be a more reliable measure of experienced pleasure and pain.

If there were such a mental state as "being satisfied with life as a whole," we would expect that respondents would be able to access it and report it

---

25 Ibid., 74–76.
26 Ibid., 75.
27 Ibid., 80.

relatively easily. Additionally, we would expect that the answers would display a certain degree of stability and also reflect non-trivial aspects of life. Finally, we would expect that the same life events would influence judgments of life satisfaction in predictable and consistent ways. It turns out, however, that global judgments of life satisfaction are so arbitrary that they yield little useful information about what sorts of things contribute to a person's happiness. This, then, makes us question whether our judgments of life satisfaction are based on anything stable or objective; perhaps, instead, they are simply arbitrary, fickle, and fleeting in nature.

Of course, that we are unreliable judges of our life satisfaction does not necessarily refute whole life satisfactionism as a theory of the nature of happiness. At best, it casts doubt on our ability to put the theory into practice in our daily lives – our ability to effectively pursue happiness. For if we are frequently wrong in judging our own life satisfaction, is this really the best guide for planning our lives? If our judgments of life satisfaction are arbitrary, this undermines their practical value for us. Reports of life satisfaction are so fraught with context-sensitive influences that it might not be prudent to plan a life according to them. These judgments might even be useless to us as a guide to personal happiness, or still worse, they might hinder our pursuit of happiness if they lead us to take on projects that undermine our future satisfactions. Certainly, as mentioned previously with respect to hedonism, if a theory has substantial barriers to its practical application, this should be a cause for concern, especially when the subject matter in question is our own happiness, which has tremendous value to us. Even more so, however, some philosophers question whether we are even *capable* of making life satisfaction judgments. In other words, apart from the question of whether we are able to *reliably* make a life satisfaction judgment, there might be compelling reasons for thinking that we *do not* and even *cannot* make such a judgment in the first place.

Do We – or Can We – Even Make Life Satisfaction Judgments?

Recall that to evaluate whether we are satisfied with our life overall, we are asked to formulate a global judgment by considering all the domains of our life we consider important, integrating these many distinct elements into a single unified judgment of our life in total. Philosopher Martha Nussbaum questions whether we really experience our life in such an integrated and singular way. She explains:

People are simply told that they are to aggregate experiences of many different kinds into a single whole, and the authority of the questioner is put behind that aggregation. There is no opportunity for them to answer something plausible, such as "Well, my health is good, and my work is going well, but I am very upset about the state of the economy, and one of my friends is very ill." Not only is that opportunity not provided, but, in addition, the prestige of science – indeed of the Nobel Prize itself – is put behind the instruction to reckon all life-elements up as a single whole. The fact that people answer such questions hardly shows that this is the way that they experience their lives.[28]

Nussbaum contends that we rarely experience our lives in this way, only infrequently – if ever – finding ourselves in a state of being satisfied with life as whole. Moreover, it would be difficult to put ourselves in such a state, for two reasons: first, it is unclear how we are to interpret "being satisfied," so what we are actually being asked to evaluate is ambiguous; and second, it is unclear how we are actually supposed to go about evaluating being satisfied with our life overall by way of the many different facets of our lives. This, then, draws out three distinct concerns with respect to survey instruments that ask subjects for their evaluation of their lives as wholes. First, subjects rarely if ever are in such a state; this is sometimes called the problem of "attitude scarcity." Second, how one understands "being satisfied" is open to interpretation. Third, it is very difficult, if not impossible, to figure out how to answer this question on the basis of many seemingly different and sometimes unrelated elements of our lives.

First, with respect to the problem of attitude scarcity, Haybron points out that we do not typically find ourselves in the mental state of satisfaction *or* dissatisfaction with our lives. While we may have an attitude of being satisfied with life when we are in a particularly reflective or philosophical mood, we are certainly not in this sort of state very often. He makes clear the problem this poses for trying to understand happiness according to life satisfaction:

This is a problem because happiness is supposed, like pleasure, to be a dimension along which human well-being varies: each of us is somewhere on the scale between extreme happiness and unhappiness, and

---

28 Nussbaum (2012: 339).

each of us could be more or less happy or unhappy than we presently are. Other things being equal, we try to make choices in life that will leave us happier, while avoiding options that will make us less happy. This is important: if it turns out that we usually aren't *anywhere* on the scale, because the relevant mental states aren't defined most of the time, then few choices will have any effect on our happiness. And any effects will be as fleeting as the attitudes themselves. Why, then, concern ourselves so much with happiness?[29]

Haybron thus draws our attention to the fact that for much of our life we do not have any attitude of satisfaction with our life, but at the same time we typically consider ourselves happy or unhappy to some degree at any given moment. So if we think that at any given moment we are more or less happy – if we believe that we are always some place on the happiness scale – then it seems as though being satisfied with life as a whole is not the same as being happy. Thus, to make the attitude of life satisfaction central to our view of happiness seems to have the unfortunate consequence of implying that most of us are not happy most of the time.[30]

Second, Nussbaum notes that even if we put aside this serious issue, there are still considerable ambiguities about what is being asked when we are questioned about life satisfaction. After all, a subject asked about her satisfaction with life might interpret what she is being asked in any number of ways. She might think of satisfaction as a feeling closely akin to pleasure, as when we say that the meal we just ate was really satisfying. Perhaps she understands the question over satisfaction to be asking whether she is content. To be satisfied in this sense is less like pleasure and more like an attitude of liking something, such as when we say we are satisfied with our town's current policies. Or perhaps, she understands life satisfaction to be an evaluative judgment that "she has done what she aimed to do." As an example of this, Nussbaum cites Mill's last words: "You know that I have done my work." Nussbaum then remarks:

> I would say that this is in one way an answer to the overall-satisfaction question: Mill is reporting, we might say, satisfaction with his life as a whole. He has done what he aimed to do. And yet it seems highly unlikely that Mill, on his deathbed, suffering from physical pain and from the fear of death that he acknowledges not being able to get rid

---

29 Haybron (2005: 292).
30 Feldman (2010) expresses a similar worry.

of, is experiencing *feelings of satisfaction or pleasure*.... While judging that his life has been on balance successful, he is almost certainly not experiencing any feelings of satisfaction or pleasure.[31]

There seem, therefore, to be many possible interpretations a subject can use when answering the question of whether she is satisfied with her life overall. So which interpretation of satisfaction does the psychologist intend? If one subject can answer according to one interpretation, and another according to a different interpretation, can we really trust that the data collected by psychological studies accurately reflect similar states in similar people? It seems as though psychological studies that rely on measures of life satisfaction are highly suspicious.

Third, how are we supposed to come up with a single number on a scale that reflects our satisfaction with our life as a whole? Philosopher Julia Annas uses an example to demonstrate this worry:

[There is] a survey that asks people to measure the happiness of their lives by assigning it a face from a spectrum with a very smiley face at one end and a very frowny face at the other. Suppose that you have just won the Nobel Prize; this surely merits the smiliest face. But suppose also that you have just lost your family in a car crash; this surely warrants the frowniest face. So, how happy are you? There is no coherent answer – unless you are supposed to combine these points by picking the indifferent face in the middle![32]

This situation reveals the absurdity of this kind of question. Yet many of our lives seem this way. There are areas of our life that we may be quite satisfied with, while there are others that could use improvement, and still others with which we are deeply unsatisfied. To think that we can simply assign numbers to each of these elements, and then average them together in order to come up with a single number that represents our satisfaction with our life *in total* seems like a ridiculous proposition. And if this is not what we are expected to do, then how do we arrive at this number? In the absence of any clear criteria, we typically answer this question on the basis of our current mood. But as we know from our own experience, our current mood is often not an accurate reflection of how our life is going overall.

---

31 Nussbaum (2012: 340).
32 Annas (2004: 45–46).

So is there any way to make these life satisfaction judgments, and to do so reliably? Are there techniques or methods we can adopt to put us into the proper state of mind required for making these judgments, and in a way that actually tracks our satisfaction with our life? If not, we might then question whether there is a better alternative to judgments of life satisfaction that we should use when assessing a person's happiness or when making choices with respect to our well-being. This worry becomes especially prominent when we consider that many people in severely dire circumstances express satisfaction with their lives. For example, many who live in abject poverty, such as those living in the slums of Calcutta, express satisfaction with life to the same degree as do college students.[33] Can we reasonably believe such people are equally happy just because they report being satisfied with life? And, if so, has happiness lost its normative power? That is, if people who are objectively doing so poorly can be happy, how valuable a life goal can it be to achieve happiness?

---

33 Diener and Seligman (2004: 10).

Chapter 7:   **It's All about Perspective**

ON NOVEMBER 18, 1978, 909 people died from an apparent mass suicide in Jonestown, Guyana. They were all members of the Peoples Temple cult who had moved to Guyana in the hopes of creating a progressive social commune free from what they saw as the injustice and inherent exploitation of capitalism. Their leader was Jim Jones, a charismatic speaker who enchanted members of the congregation with his vision of an inevitable social revolution, and who persuaded them to dedicate themselves to whatever he asked of them. Yet, as time passed, Jones became increasingly paranoid about the outside world, even going so far as to order the killing of Californian Congressman Leo Ryan, who had visited Jonestown to investigate the group. Implored by Jones, the members knowingly participated in an act of "revolutionary suicide." Among the dead were men, women, and children of all ages. They died from drinking Fla-Vor-Aid laced with valium and cyanide. The valium was to render them unconscious before the cyanide would kill them. The entire event was recorded and later transcribed by the FBI. Young children were fed the concoction by other members of the congregation, sometimes even by their own parents, having it squirted down their throats using syringes. Despite taking efforts to make the death painless, the cyanide took hold sooner than the valium, and so members watched as those around them convulsed in pain while dying. In spite of this, parents fed the potion to their children and then took it themselves. Clearly, the members of the congregation were subject to

Jones's manipulative control. They had been exploited and misled yet still remained loyal until their deaths.[1]

Is it possible that the members of the Peoples Temple lived happily? Can a person completely cede control over her decision-making to another person, voluntarily subjecting herself to the will of another, and yet be happy? In fact, if we had been able to interview the members of the congregation in order to ask about their satisfaction with life, might they have answered that they were deeply satisfied? Many people claimed that the Peoples Temple gave their lives direction and meaning, involving them in something larger than themselves, putting them in contact with the divine. They appeared joyous and vibrant, experiencing a real sense of community. All of this suggests that it is reasonable to conclude that many of them were satisfied with their lives. If so, what should we make of this?

If you are inclined to think that the cult members were not happy, why not? Perhaps the fact that we would deny that those under Jones's sway were happy, despite their claims to be satisfied with life, is because we deny that life satisfaction is identical with happiness. In other words, we could maintain that the people were satisfied with their lives, but that happiness is about something other than life satisfaction. Insofar as it is possible for someone to be satisfied with life even under such circumstances, this shows that happiness cannot mean the same thing as satisfaction. Judgments of life satisfaction do not capture our normative concerns to the degree required by a theory of happiness.

On the other hand, you might think that because they sincerely expressed satisfaction with their lives, we have to call them happy. But then in what sense is happiness *good* for us? After all, the fact that such people were happy despite knowing that they might well be asked to kill themselves suggests that their lives could have gone much better for them. Their well-being was not served by their satisfactions. In such cases, therefore, happiness does not seem all that valuable or important to a good life. For if people can be happy even when they are not in control of their life, and even when they accept orders to march to their own death, in what sense can happiness be an ideal at which we should aim?

Then again, we might be able to salvage the idea that life satisfaction and happiness are the same if we can dismiss the cult members' first-hand

---

[1] All of the information for the description of these events is paraphrased from the PBS summary of *Jonestown: The Life and Death of Peoples Temple* (http://www.pbs.org/wgbh/american-experience/features/general-article/jonestown-nov-18-1978/).

reports of satisfaction as somehow flawed. We might think that because they were brainwashed or they simply "hopped on the bandwagon" without much thought, their judgments of life satisfaction are not good evidence for answering the question of whether they were happy. Life satisfaction judgments made under conditions of delusion are faulty and untrustworthy, and so we should not trust the self-reports of the cult members. When they claim to be satisfied, maybe we should discount their claim as uninformed, biased, manipulated, or otherwise unreliable. Given their indoctrination and relinquishment of autonomy, they could not make sound judgments about their happiness. But, perhaps, if the cult members had been more informed and had more carefully considered their choices, they might have seen more clearly how deeply *unsatisfied* they were with their lives and, as a result, just how *unhappy* they truly were. Of course, to make good on this claim, we will need to explain under what conditions such judgments would be reliable indicators of happiness. That is, we would need to specify the characteristics of the appropriate perspectives within which the cult members' judgments would be authoritative.

At stake is whether a theory of happiness based on life satisfaction must treat all of a person's judgments about how her life is going as equally authoritative. According to philosophers Valerie Tiberius and Alicia Hall, the answer is no. While some life satisfaction judgments are not suitable evidence on which to assess a person's happiness, reflective judgments that are based in justified values *are* authoritative. Furthermore, introducing criteria of justification for our choice of values, and the judgments of life satisfaction based on them, preserves a connection between our evaluations of our lives and how our lives are *actually* going for us. In this way, Tiberius and Hall endorse a very tight connection between happiness and well-being, according to which a life is happy and going well for a person if she takes satisfaction in it from a suitably reflective perspective.[2] Tiberius and Hall thus defend a revised version of a whole life satisfaction theory of happiness

---

2 In her own work, as well as in her co-authored work, Tiberius tends to favor a focus on the concept of well-being. She leaves the relationship between happiness and well-being a bit vague, sometimes speaking as if they are the same, and at other times suggesting that happiness is but one part of well-being. However, everything she says about well-being could be interpreted as applying to happiness, especially since she understands a life that goes well to be one with which a person is satisfied, provided that satisfaction is suitably justified. Insofar as one takes the happy life and the good life to refer to the same thing, a possibility we have taken seriously throughout the book, Tiberius can be seen as advancing a theory of happiness. So throughout this chapter we will use "happiness" and "well-being" interchangeably, as we do not believe that anything Tiberius and Hall argue hinges on this terminological point.

and well-being, one that is sensitive to the issues of delusion or poorly chosen values brought to the fore by cases of cult membership.

Putting Things in Perspective

The judgments we make about life, according to Tiberius, depend on the particular *perspective* that we adopt. While we can adopt multiple differing perspectives on our situation, they are not equally fitting. Indeed, we realize from our own experience that we can evaluate our lives from many different perspectives. On the one hand, we often get caught up by stress from our work, or from long commutes, or from having to stop by the store on the way home to run yet another errand; when in such a mindset, it seems that our lives are not as we want them to be. Yet, in our more reflective moods, we notice that such travails are trivial compared to what so many others have had to face in life. We may, after all, be healthy, with loving families. From this perspective, our lives seem to be incredibly successful. Yet this leads to the question of which perspective is best. There seems to be no way to tell just by looking at any single life satisfaction judgment in isolation from the others whether it more accurately represents our happiness. Or, even worse, we might not think that any of our life satisfaction judgments obviously stands out as authoritative over any other.

So we need some reliable way of assessing our current life conditions. Otherwise, how could we possibly make any meaningful choices about how to live our lives? Our happiness and well-being have tremendous significance to us; each of us is very much interested in living well, and we wish the same for others. Judgments of life satisfaction play a crucial role in our well-being, since they aid us in our practical reasoning about how to live our lives. In fact, according to Tiberius, we need to make such overall assessments of our lives in order to gauge how well we are currently doing and, based on this, to make decisions and plans for our future. Hence, we do not want to rely on faulty judgments of how life is going for fear that we will make critical errors in deciding what we need to do to improve our situations.

If well-being and happiness are to be attainable, then we need to know when we are moving closer toward or farther away from them through the choices we make and the actions we take. So Tiberius argues that we need a stable basis of comparison in order to know whether any change will increase or decrease our well-being. But whether a particular choice of plans improves or diminishes my happiness will depend on which judgment of life satisfaction I use as a point of comparison. In the example above, if I use the judgment I make of my life at the point when I am stressed from my work and its long commute, then I might make the choice to quit my job before having any other means of employment or income readily available. But then I might fail to see how that choice will affect my ability to provide for my family or take vacations that I find so enjoyable. In my more reflective moments, I might judge that I am quite satisfied after realizing that my job isn't all that bad, and therefore worth keeping on account of everything else that it affords me. So, given that we can make very different judgments about the exact same life, which judgment are we supposed to pay attention to, if any? Is there any way to sort among the judgments we make to determine which one we should use when assessing whether our lives are going well?

Presumably, the best perspective will be one within which judgments of life satisfaction are reliable and so will lead to happiness more dependably than if we were instead to use judgments made from arbitrary, inconsistent, or flighty perspectives. To make the point a bit clearer, and as an argument from analogy for why we should consider perspective, Tiberius writes, "Just as we might discount visual perceptions that occur when the perceiver is wearing dark glasses or taking hallucinogens, so too we might discount a person's judgments of overall life-satisfaction when she does not occupy the proper perspective."[3] This is a fascinating analogy. After all, if we were to plan our life on mistaken visual perceptions, or if we were to trust eyewitness testimony based on false perceptions, things would not go so well for us or for others. So we specify that there are certain conditions under which we should trust (and certain conditions under which we should *not* trust) our visual impressions. Perhaps we can do the same for life satisfaction judgments: specify certain conditions under which these judgments are trustworthy, and others under which they are not. This is one project Tiberius takes on: defining the appropriate conditions under which we should be evaluating how our lives are going.

Extending the analogy with vision, the best perspective from which visual impressions are trustworthy would be that of good lighting, well-functioning eyes, and a lack of intoxicants, for example. These are constraints that we place on all visual perceptions, even though what we see is completely subjective to each. In other words, it is possible to evaluate subjective states of vision as being more or less appropriate according to

---

3   Tiberius (2003: 9).

specific criteria. Tiberius argues that this likewise holds true in the case of subjective judgments of life satisfaction. If there are no constraints, then we are back to where we started: worrying about whether our life satisfaction judgments reflect anything of importance. So what are the particular constraints we should place on our perspective so as to make judgments of life satisfaction reliable and authoritative? And how would these constraints answer to the normative worries surrounding apparent cases of satisfied cult members?

Value-Based Life Satisfaction

As mentioned already, the appropriate point of view from which to make judgments of life satisfaction will be a *reflective* perspective, one in which a person is aware of her values and has access to the information relevant to making an informed judgment about how life is going. Because of the focus on values inherent in their approach, Tiberius and Hall call it *value-based life satisfaction*. On this view, judgments of life satisfaction make use of values, which are understood broadly to include "activities, relationships, goals, aims, ideals, principles, and so on."[4] Whatever our values are, they provide the standards we use when we evaluate our lives as wholes. The more of our values our life incorporates, the better off we are. Values also provide good reasons for doing things, because they summarize what we care about. They are thus normative and action-guiding. Judgments of life satisfaction also exemplify the priority ranking of these values; after all, some values are more important to us than others.

Indeed, how we rank or prioritize our values is deeply important, since this gives direction to our lives. To this end, we want to choose our values wisely. Hence, Tiberius and Hall suggest at least two standards, which when applied to our choice of values help to ensure that they will be prudentially valuable: *information* and *affective fitness*. Information is important since "values that are sustained by false beliefs are unlikely to be stable" and are "unlikely to produce a positive emotional response over the long term."[5] Likewise, if our values are not suitably sensitive to our affective nature, then living according to them will end in frustration. Values that adhere to the standards of information and affective fitness are justified values, and judgments of life satisfaction based on them are reliable indicators of one's well-being.

---

4   Tiberius and Hall (2010: 218).
5   Ibid.

Ensuring that our values are informed is important, because we do not want to act based on values that are sourced in false or misleading information. Many people frequently act on uninformed values: they think that having the latest tech gadget will make them happy, when the truth is they will adapt quickly to the purchase; they think that becoming famous would be great, but forget about all of the loss of privacy that comes along with such fame; or they think that their health will be greatly enhanced by the latest juice cleanse or dietary supplement, even though many of the claims made by such products are not verifiable, and some are positively harmful to our health. Living according to uninformed values, as we can see, is a dangerous enterprise for our well-being (and in many cases, that of others).

As important as the standard of information is in producing justified values, it is equally important that our values fit the type of person we are. If a plan for life fails to appropriately fit the person who has it, then it will likely not lead to her well-being. That is, values may require talents, character traits, or feelings that she just does not have. There are many examples of this. Consider the tone-deaf *American Idol* contestant who is sincerely dismayed when the judges do not appreciate her talent; the man setting out to become a Catholic priest who cannot bring himself to believe in God; the wannabe doctor who faints at the sight of blood; or the woman who desires most to be a professor but who suffers from a fear of public speaking. Or as another example, consider the life of Kurt Cobain, lead singer of Nirvana. Cobain pursued his goal of becoming a rock star; tragically, however, once he achieved success, he was made miserable by it. His chosen values ended up being very ill-suited to his temperament. In the end, he committed suicide. It seems clear, then, that having values that meet the standard of affective fitness is important to living well.

In addition to these standards, we also care about how we use the information provided by our values and their relative weights. We want to make sure that our values are justified, and we care about information relevant to our ability to successfully pursue our values. For instance, many of us likely adhere (usually unconsciously) to principles or norms such as these: pay attention to what has the most importance to us; place importance on our future; pursue values that are reasonably attainable, are not incompatible, and that can be successfully pursued together; become informed about the relevant features of our values, etc. Furthermore, we tend to think that our core values ought to be maintained against peripheral values, and that we ought to spend more of our energy and resources in securing our most important commitments.

Notice, then, that there are certain standards present in a reflective perspective. In order to be justified, our judgments of life satisfaction must be based on our values, and where we fail to act according to our values, or where our values are uninformed or ill-suited to our nature, our life satisfaction judgments are apt to be faulty. Even so, the reflective perspective remains *subjective* to each person. That is, even though there are some important constraints that apply to a person's perspective when judging life satisfaction, each person's perspective will still be unique. What makes a person's life happy will vary from person to person since we do not all share the same values, especially in terms of their importance to us. The judgment as to whether a person is satisfied with his life is still made according to the values determined and accepted by him.

Moreover, the subjective nature of each person's perspective highlights its normative authority. Tiberius writes, "If theories of well-being are to be action-guiding for individuals interested in improving their lives, such theories need to connect their recommendations to things that people already take to give them reasons to act. If this were not the case, people would not take the theories as giving them advice that they had any reason to follow."[6] We want to be happy, and we care about this end. To that extent, we will be motivated by a theory only if it captures something that we care about. Otherwise, if we do not have reason to care about the values or aims that a theory endorses, what motivation do we have to adopt its imperatives? According to Tiberius and Hall, because value-based life satisfactionism is a theory that places *my* values and norms as central to happiness, then I have every reason to care about adopting it, since it represents my existing commitments – it recommends acting according to what I most deeply care about. Of course, it also recommends that I do so from a sincere and reflective perspective so that I actually make a plan for life that represents things I genuinely find important.

Value-based life satisfactionism thus has the upper hand on theories that recommend the adoption of objective standards. Values that are not already endorsed by us, but that are nonetheless imposed on us from without, will not motivate our choices. Furthermore, it would be odd for us to judge our lives according to values that we neither accept nor pursue. A person could be told to evaluate her life according to a set of objective values and even see rationally that she should be satisfied with her life, but unless she internalized these values she would be less likely to have a positive affective

---

6   Tiberius (2003: 10).

response to that judgment. For instance, if I do not value friendships but prefer solitude, quiet reflection, and my own company, then I will not be motivated to act according to the advice that one seek out activities that will bring the companionship of others. Nor will I be willing to appraise my life according to any standard of friendship; rather, I will judge my life according to whether I have had sufficient time to reflect on weighty matters.

If we apply this newly formulated value-based life satisfaction theory of happiness to a couple of examples, it will help to reveal the strengths of thinking of happiness in this way. First, there is a large body of evidence to suggest that having materialistic values leads to discontentment.[7] So if a person values avoiding discontentment, this information might help him to place a more suitable weight on the pursuit of material wealth relative to his overall system of value (provided that he values avoiding discontentment more than he values material goods). As another example, when in the throes of a new romantic relationship, people often neglect other relationships to family and friends and so sacrifice some of the things they care most about. The reflective perspective, however, helps us to overcome these forms of blindness and bias and to make more stable and reliable judgments about how to live. When we make judgments from within this perspective, we more accurately assess the importance and impact of different things on our happiness and hence can plan better for our lives.

Now that we have more carefully spelled out the conditions for authoritative life satisfaction judgments, it seems that cult members do not occupy an appropriate perspective from which to evaluate and plan their lives. The values according to which they are making life satisfaction judgments are not their own, but rather those of the cult leader. It is thus highly improbable that they are going to be affectively appropriate. After all, most cult leaders are highly idiosyncratic in their dispositions, so the values that fit their nature are also apt to be odd and unlikely to fit with other more common personalities. Second, it seems hard to believe that one could choose to join such a group in an informed way. Hence, cult members might well fail to meet the standard of information. For example, how aware were the members of the Peoples Temple that they might have to painfully poison their children as a price of membership in the group? More generally, members of many cults are enticed to join by the promise of some utopian future; but what is the likelihood of that coming to pass?

---

7   Diener and Biswas-Diener (2008: 101–05); Csikszentmihalyi (1999).

In summary, there is much appeal in the value-based life satisfaction theory of happiness. We realize it is difficult to evaluate our life as a whole without attending to those things we value. Adopting a more reflective perspective is likely to contribute more to our happiness because it provides us with the means to attend to the things we care about most sincerely. Value-based life satisfactionism is thus action-guiding and reason-giving; it also ensures that our values are justified: well-informed and affectively appropriate. On the basis of these justified values we can then tailor our choices to more fully promote our happiness and well-being. Value-based life satisfaction, therefore, addresses the concerns of philosophers and psychologists who criticize the allegedly arbitrary nature of life satisfaction judgments. While not all life satisfaction judgments are relevant to happiness, some are, and these are central to the planning of our lives – they order our current and future choices with respect to what will make us happy.

Before evaluating our satisfaction with our life, therefore, we should get into the appropriate mindset or perspective by thinking carefully about the important values in our lives. Even this is something many of us fail to do. Only after considering how the various aspects of our life shape our life as a whole are we adequately prepared to answer the question of whether we are satisfied with how our life is going overall. While we may not be satisfied with our work or our commute, as long as we are satisfied with respect to our relationships with our friends and family and our spirituality in our lives, for example, we might be willing to judge that our life is going well by and large. Provided that we make this judgment from justified values, we can trust that it reliably reflects our state of well-being and so can use it to help plan where to go from here. Finally, if we have previously adopted a reflective perspective, it is more likely that these core values and commitments will occupy some of our attention at a later point when we might not have the time to be suitably reflective, such as in the case of reacting to frequent and ongoing daily events.

Philosopher John Kekes further develops this idea of a reflective perspective. On his view, we must determine what sort of life we want and construct a plan for achieving it. This will involve ordering our various wants and commitments. Happiness then consists in having our most important wants and commitments satisfied. The idea is that while reflecting on our wants and commitments, we would also be wise to think carefully about our life's plan in general. We will want to deliberate about what is most important to us (career or family, for instance) and we will want to be sure that we are living in a way that puts us on a path for success as defined by our reflective values. Far too often, we wander through years of our life without a clear direction concerning how to improve ourselves and our circumstances. Yet if we take the time to reflect and plan carefully, we can ensure that we are doing what we can to improve the trajectory of our life.

Figuring Out What We Want

Like Tatarkiewicz, Tiberius, and Hall, Kekes agrees that happiness amounts to being satisfied with life as a whole. Moreover, again like Tiberius and Hall, Kekes believes that in order to appraise our life we must have some bench-mark or standard in mind against which we evaluate it in order to determine our level of life satisfaction. This implies that in order to formulate a judgment of life satisfaction, we need to have at least a rough idea of what it means for our life to be going according to plan. Otherwise our judgments of life satisfaction would not be tied to anything in particular and hence could be random, aimless, and erratic. Making such errant judgments of life satisfaction does not typically serve our interests in being happy and living well, and so we need to lay down some sort of strategy for living. Notice also, then, that Kekes, like Tiberius and Hall, thinks of happiness as something deeply connected to our well-being. Hence, what he has to say about living happily is also intended as advice for how to live a good life.

To be satisfied with life as a whole, a person must carefully survey her desires and evaluate which are most important to her. Once her desires have been ranked in such a way according to their priority, they become the standard for judging whether her life is going well or not. For Kekes, then, happiness amounts to the satisfaction of a very particular desire: a second-order want that my important first-order wants are satisfied. As a reminder, recall that first-order wants include things like wanting a promotion at work, wanting that attractive acquaintance to notice you, or wanting a bacon bleu cheeseburger for lunch. They are ordinary wants for specific things. Kekes suggests that happiness is not about satisfying as *many* of these first-order desires as we can; instead, happiness is about satisfying our important desires – it is about constructing the sort of life that we want. Thus happiness consists in the satisfaction of a second-order want (a want about our wants) that our important first-order wants be satisfied.

Each of us has a different collection of wants, and figuring out what our important wants are depends on knowing what we want to make of our lives. This forms the basis of our "life plan" – it determines the ranking of our wants in terms of importance. Those that are most important are the sorts of wants that we would not be happy without having satisfied, whereas those that are peripheral are wants that we could forgo satisfying and still be happy, provided our more important wants are met. Kekes continues:

> If a seeker of haphazard satisfactions can truly claim to have enjoyed a great many of them, he still cannot be said to have a happy life. For his satisfactions may be of unimportant wants or of only a few of his important wants. It is just a fact that one must choose between satisfactions. The more direction one has given to his life, the more intelligent choice is likely to contribute to his overall happiness, and the less direction there is, the smaller is the chance of achieving a happy life.[8]

Giving direction to our life requires that we consider and evaluate our values and goals, ranking them in terms of importance. According to Kekes, it is extremely unlikely that one could have a happy life without doing this. Given that not all of our wants can be satisfied, and that our short-term and long-term interests often conflict, we need to make deliberate and calculated choices about which of our first-order wants we should set out to satisfy. The only way we can do this is to formulate a strategy that reflects the relative weight and importance of each of our first-order wants to our happiness.

That we should carefully deliberate about the direction of our life suggests that happiness concerns not only the satisfaction of our desires, but also the possession of appropriate desires. That is, we want to make sure that we are pursuing only those desires that contribute to our lives being what we want them to be:

> So a reasonable man seeking happiness will ask himself two questions about satisfying any of his important first-order wants: how should I go about satisfying it? and should I want to have the kind of life in which this kind of want, rather than another, is regarded as important? The pursuit of happiness, therefore, is not just the pursuit of first-order satisfactions, but also the construction of one's life.[9]

Essentially, we need a deliberate life plan that is the product of our will. This plan is exactly what settles the question of whether any given want is important or peripheral to our overall life satisfaction, and so it is by

---

8   Kekes (1982: 361).

9   Ibid., 364.

reference to this plan that we determine which wants we should focus our energies on satisfying and pursuing at the expense of the others. The plan also reflects the sort of life we take to be valuable, since to construct it we need to consider whether a life that takes these wants as central is better or worse than a life that counts others as important. This is yet another reason for thinking that cult members, despite protestations to the contrary, are not truly happy. After all, when they are deciding to join a cult, Kekes says they should ask themselves whether the cult life, rather than some other, is really the sort of life they *should* want. The clear answer should be no. After all, to choose such a life is to willingly hand over your will to the dominion of another. In so doing, we estrange ourselves from our own lives; we abnegate our responsibility for shaping our lives according to our own identity. In fact, in giving ourselves completely over to another we lose our sense of identity. According to Kekes, we cannot, therefore, be happy.

Being Committed

Kekes states that when we have decided (or discovered) where a particular want figures into our system of wants, we have made a *commitment*. Commitments function as standards by which wants are judged. There are three types of commitment: unconditional, defeasible, and loose. The more important the want is to a person being or becoming the type of person he would like to be, the higher it will be on the list.

"Unconditional commitments" are, as the name suggests, the most central commitments to our lives. They are so central to our happiness that they will not be sacrificed for other commitments. When an unconditional commitment is dishonored, it comes at great psychological cost:

> There is a crisis, we do something, and we realize that we cannot come to terms with what we did. The man we have considered ourselves being would not have done that. We did it, so we are not the man we took ourselves to be. The result is that an abyss opens up at the centre of our being.... There are many examples of what happens when unconditional commitments are violated.... [One] is the tragedy of many survivors of concentration camps who suspect that they survived, at the expense of others who did not, because they accommodated themselves to unspeakable evils which the dead, their betters, rejected.[10]

---

10 Ibid., 365.

According to Kekes, unconditional commitments are reflective of our identity in the sense that they represent the type of person we take ourselves to be, or the type of person we are aspiring to become. To violate an unconditional commitment would be to act against our own sense of self – it is, therefore, a profoundly alienating experience. To act against our unconditional commitments betrays a lack of integrity. Indeed, Kekes suggests that no reason could override our unconditional commitments, since they are already the most weighty reasons for our actions.

As an example of how deeply unconditional commitments run, Kekes offers the life of Sir Thomas More. More was a lawyer, philosopher, statesman, and, most notably, a close advisor of King Henry VIII. According to Kekes, More was executed for not being willing to falsely swear an oath. In particular, he would not swear the Oath of Supremacy, which sought to establish King Henry as the head of the Catholic Church in England. More, a devout Catholic, refused. His unconditional commitment to his faith meant that he was tried and beheaded for treason. More's famous last words from the scaffold were, "I die the King's good servant, but God's first." Not even to save his own life or to care for his family, whom he left alone, would More violate his commitment to a certain kind of moral piety, and this is precisely what made More the man that he was. Others might well have decided to falsely swear the oath, but that is the whole point: "that decision could only have been made by another man…. More, however, was what he was, because he placed his commitment to God above his commitment to his family."[11]

Of course, sometimes our unconditional commitments can change, but such a change results in a "drastic alteration of a man's life and view of himself."[12] For example, although More was unconditionally devoted to God for most of his life, it is not unimaginable that witnessing the political charades of kings and popes could have led him to undergo an atheist conversion. In such a case, his unconditional commitment to God would have changed, as he would no longer have been able to devote himself to something he did not believe in. Yet his sense of self and of the world also would have changed; he would not be *that kind of person* anymore. In such circumstances, he might have rethought his commitment to family. But if he had done so, he would not be the Thomas More we know about. He would have been a different man made of different stuff. This implies that

---

11 Ibid., 366.
12 Kekes (1982: 366).

what it means to live a happy life will differ with each individual, as each person has a unique set of prioritized wants. Some of us, for instance, would choose differently than More did. Our choices in life are representative of *our* identities, not his.

"Defeasible commitments," according to Kekes, guide our everyday lives. They include obligations we might have as a matter of our values, social roles, family, career, or other life choices. Defeasible commitments are normally honored, but they can be overridden by other competing defeasible commitments. In cases of conflict, we appeal to our unconditional commitments to determine which defeasible commitment is more essential to our happiness. For example, there are often conflicts between love and self-interest. Love sometimes requires that we sacrifice what is best for us personally, as when a parent continues to financially support an adult child who is unable to secure employment. The story of Robin Hood provides a good example of the conflict between commitments to law and charity. Robin Hood resolved the conflict in the direction of charity: stealing from the rich to give to the poor. Perhaps he did so by appeal to an unconditional commitment to equality.

Finally, "loose commitments" are on the periphery of our lives. If such commitments went unsatisfied, we would not feel as though a central aspect of our lives was missing. Typically, they take the form of being a particular way of meeting a defeasible or unconditional commitment. They might include such things as being on time to appointments, not taking personal calls during working hours, paying bills when they are due, exercising, and taking the dog for a walk.

As an example of the three-tiered structure of commitments and how they work together, consider the example of a man named Alan. He is deeply and unconditionally committed to being charitable. Still, a commitment to charity may take many different forms. Sometimes it means financial support, at others it means volunteer work, and at still others it means being forgiving of moral shortcomings in others. His commitment to being charitable is fundamentally important to his happiness, but the form that his charity takes is of secondary importance. He does not necessarily need to be charitable in a particular way, or in all ways, in order to satisfy his commitment. In Alan's case, one way in which his unconditional commitment to charity manifests itself is in a defeasible commitment to his local Masonic Lodge. This commitment is defeasible because it might be overridden, but also because his commitment to charity can take other forms. His commitment to his local Masonic Lodge also comes with many loose commitments. He obliges himself to making weekly meetings; he may run for office; he pays his dues; and he speaks well of the Freemasons to his friends and acquaintances. That these are the particular forms his fealty to the Lodge takes is quite insignificant to his overall happiness. It is more important that he is achieving the satisfaction of his most important and central commitment to charity. Others committed to charity might not join an organization such as the Freemasons. Yet, for those who do, their membership will require obligation to loose commitments relative to the culture of the group.

One implication of Kekes's view is that a person can put up with a great deal of pain and still have a happy life. Physical and psychological suffering (even when experienced frequently) may be outweighed by other important first-order wants, such as the pursuit of scientific knowledge, as in the case of Stephen Hawking. There are other apt examples that fit this mold as well, including marathon runners who suffer extensive exhaustion and yet feel intense satisfaction upon achieving their goal; or Job who lost everything and yet because he prioritized his piety and devotion to God, could be said to have lived happily; or even hunger-striking Gandhi, who sacrificed his own health for his commitment to seeing the social injustice of British colonial rule end for his fellow citizens in India.

To summarize, Kekes argues that to be happy is to experience the satisfaction of a particular second-order desire: that one's important first-order desires be satisfied. Of course, to judge whether or not our important first-order desires are met, we need to know how to discriminate among desires, picking out the important from the unimportant, and this, in turn, requires a plan for our life. A life plan is a three-tiered structure of commitments that establishes the sort of person we are aspiring to become. If our commitments are left unfulfilled, then our aspirations are frustrated and we are not happy. Moreover, happiness is unique to each person, reflecting each person's individuality.

Things to Avoid in Planning a Life

Even though happiness is unique to each person, Kekes argues that there are better and worse ways of formulating a life plan. In particular, there are two broad categories of errors we make in developing life plans. First, a plan can suffer from internal defects such that its realization will be impossible, or at least highly improbable. Second, there can be external impediments to the implementation of one's plan. Whereas internal defects are problems with the plan itself, external impediments come about through trying to live according to a plan that runs counter to prevailing legal, moral, and cultural norms. Kekes thus offers some warnings we would do well to take note of when constructing our own plans.

There are several internal defects from which a life plan could suffer, according to Kekes. One shares an affinity with the standard of affective appropriateness already discussed in connection with value-based life satisfactionism. In particular, Kekes notes that to choose a life plan that does not fit with one's temperament, talents, and feelings sets one up for frustration, unhappiness, or even worse. Kekes identifies other possible internal defects as well. For instance, a plan could suffer through containing incompatible elements. That is, a person could have unconditional commitments to two mutually exclusive wants. Because both cannot be satisfied, a person's happiness will suffer, as one of the person's most central wants will necessarily be frustrated. Perhaps a parent who joined the Peoples Temple could illustrate this problem. Committing oneself unconditionally to Jim Jones appears to have conflicted with the commonly understood unconditional commitment of a parent to his or her child. Another good illustration is the case of a woman wanting to be both an accomplished ballerina *and* an active officer in the Marine Corps.[13] Perhaps for reasons of family tradition, the woman had always planned to enlist in the Marines, but she has also discovered a passion for the ballet and has found out that she is quite talented. In this case, it seems difficult to imagine how these two commitments could be successfully balanced and satisfied in a life. After all, dedicating the necessary resources to one of these time-consuming, labor-intensive careers precludes having the ability to devote energy and effort to the other. Therefore, it would be highly difficult to fully realize this sort of life plan – one that is dually committed to incompatible commitments.

Another internal defect would be if one's plan were humanly impossible to achieve. Even if one can make some progress, there are some ends that simply cannot be achieved. Perfectionists are a good example, as it is impossible for a perfectionist to actually achieve this commitment. What is more, even if one could come close to achieving perfection, it does not seem to yield any satisfaction, as studies have shown that perfectionism is highly correlated with lower self-reported life satisfaction.[14] Therefore, being unconditionally committed to the ideal of perfection seems to undermine happiness, so one would do well not to include it in a life plan.

---

13 This example is based on one from Annas (2004: 47).
14 See, for example, Diener and Biswas-Diener (2008: 195).

Finally, a plan might include unconditional commitments capable of only transitory satisfaction. The character of Don Juan is a good example of this. Being unconditionally committed only to sexual conquest means that eventually he will be frustrated. After all, it is in the nature of bodies to wear out, and so he will sooner or later be incapable of satisfying this aim. Or consider those who are so committed to outward appearance that they make it a central desire to always appear young and beautiful. These people are guaranteed to have their desires thwarted as they age. They might attempt to hold on to youth and beauty by spending thousands of dollars on artificial remedies including ointments, oils, creams, and plastic surgery; but eventually youth and beauty give way, so one had better find other commitments in life.

A plan can also fail due to conflict with its external environment. For example, a person's plan can be radically out of step with one's times. The life of Don Quixote, the titular character from the novel by Miguel de Cervantes, seems to illustrate this point nicely. Deeply committed to the ideals of chivalry and knighthood, and to a code of principles that are radically out of step with his times, the beleaguered Don Quixote engages in frustrated quest after frustrated quest. Clearly, although he chose his own plan of life, and although he has engaged earnestly in its pursuit, because he is living with ideals that clash with his cultural environment, he is bound to be unhappy. Imagine, for instance, trying to live according to Victorian ideals in twenty-first century America: you would likely be the object of scorn, ridicule, and mockery everywhere you went. This was the plight of Don Quixote, whose commitments opened him to abuse by those he encountered.[15]

Alternatively, one may also construct a plan that ignores the legal and moral constraints imposed on one by society. This, too, as noted in Chapter Three, would frustrate the realization of one's plan and prevent one from becoming fully happy. A fine example here is the lead character from the

---

15 Kekes (1982: 372). However, some have argued that Don Quixote, far from being made unhappy while living according to values deeply out of tune with his times, was actually happy only during this time. When he was "cured" of his mental affliction, he was made unhappy. Nevertheless, Kekes's point still remains. First, Kekes is suggesting only that it is less likely for a person to achieve his life-plan if that plan includes swimming against the tide of social norms, not that it is impossible. Second, even in the story, Don Quixote was unable to successfully fulfill his life plan. The world got to him. They "fixed" his troubled mind. As a result of failing to live out his plan due to the impinging requirements of social norms and expectations, Don Quixote's life was ultimately unhappy.

cable television series *Dexter*. Dexter Morgan, played by Michael C. Hall, is a blood-spatter expert for a local police department by day, but a serial killer by night. Although he attempts to maintain a sense of justice by practicing a gruesome form of vigilantism – killing only those whom he believes are guilty of terrible crimes – he nevertheless has a plan that is at odds with the legal and moral norms of his culture. Hence he suffers, as he must always be on guard not to be exposed. Kekes argues that anyone in this position is unhappy:

> A man whose life-plan involves frequent violation of the legal and moral standards of his society cannot be happy; this is so even if he rejects these standards. Systematic life-long dissimulation and lying are required for living at odds with one's society. Trust, relaxation, and intimate personal relationships are impossible, for one's true sentiments must always be hidden.[16]

It is important to note here that Kekes is *not* arguing that there is one true morality that must be part of every person's plan if they are to be happy. It does not matter to the case whether we believe Dexter's actions are just. Because he is not acting in conformity with the prevailing attitudes of society, he must hide himself or risk being ostracized or jailed. These are sources of stress regardless of whether he is in the right. Nevertheless, Kekes suggests that, as a matter of prudence with respect to happiness, it is wise not to formulate a plan that requires constant violation of the legal and moral norms of one's society, as it will lead to constant struggle. We either have to lie to others, preventing genuine interaction and relationships with our fellow human beings, or face serious sanctions.

Even if one takes pains to plan a life carefully, making sure one's plan is not impaired by either internal or external defects, this is still not enough for happiness. It is not enough, states Kekes, that a person has a careful life plan and that he is making significant progress toward meeting it. It is not even enough that his judgment that he is satisfied with his life is true. He *also* needs to have a reason to believe, and no reason to doubt, that this will continue into the future; he must believe that his satisfaction with life will remain true as his life unfolds. We can think that this will be the case, and yet we may still be wrong. In order to be truly happy, we need to be able to reliably judge that our most important first-order wants have already

---

16 Ibid.

been satisfied, or that we are making decent progress toward their satisfaction, and that this will continue to be the case.

Is Being Satisfied Enough?

According to whole life satisfactionism, our happiness consists in our satisfaction with our lives as wholes. Previously, we considered worries about simple versions of this view that prompted philosophers like Tiberius and Hall and also Kekes to articulate some constraints upon the perspectives from which we evaluate our lives and the plans we construct to direct them. In particular, we were concerned that there were no sound criteria that would allow us to know that a judgment of life satisfaction is authoritative and that it reliably reflects things of value in life. Still, while adopting such constraints might well fortify life satisfaction theories against certain normative concerns, it comes at a cost. How often do people actually find themselves in a suitably reflective perspective? How often do we occupy this point of view when deciding how to live? On the value-based life satisfaction view, the only way to reliably determine whether or not I am happy is to appraise my life overall from within a reflective perspective. Judgments that are not made from a reflective perspective are not fitting evidence of my happiness or unhappiness. To the extent that I cannot put myself in the reflective perspective, I am not in a position to determine whether or not I am happy, as I will not have the proper evidence upon which to base this conclusion.

However, adding these constraints to our life satisfaction judgments and life plans will mean that most people rarely evaluate their life satisfaction in an appropriate way. How many people have actually taken care to think through their values in order to determine which are core as opposed to peripheral, or which meet the standards of information and affective appropriateness? If happiness and well-being are constituted by life satisfaction only when they meet these constraints, then most people have never found themselves *anywhere* on the happiness scale. And even those who have approached their happiness in such a careful and deliberate way would have to admit that they are *rarely* in the sort of perspective required to make reliable judgments of life satisfaction. In other words, placing constraints on our life satisfaction judgments generates an even more worrisome version of the problem of "attitude scarcity" mentioned in the previous chapter. Earlier, Haybron and Nussbaum questioned whether we ever find ourselves in a state of being satisfied with life as a whole. It would be even more unlikely that we find ourselves in a *reflective* state of being satisfied with life as a whole. Given this, we might question the practical value of this revised formulation of whole life satisfactionism.

Tiberius admits that some of us are less reflective than others, but she holds that the reflective perspective need not be explicitly conscious. In other words, many of us adopt a perspective without being aware that we are so doing. As an analogy, all of us seem to follow certain rules of grammar in normal conversation, but how many of us are consciously aware of the rules that we follow? In the same way, some of us might be more or less in the reflective perspective without having to know that this is the case. Tiberius elaborates: "People do have values and norms of reflection, even if they are not terribly articulate about them, and we can and do improve our perspectives without thinking very explicitly that this is what we are doing."[17] She also adds that, insofar as the reflective perspective is defined by the values, weights, and standards that *we* accept, it does not require that our perspective be overly intellectual. Additionally, Tiberius is clear that while we need to be informed, our perspective need not involve complete information. People can use any level of reflection to improve their perspectives and help plan their lives better, such as by learning from others or from data gathered from empirical studies. What matters is that we give enough proper consideration to what is important to us.

Yet there are further worries with thinking of happiness as satisfaction with life. For instance, what about cases in which we take satisfaction in our lives even while we are emotionally distraught? Perhaps we are satisfied *because* we are melancholy. It is certainly possible that our satisfaction with life and our emotional states can sharply diverge from each other. Maybe our plan for the evening is to wallow in a sad movie, crying at the heartbreaking ending that befalls the tragic hero. As we watch the movie with our box of tissues nearby, we might think to ourselves, "This is exactly what I wanted with my evening." What do we say in these cases? Will our satisfaction be sufficient to render us happy in spite of experiencing depressive emotionality? Or are we satisfied even though we are unhappy? Which is the most natural response? It seems that a defender of life satisfactionism would have to answer that we are happy; nonetheless, to many this seems quite counterintuitive. How can we be happy while being miserable? Haybron formulates this concern with respect to a tortured artist. He writes:

---

17 Tiberius (2003: 12).

On the most natural reading of the view, it is perfectly possible for someone to be satisfied with her life even though she is depressed or otherwise emotionally a shambles. Indeed, this possibility would seem to be an *attraction* to many: the tortured artist might think emotional matters unimportant, or even that it is *good* to be depressed, and thus be satisfied with her life. Her life is going well by her lights, as she is getting and doing what matters to her. Be that as it may, it is deeply counterintuitive to regard such an individual as being *happy*.[18]

Haybron then argues that in those cases where our life satisfaction diverges from our emotional state, happiness and well-being will track our emotional state rather than our life satisfaction. Thus he thinks that the work of happiness is being done by our positive affect, and any connection our happiness shares with our life satisfaction is merely secondary.

As an alternative example, consider the romantic poets and their view that to truly live fully, we need to experience our emotional life in all of its vividness, including those states such as melancholy or misery. We should not run from these states, but rather dive into them as part of an exploration of the human condition. For example, reflect on John Keats and his poem in praise of sadness, "Ode on Melancholy."[19] In the second stanza he writes:

> But when the melancholy fit shall fall
> Sudden from heaven like a weeping cloud,
> That fosters the droop-headed flowers all,
> And hides the green hill in April shroud;
> Then glut thy sorrow on a morning rose,
> Or on the rainbow of the salt-sand wave,
> Or on the wealth of globed peonies;
> Or if thy mistress some rich anger shows,
> Emprison her soft hand, and let her rave,
> And feed deep, deep upon her peerless eyes.

One would be hard pressed to describe Keats as a happy man, but at the same time he seems to revel in his melancholy. In the poem he suggests that to fully live, to experience true joy, we must dive passionately into all experiences, including depression and grief: to feed upon our sorrow

---

18 Haybron (2005: 291); emphasis in original.
19 Keats (1993: 795).

nourishes the soul. Keats might then describe himself as satisfied with his life only if he experiences this unhappy emotion in its full intensity. In spite of his being satisfied, then, we would consider Keats unhappy. If so, then a person can be satisfied and yet unhappy – in fact, satisfied *because he is unhappy*. We might therefore question whether life satisfaction and happiness are the same, wondering, instead, if our happiness is more tied to our emotional life.

Nussbaum also questions whether life satisfaction has any significant *value* in our pursuit of the happy life. Happiness seems to be something that is good for us, but there are many occasions when being satisfied is quite bad for us. First, sometimes people can be satisfied with their circumstances when they are actually quite grim: consider a woman who has suffered lifelong abuse, but because she perceives there to be no other option she has not only become accustomed to it but also accepted it. As Nussbaum has cataloged, women who live in sexually oppressive cultures will report satisfaction with lower levels of education, freedom, and political rights, and even physical health, because they have come to internalize the standards of their community, believing they deserve no more.[20] Or one could experience satisfaction as a result of a mistaken view of one's situation, such as the case of a person whose spouse is secretly unfaithful. Additionally, even if it is a significant value, happiness might be outweighed by other, *more significant* values. For instance, we might think that service to our country, fighting for justice or social change, practicing compassion for others, striving for a difficult goal, or experiencing risk and suffering could each be more important than attaining a state of satisfaction with our lives. To the extent that we keep our focus on satisfaction, we might fail to honor other commitments or obligations. We might even end up with nothing worth living for.

Finally, sometimes those who are satisfied have no motivation to strive to be better. If this is true, then to be satisfied might well be bad for us since we will not work to better ourselves or our situation. Instead, we may find ourselves becoming apathetic toward the project of shaping ourselves into better people and resting content with rather poor circumstances. In these ways, being satisfied can actually be harmful to our overall pursuit of the happy and good life. It seems that being *dissatisfied* might offer more motivation to change our direction in life for the better. This might then make us question the importance of being satisfied with life for our happiness and well-being.

---

20 Nussbaum (2012: 350).

Revisiting the Cult Experience

One of the advantages of value-based life satisfactionism is that it appears to explain our intuition that the life of a cult member is not a happy and good life, even from within a subjectivist framework. In other words, one of the strengths that such a view appears to have is that it can accommodate our thought that each person's happiness is up to that person, while at the same time showing how people can still go wrong in their pursuit of subjective happiness because there are certain conditions of reflection placed on the choice of one's life plan.[21] This, in turn, affords value-based life satisfaction the normative authority missing from other forms of life satisfactionism. Of course, these supposed advantages accrue to the theory only if it is actually able to rule out cult members from being happy. But is this actually the case?

It seems that at least with regard to the Peoples Temple cult, Tiberius, Hall, and Kekes are able to explain the intuition that such a life is not happy and good. As previously explained, the members did not meet the standards of information and affective fit. After all, they were under the impression that their move to South America was in the service of building a utopian society – they did not join and move so far from their families in order to commit suicide. Furthermore, Jim Jones manipulated them into giving up control over their own volition. Then again, perhaps Peoples Temple is not representative of all cults. Is it possible that one could meet the standards imposed by value-based life satisfactionism and yet still choose to join a cult and thereby live a happy and good life?

Consider, for example, the Heaven's Gate cult. Led by Marshall Applewhite and Bonnie Nettles, the cult required members to live an extremely ascetic lifestyle, forcing them to give up all material possessions, share everything communally, and follow a strict code of behavior. Some male members even underwent voluntary castration. Moreover, Applewhite preached that human bodies were but mere vessels, which when properly controlled could help members to evolve to the "Next Level." To reach the Next Level, in 1997, 39 members of the cult, including Applewhite himself,

---

21 Our concern here is, again, with those cult members who claim they were satisfied with their cult lives and whether a theory of happiness and well-being should take those claims at face value. To be sure, there are other cult members who were clearly unhappy in the cult life: on the basis of their own statements, they did not take satisfaction in their lives. In many cases, this was due to increasingly strict standards being placed upon them that were not in place when they had initially joined. In fact, in many cults, mass suicides are precipitated on the basis of increasing paranoia by the cult leader, whose behavior becomes erratic and oppressive.

shed their human "vehicles" by committing suicide through a combination of ingesting barbiturates and vodka. To ensure success, they also asphyxiated themselves with plastic bags. When the bodies were found, each was dressed in a black shirt, sweatpants, and new Nike sneakers, and each had a purple square handkerchief spread smoothly over their faces. The mass suicide was motivated by the belief that an approaching comet known as Hale–Bopp was being followed by a spaceship that would pick up the souls of the cult members once they released them from their earthly bodies.[22]

Now, is it possible that at least some of the members of Heaven's Gate were satisfied with life? Would they meet the conditions set forth by value-based life satisfactionism? There is some reason to think that the answer to both of these questions is yes. Because life satisfaction judgments, even when suitably justified, are subjective to each person, it is at least possible that *some* of the cult members were happy. Interestingly, two other Heaven's Gate members not present during the mass suicide voluntarily committed suicide on their own in the service of joining their former members in the Next Level just months later. Other members of the Heaven's Gate cult who did not participate in the mass suicide were interviewed some time later. Even after a chance to live back in the normal world with opportunity for distanced reflection on what transpired, and even after having gathered more information, some of these members expressed that they were completely happy during their membership in the cult. One member, Rio DiAngelo, even remarked that he was happy for those who moved on and expressed the wish that he had joined them. DiAngelo still remains committed to the Heaven's Gate cult life, waiting for his turn to be picked up by the spaceship.

Furthermore, for many of the cult members, the cult life *is* what affectively fit them. The *normal* world did *not*. This is often why people join cults, because they haven't been able to find meaning in the humdrum of ordinary living and so become disaffected by mainstream society. For example, according to his mother Nancy Brown, member David Moore decided at age 19 to join Heaven's Gate because he couldn't ever picture himself just living the kind of life that most people did. It appears, then, that for David, living a "normal" life did not fit his affective nature. It left him unfulfilled, and so in his search for meaning and direction, he joined the group. In the end, David was among the 39 cult members who died.

---

22 All information on the Heaven's Gate cult is taken from the BBC television series *Inside Story: The Cult*, dir. Rachel Coughlan (1997).

You might imagine that Nancy would, as a result, resent her son's membership in Heaven's Gate. But, to the contrary, she says, "It is hard to be sad for David about the ending of his life. I am sad for me and his family because we won't get to see him again. But ... he looked like he died peacefully. David lived his adult life doing what he wanted to do with people who loved him and so who's to say whether this was a bad life." David's mother recognizes that her son languished under typical social norms and values, but that he flourished within the self-control and discipline of the cult. She notes that he was among people who loved him and whom he loved. The cult life suited him well. It seems, then, that even value-based life satisfactionism does not rule out the possibility that on rare occasions the cult life can make some people happy.

Still, we might believe that insofar as someone sets a plan for life that involves his death, he cannot be considered to possess happiness or wellbeing. Then again, as another member of the Heaven's Gate cult states of those who committed suicide, "They died for exactly what they believe in. People die for their country. People die for their spouses and friends. People die for all kinds of reasons, and dying for your belief system is a valid reason to die as long as you don't hurt anyone else." In fact, how different are they really from someone like Thomas More, who also implicitly chose his own death based on his belief system? People have died for far less, and so it might be an unfounded assumption to believe that it must always be a bad thing to willingly choose a path that will prematurely end your life. Even if they could have lived longer, many Heaven's Gate members felt that their time was filled with much meaning and satisfaction. And as noted in the previous chapter, we don't just count a life as a good one simply on account of its length. Many people who have lived lives that have ended sooner than expected, such as Martin Luther King, Jr. or Jesus, are still thought to have lived exemplary lives.

So what are we to make of this? It seems that value-based life satisfactionism allows that *some* cult members are living happy and good lives. Yet if you are convinced that one cannot live a happy life while also being a cult member, then it seems as though you must reject value-based life satisfactionism. Although it initially seemed plausible that, by putting constraints on the life satisfaction view of happiness, we could explain the intuition that one cannot be happy while in a cult, upon further investigation it now appears that at least some cult members meet all the conditions that Tiberius, Hall, and Kekes place on them and so turn out to live good and happy lives according to these views. If this conflicts with your belief that such a life could never be a happy one, you must reject the idea that happiness resides in one's satisfaction with life.

On the other hand, if you are not troubled by the possibility that cult members could possibly live happily, there is a different issue to worry about: if a cult member can be happy, even while being manipulated and when being a member leads to his suicide, then what is the value of happiness to well-being? That is, if one can join the Peoples Temple or Heaven's Gate and still be considered happy, then isn't it the case that happiness is sometimes bad for us, and therefore cannot be the same as well-being? In such a case, what we really value is the good life, and so the correct conclusion to draw from the cases of cult membership is that, although they might be happy, happiness has little to do with what truly matters in life: living well. What these considerations imply is that there might be something faulty with a subjective theory of the happy life. They might *also* imply that there is something problematic about a theory of the good life that relies primarily on the subjective state of satisfaction.

As a result of the worries highlighted by Nussbaum, Haybron, and the Heaven's Gate cult, there is some serious cause for concern regarding both the concept and application of satisfaction. First, we might question whether we ever find ourselves in a state that is "being satisfied with life as a whole." And even if so, there are normative concerns regarding the value of such a mental state. Contemporary psychologists and many philosophers just assume that life satisfaction is positive. However, as just noted, life satisfaction might very well be *bad* for us. We cannot simply maintain that the experience of satisfaction is unproblematically good for us, and so more needs to be said about this purported element of happiness and well-being. These considerations, then, give us some reason to think that there may be more to our happiness beyond our satisfaction. They may also give us pause with respect to whether life satisfaction can be a plausible account of one's well-being. Can satisfaction with life alone capture what we mean by a life that is going well for us? Perhaps, in order to explain our intuitions that happiness and well-being cannot be served by living as brainwashed automata, we are going to have to rely on at least some objective standards for the happy and good life. At the very least, our considerations of cult members indicate that in order to live a happy and good life, we might think it necessary to be autonomous and fully informed about our situations. In the coming chapters, we will look carefully at the notion that there are objective standards for the happy life, taking seriously the possibility that what is good for one is good for all.

Part IV: Happiness
              as Eudaimonia

Chapter 8:   Is Ignorance Bliss?

Imagine a machine that could give you any experience (or sequence of experiences) you might desire. When connected to this experience machine, you can have the experience of writing a great poem or bringing about world peace or loving someone and being loved in return. You can experience the felt pleasures of these things, how they feel "from the inside." You can program your experiences for tomorrow, or this week, or this year, or even for the rest of your life. If your imagination is impoverished, you can use the library of suggestions extracted from biographies and enhanced by novelists and psychologists. You can live your fondest dreams "from the inside." ... The question is not whether to try the machine temporarily, but whether to enter it for the rest of your life. Upon entering, you will not remember having done this; so no pleasures will get ruined by realizing they are machine-produced. Uncertainty too might be programmed by using the machine's operational random device (upon which various preselected alternatives can depend).[1]

ROBERT NOZICK'S EXPERIENCE MACHINE is one of the most widely discussed and compelling thought experiments in philosophy. In this scenario, you are presented with an extremely powerful and reliable machine that can provide you with *any* experience you would like, whether you

---

1   Nozick (1989: 104–05).

choose experiences that offer you pleasures, pains, satisfactions, or dis-satisfactions. For instance, you might want to program the complex experiences of loving someone and being loved, or completing your college degree, or protesting against certain governmental policies, or perhaps winning a hard-fought tennis match. Everything you experience in the machine is entirely up to you. You can decide how much of anything you want to experience, and in what order different events take place. You can even include elements of uncertainty with some randomly generated experiences so as not to get bored. Most importantly, once inside the machine you will not remember making the choice to enter, and so each experience will feel completely genuine to you. How it feels "from the inside" will be the same as if you were still living in reality. Since it is a thought experiment, don't focus on whether or not this machine is currently technologically feasible. That misses the point. Instead, assume such a machine *were* possible. The question is whether you would enter this machine for the rest of your life.

Do We Value Things outside Our Subjective Experience?

Nozick assumes that most would not choose to enter the machine, no matter how dependable and faithful it might be in terms of providing pleasurable and satisfactory experiences. But why? What is it that prevents us from plugging in? Or, as Nozick asks, "What else can matter to us, other than how our lives feel from the inside?"[2] Whichever reasons we offer, ultimately the choice of whether to plug in is a question of *value*.[3] Our answer depends on whether plugging in to the Experience Machine would constitute the best kind, or one of the very best kinds, of life. For if happiness is simply the experience of certain mental states – such as pleasure of both higher and lower kinds, or satisfied desires, including being satisfied with one's life as a whole – these mental states can be generated by the machine, and so we could be happy in the Experience Machine. Our choice not to enter the machine implies that we must value something more than just how things

---

2 Nozick (1974: 43); italics removed from original.
3 Certainly, there are also epistemological and metaphysical questions surrounding the Experience Machine, such as: "Can you know you are not already plugged in?" and "Don't the machine experiences themselves constitute a real world?" (ibid., 105). But with respect to happiness and well-being, the important question is one of value: would living in an Experience Machine be one of the very best kinds of lives? For our purposes in the book we will mostly focus on this question of value.

feel from the inside. Consequently, either there are more important things in life than happiness, or we have the wrong understanding of happiness. In other words, if we believe that happiness consists in either experiencing pleasure or being satisfied with life, then plugging into the machine will guarantee us happiness. So why not plug in? Is it because we are afraid that we wouldn't *really* be happy? If so, we might question whether we ought to think of happiness as simply feeling pleasure or being satisfied with our life. Perhaps it requires more than how we experience life. On the other hand, maybe we are willing to grant that the machine would, in fact, make us happy, yet we still wouldn't want to live that kind of life. If this is the case, we are assuming that there is more to a good life than being happy.

Nozick claims that it is the second explanation that best captures our reluctance to plug in: there are more important things in life than happiness. "We care about more than just how things feel to us from the inside," writes Nozick. "There is more to life than feeling happy."[4] That is, although our subjective experience of life is important, we value more than just how things appear to be going – we want them to actually *be* the way we want, and not just *seem* to be that way. It is true, argues Nozick, that one could experience happiness while in the Experience Machine. For, according to him, happiness is the same as life satisfaction, which is a subjective mental state. Nevertheless, there is more to life than happiness: there are other things we value, and at least sometimes we will forgo happy experiences in order to secure them. Notice this implies that the happy life and the good life are *not* the same. In fact, although happiness might be one ingredient in a good life, Nozick argues that it is not the only one; it's not even the most important one at that. So what are these other ingredients? What else do we value? According to Nozick, a good life is a life that is very good for the person living it, "in whatever dimensions he considers most important and whatever dimensions *are* most important."[5] The Experience Machine reveals at least three dimensions we care about in addition to positive subjective experience: authenticity, genuine relationships, and autonomy. A life that lacks any one of these could be going better for the person living it.

The Value of Authenticity
Nozick thinks that few of us actually believe that all that matters in life is our subjective experiences. Most of us think there are other important

---

4   Nozick (1989: 106).
5   Ibid., 113.

elements. For example, he states that we would not wish for our children a life of great satisfactions that depends on well-crafted deceptions they never detect. That is to say, we would not wish a future for our children in which they have a seemingly "loving" family on the surface, yet under the surface a secretly unfaithful spouse and children who are very careful to conceal their spite. Nor would we wish them perceived success under false pretenses. This is not what we want for ourselves or our children. Nozick writes:

> That person is living in dream world, taking pleasure in things that aren't so. What he wants, though, is not merely to take pleasure in them; he wants *them to be so*. He values their being that way, and he takes pleasure in them because he thinks they *are* that way. He doesn't take pleasure merely in *thinking* they are.... Nor do we merely want the added pleasurable feeling of being connected to reality. Such an inner feeling, an illusory one, also can be provided by the experience machine. What we want and value is an actual connection with reality.... To focus on external reality ... is valuable *in itself*, not just as a means to more pleasure or happiness.[6]

What we want is not merely to be pleased or satisfied by our experiences; we want them actually to be going the way we want. This reflects our commitment to the value of authenticity: we want our experiences to genuinely reflect our life as it actually is. In fact, our taking pleasure in the circumstances of our lives seems parasitic upon our believing that they are authentic. Even more, Nozick explains that the problem is *not* that we desire a connection to reality that the Experience Machine does not give us; instead, a connection to reality is important *whether we desire it or not*. Thus, there are things that are important to us apart from getting what we desire. If this is true, then there must be some things that are *external* to our conscious experience that are important to the good life.

Nozick further explains: "What we want, in short, is a life and a self that happiness is a fitting response to — and then to give it that response."[7] While we can have happiness when it is not a fitting response to our life, we want the life in which our happiness *is* fitting. That is, we want not just the experience of happiness, but the life in which that happiness is appropriate. This requires that we *earn* our pleasures and satisfactions. When they are

---

6   Ibid., 106; emphasis in original.
7   Ibid., 117.

given to us without effort on our part, then they are not achievements and so lose their value. This is another reason why Nozick thinks we care about more than just happiness when thinking about our lives.

The Value of Genuine Relationships

The Experience Machine thought experiment also reveals the value we place on genuine relationships with other human persons, and not just interactions with sophisticated computer programs. According to Nozick, we do not just want to feel as though we know other people intimately and they also know us well; we want it to be *true* that we are speaking with, interacting with, loving, respecting, and caring for other real people, rather than simulated automata. He states, "One of the distressing things about the experience machine, as described, is that you are alone in your particular illusion."[8]

Then again, perhaps, this conclusion is too quick. Many people today have formed apparently serious relationships with simulated programs. Some have even taken these relationships to the utmost limit by publicly marrying video-game characters. For instance, a Tokyo man who goes by the name of Sal decided to marry what he refers to as his "dream woman," the avatar Nene Anegasaki from the Nintendo DS game *Love Plus*. When asked about whether he can love an electronic device, Sal admits: "I understand 100 percent that this is a game. I understand very well that I cannot marry her physically or legally." Yet, he says, "I love this character, not a machine."[9] Cases like this raise a fundamental question about the nature of human relationships: can you actually feel fulfilled as a human being if you know you are engaged in a "loving" relationship with a mere computer program? Many are convinced that you cannot.

Yet what about a relationship with an artificially intelligent android, such as those from the famous Philip K. Dick novel *Do Androids Dream of Electric Sheep?* (1968), the inspiration behind the 1982 film *Blade Runner*? The story is about bounty hunter Rick Deckard. One subplot of the movie version of the story involves Deckard falling in love with the android Rachael, who appears and acts "more human than human." But is it really even possible to knowingly fall in love with a non-human android? A robot? This raises interesting questions about the nature of personhood and the limit of human relationships.

---

8 Ibid., 107.

9 See http://www.cnn.com/2009/WORLD/asiapcf/12/16/japan.virtual.wedding/index.html.

Would it matter if the computer program or the android has achieved some form of artificial intelligence according to which we could attribute it personhood? That is, would we be more willing to believe that someone could genuinely love a non-human artificial consciousness so long as we also thought that consciousness was intelligent? Must we actually connect only with other human persons specifically? It seems clearly not. Accordingly, if the Experience Machine's programs were sophisticated enough, perhaps it could preserve for us the value we have for genuine relationships. Apart from the question of which beings might possess intelligent minds, it seems clear that we desire to *actually* be related to such beings (and not just seem to be), which is a value for something beyond our simple experience of life.

Apart from these difficult questions over personhood, video games and the Internet have also provided opportunities for real human beings to communicate with each other by way of online virtual characters, which often act and appear nothing like the humans who play them, or in some cases, who create them. Indeed, many people today spend a large portion of their lives as role players in video games, regularly interacting online with real people by way of their virtual video-game avatars, but these are people they will never physically meet. Some of these games include multiplayer online role-playing games such as *World of Warcraft*, with clear objectives and rules, while others, such as *Second Life*, seem geared toward providing outlets for alternative social interactions. Indeed, more and more people today claim they only feel comfortable expressing themselves in a virtual world rather than in physical reality. All of this suggests that the character of human connections is changing. Once again, this raises interesting issues surrounding the nature of relationships. It might make us question whether we value sharing our experiences with others *more than* we value the actuality of those experiences. On the other hand, perhaps it simply changes what we consider "actuality"[10] to be.

Either way, however, Nozick argues that most of us prefer true genuine human relationships based in an actual connection to reality. Even if everyone we care about were also plugged into the Experience Machine and provided with the same illusion so that our experiences were coordinated (similar to interacting with avatars in a virtual reality), we would still

---

10 The idea here is that the experiences within the machine might also constitute another kind of world, in which case there might be many realities and ways to construe "actuality." The thorny issue of realism is beyond the scope of this book.

choose not to plug in, because we value *both* sharing our experiences with others *and* actuality. If there were real people behind the simulated avatars – rather than the simulation merely being a function of programming – would we find this shared experience as objectionable? Nozick admits that while it would be less objectionable, it would be objectionable nonetheless.

The Value of Autonomy

Nozick also notes that once we are in the Experience Machine, we would lose the ability to make truly *free* choices about how to live our life. We want our life to be the product of our own creativity and will. We do not want simply to feel from the inside as though our life is the product of our individual volition; we want it actually to be that way. And while it is true that we can program our entire set of life experiences prior to entering the machine, once we are in the machine we are no longer able to exercise any agency over the choice of our experience, even if it seems to us that we can. In other words, we care about our autonomy.

On the contrary, though, we might doubt that we are in fact the product of our own will *outside* of an Experience Machine. How do we know that we even have free will? We may feel that our will and volition influence our lives, but maybe the "choices" we make are really just a product of many complex chemical and electrical interactions going on in our brains. We want to believe that this is not true – that we *do* have free will – but if we do not actually make any genuine choices, then does Nozick's claim here show that the Experience Machine is any less valuable than reality, at least in this regard? Regardless, determining if and to what extent humans enjoy free will is a deeply complicated question that itself would require volumes to explore. In the end, it is hard to know what is and is not compatible with the exercise of free choice.

Even putting to the side the difficult philosophical questions over free will, there is an important insight captured by Nozick's remarks about freely choosing: namely, that entering the machine removes all ability to explore reality, and respond to it, alter it, and thereby create new actuality ourselves. It seems that we lose our agency to act in the world after plugging into the machine. We become passive consumers of our experience rather than actively living our lives. And without the capacity to make these kinds of choices and to connect with reality in these significant ways, we might question what is left to define ourselves – who does our "self" become in the machine? In an earlier formulation of his Experience Machine thought experiment, Nozick explains:

> A second reason for not plugging in is that we want to *be* a certain way, to be a certain sort of person. Someone floating in a tank is an indeterminate blob. There is no answer to the question of what a person is like who has long been in the [machine]. Is he courageous, kind, intelligent, witty, loving? It's not merely that it's difficult to tell; there's no way he is. Plugging into the machine is a kind of suicide.[11]

In what sense are you a person when you are in the machine? Do you have an identity? You seem more vegetative than active. You effect no change in your life or the lives of others. You achieve nothing, produce nothing, engage in no meaningful activity. What then are you?

Furthermore, in what sense can we be considered moral persons once we enter the Experience Machine? While one might initially think that fighting to reduce world hunger or promote world peace would represent a "nobler" programming choice for one's life inside the machine, we would not actually be affecting the real world in any meaningful way. While we thus might experience ourselves as moral agents, we would not actually be so. Seen in this way, it would be no less laudable to program a lifelong hedonistic binge full of sex and drugs than to choose to have nobler experiences; either choice would have the same impact on actuality: none. Imagine if Dr. Martin Luther King, Jr. had decided to fight for civil rights for African Americans only inside the Experience Machine. Would he be praiseworthy then? His decision to embark on the arduous struggle for freedom is a value he prized above his own subjective experience. And it would not have been enough that he merely experienced marching with hundreds of thousands of protestors or delivering powerful sermons. His goal was to effect real change in the world, which he did, and this is why he is admirable as a moral exemplar for others.

The fact that we are worried about the kind of person we would be in the Experience Machine shows that we are not only concerned with how our time is filled. We fundamentally care about what *we are*:

> We are not empty containers or buckets to be stuffed with good things, with pleasures or possessions or positive emotions or even with a rich and varied internal life.... The view that only happiness matters ignores the question of what *we* – the very ones to be happy – are like. How could the most important thing about our life be what

---

11 Nozick (1974: 45).

it *contains*, though? What makes the felt experiences of pleasure or happiness more important than what we ourselves are like?[12]

Nozick concludes that we learn that something matters to us more than merely our experiences after we think about the Experience Machine and then realize that we would not use it. We value things in our lives and about ourselves that are not, strictly speaking, part of our happiness. Perhaps Nozick is right to conclude that there is more to life than happiness.

Are We Talking about Well-Being or Happiness?

According to Nozick, the Experience Machine helps us to see other important elements of a good life. Happiness is certainly included as an element in well-being; however, it is not the only one, and it may not even be the most important. Nozick writes:

> Of course we wish people to have many such moments and days of happiness.... Yet it is not clear that we want those moments constantly or want our lives to consist wholly and only of them.... We want experiences, fitting ones, of profound connection with others, of deep understanding of natural phenomena, of love, of being profoundly moved by music or tragedy, of doing something new and innovative, experiences very different from the bounce and rosiness of the happy moments.[13]

Essentially, happiness is important in part as an appraisal of one's life, but without these other things that we value – such as authenticity, genuine relationships, and autonomy – any happiness we experience has less value. According to Nozick, "A life cannot just be happy while having nothing else valuable in it. Happiness rides piggyback on other things that are positively evaluated correctly. Without these the happiness doesn't get started."[14] Thus, for Nozick, it would be a mistake to interpret authenticity, genuine relationships, and autonomy as constituents of happiness itself, as he appears committed to the view that happiness is satisfaction with one's life overall. Instead, these other elements are constituents of a good life, and they can impact our well-being whether they enter our consciousness or not.

---

12 Nozick (1989: 102).
13 Ibid., 117.
14 Ibid., 113.

On the other hand, one could argue that happiness requires some non-psychological components. On this view, being happy is more than being in a particular mental state, but it also requires having a life that is authentic, autonomous, and so forth. In fact, this is how Martha Nussbaum interprets the lesson of the Experience Machine. She takes Nozick's thought experiment to reveal that happiness is "something like flourishing human living, a kind of living that is active, inclusive of all that has intrinsic value, and complete, meaning lacking in nothing that would make it richer or better."[15] In being inclusive of all that has value, happiness would be about whatever enriches life, and so, if the Experience Machine does not offer us a life complete with all that has value, then it cannot offer us happiness.

Notice, then, that the lesson of the Experience Machine can be interpreted in one of two ways. Either we can take the thought experiment to show that there is more to the good life than happiness, which is Nozick's conclusion. Or, if we think that happiness is the same as well-being, then this calls into question an assumption that has up until now been taken as an obvious truism: happiness is wholly concerned with our psychological experience. In fact, the thought experiment might reveal that there are at least some non-mental constituents important to happiness. Interpreted in this second way, the Experience Machine reveals that there must be more to happiness than how it feels from the inside. Instead we should accept that happiness is about *more* than how we experience our lives. Like the case of Truman discussed in Chapter Two, the Experience Machine forces us to reckon with two competing intuitions about the nature of happiness. Cases of radical deception seem to challenge us to choose between thinking that happiness is only about how we experience our lives – and so we can be happy even while being deceived – and thinking that our happiness can be affected by things of which we are totally unaware – and so we might well be quite unhappy despite our feelings to the contrary. So which is it? Should we conclude that there is more to life than happiness, or that there is more to happiness than what is on offer from the Experience Machine? Perhaps exploring other cases of deception can help to settle which of the two interpretations should be given up for the other.

---

15 Nussbaum (2012: 342). See also Nussbaum's n. 18.

Can We Be Happily Deceived?

Consider another example of deception. Imagine a man who deliberately reflects on his life in order to determine what will make him happy, and he decides that he would like to live a life in which he is loved and respected by his close friends. Moreover, he adds that he would hate to have friends who only pretend to like him, and in that case he would prefer to know about this rather than live with fake friends. Now further imagine that this unfortunate situation actually comes about: the man's supposed friends in reality despise him, all the while giving him every reason to think this is not the case. The man is unaware that one of his worst fears has been realized. Now is this man happy? Is ignorance bliss?

Philosopher Richard Kraut explains that we are pulled in both directions by cases like this. They seem to highlight a tension between two common ways of using the term "happy":

> We are not at all reluctant to say that the deceived man *feels happy* about his life. But we are quite reluctant to say that *the life he is leading is a happy life*. And we are at sea when we have to decide whether he is *happy*; the word "happiness" seems to lean in two directions, sometimes referring to the *feeling* of happiness, sometimes to the kind of *life* that is happy.[16]

We see, then, that one natural way of talking about happiness refers to our feelings and attitudes – pleasures and satisfactions – while another refers more broadly to our lives overall. Both uses of "happy" and "happiness" seem commonplace in ordinary language, yet they can be at variance with each other. In other words, it is possible to simultaneously judge someone as both "happy" and "unhappy" if one is using the first term to represent his pleasure or satisfaction but employing the second term to refer to his life. So which use is more appropriate? Which is more accurate?

Those who say that the man is clearly happy seem committed to the view that happiness consists only in a subjective mental state. If that man thinks he is happy, then he is, regardless of the fact that what he most fears has come true. If he is unaware of this fact, it cannot influence his happiness. Kraut draws an analogy with fear: "Just as unfounded fear is still fear,

---

16 Kraut (1979: 179); emphasis in original.

so unfounded happiness is still happiness."[17] Kraut admits that there is a compelling intuition that the man is happy. Perhaps his happiness is not "true" or "authentic," but it is still happiness. To draw out this intuition, he asks us to imagine later that the man becomes suspicious of his friends, now wondering what they really think of him. Kraut asks: "Would we say that he is finding out whether he is really happy? Wouldn't it be more natural to say that he is finding out whether his happiness has been based on an illusion?"[18] In other words, it seems natural to think that the man is not denying his happiness; rather, he is only attempting to discover whether that happiness is well-founded.

Yet our intuitions in the case also pull us in the other direction. It seems that we are also tempted to think that the man is not happy despite his feeling so. Philosopher Richard Taylor admits that, though we often say that such a deceived person can be happy, we don't really mean it:

> We tend to be tolerant of error here, for its only victims are the possessors of it. Another person's dashed expectations seldom threaten our own. And we are therefore content to suppose that if someone seems to himself or herself to be happy, perhaps he or she really is happy after all. But one can see how shallow this is by asking whether one would really wish to *be* that other person.[19]

Although we might judge our deceived man happy in some sense, Taylor thinks we likely have not taken the time to carefully and sincerely formulate our judgment. We do not wish his life for ourselves any more than we would like to plug into the Experience Machine. His is not an enviable life. What this reveals is that when we reflect on such cases, we come to think that happiness based in massive deception is no real happiness at all. Happiness seems, therefore, to include the requirement that it be based on authentic or veridical experience. Perhaps we don't think the man is really happy because we imagine that were he to find out, he would be made deeply unhappy.

Kraut, too, thinks we are reluctant to believe that victims of radical deception can be happy. He points out that one powerful explanation of our skepticism is that the man himself places a standard of authenticity on his

---

17 Ibid., 178.
18 Ibid.
19 Taylor (2002: 208).

own happiness. More specifically, he states that his happiness lies in genuine friendship, not illusion. Thus, *judged by his own standards*, the man would not consider himself to be happy were he to become aware of the illusion. It matters little that he is in the same psychological state he would be in were he to have genuine friends. Kraut explains what we can learn from this example:

> Evidently, when we ask someone, "What will make you happy? What is your idea of happiness?", we are *not* requesting that he specify the conditions under which he will be in a certain psychological state. It is *not* like asking, "What will make you angry?" Rather, it is inquiring about the standards he imposes on himself, and the goals he is seeking. And this makes us hesitant to say that the deceived man is happy or has a happy life. Judged by his own standards of happiness, he has not attained it, though he is in the same psychological condition he would be in if he had attained it. Merely being in that psychological state is not something to which he attaches any value, and so it is odd to say that he has attained a happy life merely by being in that psychological state.[20]

This way of looking at the deceived man emphasizes the aims and values that he endorses rather than simply the feelings he experiences. This, however, implies that the question of happiness is really a question of value; *happiness is an evaluative term*. Thus, those who are tempted to say that the man was never happy might be thinking of happiness more in terms of whether one's life measures up to one's standards, rather than as a description of how one feels. These standards may include one's feelings, to be sure, but they will also likely include one's fundamental values, projects, and goals, among other things.

To further explore this issue, let's consider a similar situation, but one where the person subjected to deception actually comes to find this out. Kraut asks us to imagine a cruel trick. Someone is voted the most popular student in his high school; however, it is all a ruse. In fact, his fellow students do not like him at all but think it would be amusing to toy with his emotions. He is just gullible enough to take the vote at face value. After a day of immense joy and euphoria, he discovers that he has been duped. Years later he is asked what the happiest day of his life has been. If that one

---

20 Kraut (1979: 178–79); emphasis added.

day in high school was the day he felt most intensely joyous – the day when he *experienced* his life to be most happy – must he answer that this was the happiest day in his life? Kraut answers, "I think not. I can understand his saying that it was actually the unhappiest day of his life, however happy he felt."[21] On the one hand, he was elated by his unexpected rise in popularity, and the feeling of euphoria cannot be denied after the fact – it is not as though he did not experience it. On the other hand, according to Kraut, his life was not made happier by this experience. It even makes sense to think this was one of his most *unhappy* days, despite his positive state of mind on that day. He would judge it so because he now recognizes that his aspirations were going unfulfilled and that his standards for his life were not being met. This seems a perfectly plausible and reasonable conclusion to draw.

Essentially, Kraut argues that a happy life – or a happy day – is not simply a matter of the intensity of the episodic pleasures or satisfactions. Instead, it has to do with one's aims – with the standards that are applied to one's life – and with how one's life is shaping up overall, which may have little to do with episodes of pleasure or satisfaction. Kraut argues that we typically mean by happiness more than just a certain state of mind. We often refer to an individual as happy when his life meets a certain standard. In fact, apparently happy psychological states might very well be bad for us if they are rooted in deception. In those cases, they might actually signal *unhappy* days or lives. Once again, then, we see another reason for thinking that happiness is not merely momentary or episodic, but rather something built from these episodes within a larger context of purposes and goals. A happy life is not a function of all the "happy" moments within it. When happiness is understood in this way, it is easy to see that those who are radically deceived are living unhappy lives, which offers support for the second intuition that happiness is about more than just our experience of life. We trust the man's later judgment that it was an unhappy day, which shows that we believe that one can be mistaken in the moment with respect to whether one's standards for happiness are being met. Indeed, in cases where we come to later realize some deception earlier in life, many of us would in fact rewrite our history, claiming that we were not happy after all, even though we thought we were.

Yet what if the high-school student had chosen different standards for his happiness? It seems possible that he could still judge that particular day the

---

21 Ibid., 179, n. 22.

happiest day in his life, claiming that he doesn't mind having fake friends or falsely winning popularity contests. All he cares about is whatever experience happens to give him the most pleasure, regardless of what it is and whether it is disingenuous. Would we then be inclined to think that he is actually happy? Or would we think that since we would not choose such a life for ourselves, he can't really be happy? But why wouldn't we choose such a life for our own? Is it because we think that he has chosen mistaken standards by which to live, pursuing the wrong things in life? Should he instead care about authenticity and having genuine connections to others, for example? Otherwise, what kind of life is that to live? This might lead us to think that the standards for happiness are more objective.

Kraut notes that just as the deceived but unaware person might experience his life as though it were happy and yet actually be unhappy, it is an illusion to hold false beliefs about what goals we should pursue. We can be mistaken in the standards we choose for ourselves, and in how we apply them to our own life. Moreover, claims Kraut, this is equally a case of deception, though a fraud committed by oneself rather than by others. He elaborates:

> If a person wants to lead the best life he is capable of, but is deeply mistaken about what this life consists in or how it is to be accomplished, then he is in as sorry a state as the man who is deceived into believing that he is loved by his friends. Both think they are leading a certain sort of life, but they are far from it, and so neither is living a happy life – though they may *feel* happy.[22]

The funny thing about being wrong is that it feels a lot like being right. We can be mistaken with respect to our own standards for happiness and yet be none the wiser.

And if we do not believe that we can go wrong with respect to choosing our standards, then some of our behaviors seem odd, to say the least. If we can never be wrong about the standards for our happiness, then why do we seek advice from others? Why do we listen to philosophers or go to psychologists or buy books on how to improve our happiness? If happiness is completely a matter of the standards you set for yourself, and if you can never err in your choice of standards, then looking to others for guidance would likely be useless. It would be like looking to others to determine

---

22 Ibid., 185.

what foods will taste best to you, or asking others what your favorite color should be. Any answer they give would be, at best, a guess based on their own tastes. On the other hand, if we can be deceived about what are the best ways to live in order to achieve happiness, then asking help from others, especially those that seem to be doing well, makes a lot more sense.

Then again, as noted in the previous chapter, objective standards that are imposed on us will not motivate our choices if they are not endorsed by us. They will also hold little weight in how we evaluate our lives. They will thus fail to be normatively compelling. Telling the high-school student that he should value authenticity will do little to change his mind if he has already thought about his standards carefully and sincerely does not mind having fake friends or disingenuous experiences.

Additionally, we might think that some deception is a good thing, and that our happiness may even depend on minor deceptions. For example, we may know that our spouse or friend is lying to us when they remark that we look nice just after being prompted by us with the question. Even so, our happiness is better served by the lie. We ourselves tell these same fibs to others. We realize that being a good friend might mean, at least once in a while, being less than perfectly honest and so we use minor falsehoods such as these to make our loved ones happy. Further, we like to think that we are above average in looks, intelligence, and other similar qualities. But obviously we can't *all* be above average. We'd like to take credit for being these ways even if we realize somewhere deep down that it may not be true. And so, it seems, we even deceive ourselves in order to prop up our happiness. Or consider another question: how many people want to know what their parents *really* think of them? For many people, the desire to fulfill their parents' expectations and make them proud of the way they've lived their lives forms an important basis of their happiness. They would rather live with the idea that they are making their parents proud than find out that their parents view them as an incredible disappointment. In fact, there are so many other ways in which our happiness depends on well-crafted minor deceptions. To be sure, we might not think that someone so radically deceived as those in the cases we have been considering is happy. But, at the same time, we also are not willing to think that only a life of utter honesty can be happy. To the contrary, we might think that a happy life includes some amount of helpful deception.

Even so, it does seem that cases of deception suggest that happiness is an evaluative term; in other words, the question of happiness is a matter of what has value. And in these cases we've considered, it does seem pretty clear that the deceived men are living lives that could have gone much better for them. Cases of deception, therefore, compel us to directly confront the question of what exactly is the nature of the relationship between the happy life and the good life. Are they the same?

Are Happiness and Well-Being the Same?

While nowadays we may agree that most of us want to be happy and that we do things in the service of happiness, we might be reluctant to think that happiness is the same as well-being. Instead, we seem more comfortable claiming that there is more to a good life than happiness. In fact, what many take the Experience Machine to show is that happiness is best understood as having only very little value, if any, to a life of well-being. Philosopher Julia Annas explains this common way of thinking: "It is much more likely that, if we had a plausible candidate for happiness, but it were pointed out that this candidate lacked something important to human life, the response would be that there is more to life than happiness."[23]

Again, this kind of response likely results from thinking that happiness is about how we experience our lives and that it cannot, therefore, be affected by things of which we are unaware. In other words, happiness is a subjective state where I am the authority: if I think I am happy, I am. But this way of thinking deprives happiness of any authority to rank or judge lives. It would also mean, as demonstrated by the cases of radical deception, that being happy might even be bad for us. But is that right? Or does this overlook the possibility that there is a close connection between happiness and the good life? If there were such a close connection, then we should conclude that ignorance is not bliss. In fact, it never could be, since ignorance is bad for us, and therefore it cannot be a source of happiness. Perhaps, then, happiness is actually about more than how we experience our lives.

According to the theory of eudaimonism, happiness refers to our complete end and the living of an excellent or flourishing life. It therefore rejects the idea that to experience ourselves as happy is all it takes to be so. Our experience in the moment is not authoritative. Clearly, we would trust the high-school student's later judgment that it was actually an unhappy day because he learned more information surrounding his circumstances. In particular, he realized that his experience was not happiness because it was deceptive. This shows that to know our life is going well requires more

---

23 Annas (1998: 45).

than just information from immediate experience. More likely, we cannot know until later in life whether our life has been lived in an excellent way. And as noted above, we also realize that it is possible that we can be mistaken in the moment not only about whether our standards are being met, but also with respect to the standards we choose for our lives.

On the basis of these considerations, we might think that eudaimonism more correctly captures what we think is important about and essential to happiness. We should be careful to point out, though, that even on eudaimonism, our experience of life is quite important. Eudaimonist accounts of happiness – those that most closely identify the happy life and the good life – include all the pleasures and satisfactions that contemporary happiness thinkers care about anyway. For example, when Aristotle talks about eudaimonia, he refers not only to the individual's life as flourishing in objective ways, but also to the fact that the individual will typically be in certain positive states of mind. After all, your experience of life is one aspect of your nature according to which you can flourish. The good life, the life that is worthwhile, will include the pleasant life. This leads Kraut to state, "To think that happiness just involves a psychological condition and that eudaimonia does not is to get both concepts wrong."[24] Happiness includes our inner mental life, but it also includes more than that. The difference is that eudaimonism treats how pleasures or satisfactions are formed, as well as what they are based on, as obvious matters of concern. This underscores the extent to which eudaimonists assume the evaluative nature of happiness. To call someone happy is to say something about the appropriateness of her mental experience: not merely that she feels pleasure or satisfaction, but that she feels pleasure or satisfaction as she *should*.

Another reason we might think that happiness cannot simply be a function of pleasures and satisfactions concerns the notion of achievement. Recall that the Experience Machine can provide a person with all the states of pleasure and satisfaction she desires. This means that, rather than put in the hard work to earn our happiness, it is possible that something (or someone) could do all the work for us. But how many of us actually think that happiness is something that can be just *given* to us? Further, how many of us think that pleasure or satisfaction alone will make us happy, regardless of how we obtain it? What if it requires that we relinquish our agency or liberty? Additionally, we want many things out of life. For example, we might want a high-paying job, a nice house, relaxing vacations, a comfortable

---

24 Kraut (1979: 168).

retirement, and so on. To be sure, the Experience Machine can give us all these things. However, Annas questions whether we just care about getting these things, or whether we care more about the kind of life we live in which we have these things. That is, we think of a happy life as one in which we have these things as *achievements* – that we have lived in such a way that we *earn* them as a result of the life we have made for ourselves. We don't just want the stuff; we want the life in which our stuff is a proper reward for our efforts.[25]

Moreover, thinking of happiness as an achievement – and therefore something not available from an Experience Machine – also makes sense of thinking of happiness as a purpose or end. If the Experience Machine can give us happiness with no effort on our part, then how can happiness be our purpose or end? That is, how can one's purpose in life be something so easy to get? According to Annas, when we think more carefully about our life and how the concept of happiness fits within it, we see that it connects with our practical interests; it connects with other things we value. We realize that episodes of pleasure or satisfaction are not valuable in themselves. They are valuable only insofar as they are nested within an overall framework of aims and goals. Happiness orders this network of value. It is an organizing end in our life: our *telos*. We make plans, both short-term and long-term, with the goal of increasing our happiness. Pursuing happiness gives structure to our life as it sets a target at which to aim. This explains why happiness has such a strong normative pull: as a normative notion, it helps to govern our conduct, offering reasons and motivations to act in some ways rather than others. That happiness has such normative force is a compelling reason for thinking that the happy life and the good life are the same. Just as with well-being, happiness serves as the goal of our projects in life and so gives our life a direction.

Therefore, if happiness is normative in the way just described, then it would seem odd if it turned out only to involve experiences without regard to whether they are the products of deception or are otherwise ill-gotten. For instance, if happiness is merely episodes of pleasure and satisfaction, then it certainly seems quite odd that we wish people happy new years, happy marriages, and happy lives. Or, as mentioned before, consider that when we look into the crib at our newborn baby and wish for her a happy life, we are not simply wishing her a life full of good-feeling moments with many experiences of satisfaction. Such experiences can, even if unlikely, be

---

25 Annas (2004: 50).

the product of drugs (like Aldous Huxley's "soma" from *Brave New World*), virtual or hyper-realities (such as an Experience Machine), evil acts (as with Ted Bundy), or elaborate deceptions by others. Kraut further argues that these episodes of pleasure or satisfaction could even accompany a life characterized by terrible circumstances, such as severe mental disability, slavery, or extreme incapacitation of some kind, like a lobotomy of one's brain. And if this is true, then it does not make sense to wish such happiness on others. It seems more likely that we mean much more than that the person experience positive psychology; we mean something much less trivial. Rather, we are wishing for our child to live a life that goes well as a whole, and for her to be the kind of person she aspires to be. And we are wishing for our child to find success in attaining what she values, provided that her choices are not restricted by unfortunate circumstances. Thus, wishes for happiness seem to include the idea of a life that excludes major misfortunes. And this is why, Kraut argues, we mean essentially the same thing when we wish for a baby to have all the best and when we wish for a baby to lead a happy life.

Hence, contrary to mental state accounts, there are other more robust and important senses of happiness that capture and explain more satisfactorily why we plan our lives around achieving it, and why we think that a happy life is good for the person who lives it. In particular, happiness is about achieving for ourselves the sort of life we aspire to. It is about successfully living up to our values and ideals. To be happy is to have achieved one's most important goals. We thus see happiness as *purposive* and *unifying*. Why am I choosing to do this rather than that? How does this fit with the rest of my aims? Annas calls these ways of thinking about life *global*: thinking of my life as a whole, given my goals and the way they fit together. According to Annas, what this shows is that happiness is something valuable, and it has to do with our lives as wholes, not just segments or parts of it. It therefore is an achievement: a sort of fulfilling of our positive potential or flourishing. To be happy is to have lived excellently.

Annas offers an interesting example to motivate her claim that with respect to happiness, what matters is the living and shaping of our lives, not our feelings or desires. She imagines a woman who lost her job as a result of whistle-blowing on corrupt practices. She writes:

> One onlooker may say that she has ruined her prospects for happiness; now she is unemployable, and all her training and ambition will go to waste. The other may say that she would never have been happy had she not acted as she did; had she failed to live up to her values, her

life would have been infected by hypocrisy. This is a dispute about happiness that could not be settled by reports about her feelings or desire-satisfaction.[26]

Notice that the first response to this situation is not concerned with feelings or desires. It does not state that the woman will be unhappy because she will feel regret or experience depression as a result of losing her job. Rather, it relies on the fact that the woman will no longer be capable of making use of her talents – talents she has spent some measure of time developing in herself. Because she is no longer employable, all of her training and ambition have been for nothing, and so her happiness is ruined. Likewise, the other response says that she could not have been happy by remaining in the position (and thus making good use of her developed skills), because her life would have been infected by a moral failure. To fail to live up to one's values signals a lack of integrity. This all seems a rather natural way to speak about this case, and as Annas points out, nowhere in this dispute about the woman's happiness can we find any concern for her feelings or satisfactions. Thus happiness again seems something more.

Thoroughly contemplating cases of deception, along with the ways in which we use the term "happy" to wish good on others, offers many reasons for thinking that happiness is the same as well-being. We think of happiness as arising from living in some ways rather than others, and it is something we have to earn rather than something that can be just given to us. To live happily is to live a prosperous life. Given that it is about the *living* of life, and not merely the *experiencing* of life, happiness seems to be about what makes a life go best – what is of value in the living of a life. We have already considered authenticity, autonomy, genuine connections with others, and achievement as important dimensions of living happily. But are there other ways to live that add value to a happy life?

What of Moral Virtue?

On the view that happiness and well-being are the same, we have already begun to build a list of what makes a life go best – of how one must live in order to be happy. Because the components of the list go beyond mere subjective experience, such views are sometimes referred to as *objective list theories* of happiness or well-being. An objective list theory is one form

---

26 Ibid., 49.

that a eudaimonist account of happiness might take. After all, according to eudaimonism, to be happy is to flourish as a human person, to fulfill your positive potential. Objective lists attempt to specify the domains in your life according to which you do better or worse. The better you excel along each dimension, the more you will prosper as a person. Beyond those already identified, what are the objective elements of life that can contribute to it going well and being happy?

If happiness is about what has value in life, and if we are building a list of the important domains along which humans can fare better or worse, then it seems clear that we might want to consider the moral domain. In fact, thinking back on the Experience Machine, you might have thought that one reason for not plugging in was notably absent from the discussion. For many, the reasons not to plug in have little to do with authenticity or autonomy. Rather, some choose not to enter because they believe they have obligations to those who would be left behind, obligations that override any private interests we might have in experiencing pleasures and satisfactions. If this is the reason you were reluctant to plug into the machine, then maybe you think a dedication to the moral life is a deeply important aspect of what it means for a life to go best. So should we include the moral life in our list of things that contribute to a happy life? That is, what exactly is the relationship between the moral life and the happy life? Must the happy life include moral virtue?

Chapter 9:   Happiness, Moral Virtue, and the Purpose of Life

IN PLATO'S *Republic*, GLAUCON, a central character of the dialogue and Plato's real-life older brother, argues that a person can be happy even while lacking moral virtue. In fact, he suggests that being moral is often contrary to living happily. To make his case, Glaucon recounts the fates of two different men. One of the men is truly just and virtuous, living a life of piety and nobleness with the desire to *be* and not simply to *seem* just, yet he nevertheless has the false reputation for being unjust. The other is the converse: a thoroughly vicious man with the highest reputation for being virtuous. Of course, the two men suffer radically different fates in life. According to Glaucon, the just man with the false reputation is frustrated throughout life, and in the end he "will be scourged, racked, fettered, will have his eyes burnt out, and at last, after suffering every kind of torture, he will be crucified."[1] One might even imagine that Glaucon is describing the life of Jesus, who lived a wholly virtuous life only to be crucified on account of false charges that he claimed kingly powers against the Roman Empire. The unjust man, on the contrary, with his pristine reputation lives a life of fortune, prestige, and power, having every advantage. He can even curry favor with the gods, according to Glaucon, as he is more capable of offering sacrifices and doing his duty, all the while being vicious and unjust in private.

Which of the two lives is happier? Glaucon thinks the choice is clear: "a better provision is made both by gods and men for the life of the unjust,

---

1   Plato, *Republic* II.362a.

than for the life of the just."[2] Socrates, Plato's teacher and mouthpiece in the *Republic*, contends to the contrary that it is not at all obvious that the unjust man lives a happier life. In fact, he believes the opposite to be the case: the virtuous person will always be the most happy, whereas the vicious person will always be the most wretched and miserable. Who is right? At first glance, it seems that Glaucon has the stronger position. After all, the vicious man is afforded all sorts of power, wealth, and honor due to his reputation, not to mention the fact that he is not made to suffer public execution. It is hard to see how his life could fail to be the happier of the two. Nevertheless, Socrates is convinced that the advantages the unjust man enjoys are of little value to the truly happy life. In fact, the only thing that matters to happiness is the life of virtue. If Socrates is correct, then the vicious man's life is missing the only thing of importance, while the just man's life has it in spades. Let's explore this claim.

As a eudaimonist, Plato holds that to be happy, a person's life must be going well for her, where this means that she is flourishing or living an excellent human life, or that she has achieved certain goods or developed certain capacities. In other words, she must live well and in a way that lacks nothing of ultimate importance. According to eudaimonism, the fact that the just man experiences a loss of reputation and endures much suffering does not automatically mean that he is unhappy, since this would be to assume that happiness reduces only to our experience of life, something that eudaimonists reject. Instead, especially in light of our discussion of radical deception from the previous chapter, it seems plausible that there are things important to happiness beyond our psychological experience.

In this chapter, we will be considering perhaps the two most widely known eudaimonist accounts of happiness, those of Plato and Aristotle. According to both ancient philosophers, achieving happiness or a life well lived is the *purpose* of life. For example, Aristotle writes, "all knowledge and every pursuit aims at ... the highest of all goods achievable by action ... happiness."[3] To think of happiness in this eudaimonist sense is to recognize that it is the ideal and goal of all our actions. We plan our lives with the aim of achieving happiness. However, the ancient Greeks do not merely say that happiness is an end at which we aim, as one among many. In fact, they don't even stop at saying that it is our only end. They claim that happiness is a *complete end*. To understand happiness in this way implies that the happy life

---

2   Ibid., II.362c.
3   Aristotle, *Nicomachean Ethics* I.4.

is missing absolutely nothing of significance. It is an exemplary human life, a life that displays a fully developed, realized, or perfected nature.

Moreover, to claim that happiness is our final and complete end means that happiness is our *telos*. A *telos* is our unifying purpose, our ultimate overarching end; it structures our values and projects in life; we plan everything around it; it gives both reason and direction to our behavior. This allows us to make sense out of much that we pursue. Many of the desires we have seem to make sense only within the context of larger, more inclusive aims. Our goals are thus nested: they fit together to shape a conception of our lives as wholes. As a result, philosopher Julia Annas claims that we realize that

> what faces me is not just a series of actions trailing into the future, but a task, namely the task of forming my life as a whole in and by the way I act. I then have, even if in a vague and muddled way, a conception of my life as a whole and of the overall way my endeavors are shaping it – my *telos* as the ancients put it.[4]

So our project is to build a worthwhile life through our choices and actions. Being mindful of our overall aims, we actively shape our lives by unifying our daily activities into an integrated whole. Aristotle argues, "Everyone who has the power to live according to his own choice should ... set up for himself some object for the good life to aim at ... by reference to which he will do all that he does, since not to have one's life organized in view of some end is a sign of great folly."[5] It is not impossible for us to wander blindly through life, but then what will we have made of ourselves? What value does such a life have to the one who lives it? It seems a rather foolish waste.

Nevertheless, saying that happiness is the complete end at which our lives aim does not yet fill in the details of what it means to be happy. Happiness could still be understood in a number of ways. In fact, Plato and Aristotle disagree with each other over the nature of happiness. Nevertheless, they both accept that to give an account of happiness is to give an account of the ideal human life. They also agree that moral virtue is essential to the happy life, though to what extent is a matter of dispute. And finally, both accept that at the very least, as a complete end, happiness cannot be reduced to the experience of pleasure or satisfaction. So what does a flourishing human life look like? In other words, what makes for an excellent life?

---

4   Annas (2004: 48).

5   Aristotle, *Eudemian Ethics* 1214b, 6–14.

To answer the above questions, perhaps it would help to consider what makes other things excellent. For example, we might ask, what makes a knife an excellent knife? What criteria must it satisfy to be counted among the best of knives? We seem to evaluate knives according to the following criteria (perhaps among others): durability, sharpness, balance, and ergonomic fit. The more elements of this list a particular knife has, and the higher the degree of each it possesses, the better the knife. A knife that dulls quickly, is poorly balanced, and is awkward in the hand is a bad knife, whereas a knife that meets all of the criteria is an excellent knife. Of course, the perfect knife — if such a knife exists — is the knife that meets all the criteria to the highest degree possible.

What leads us to select these criteria as appropriate ways of evaluating a knife? We hit upon these as the features of a good knife by way of first recalling what a knife is for: what its purpose is. A knife is designed for the purpose of cutting things, and so whatever features of a knife allow it to perform its function more fully are criteria we use to judge the goodness or badness of particular knives. We do this with many ordinary objects. For instance, we evaluate automobiles according to fuel efficiency, safety, reliability, and design. Why? Because each of these elements, we assume, contributes to an automobile's more fully fulfilling its purpose of capably transporting persons. This means that to determine the properties of an excellent knife or car we need to first determine or have in mind the object's purpose; and it is in regard to this purpose that we can determine what features it must have in order to more fully achieve it.

Of course, we need to be careful in how we understand both the purpose of a knife and, accordingly, those features that lead to its being excellent. After all, what it means for a paring knife to fit well in the hand is different from what it means for a carving knife to do so. Likewise, what counts as sufficiently sharp will be different if we are considering a butter knife instead of a utility knife. Particular knives have specialized purposes, so it makes sense that the properties of a good knife will be relative to these more focused uses. Nevertheless, we can still generalize the criteria for excellent knives in the way we have, since whatever else their specialized purposes may be, *all* knives are designed to cut things. This requires a set of general properties, which will be manifested in slightly different ways depending on the knife's specialized purpose.

By like reasoning, if our purpose in life is to be happy, then we should try to determine which aspects of life allow us to more fully achieve happiness; and whatever aspects these are, they will be closely linked to our nature as human beings. Yet some might think it really odd to suggest that human beings have a purpose. While it is quite natural to understand artifacts like cars or knives as having purposes, this is only because they have been intentionally designed for some function or use. It is less clear, however, that we can make sense of a human person as having a purpose. To think that we do seems to suggest that, perhaps, like artifacts, we were designed by some intelligent being to serve some function. Of course, this would require a specification of who and why. Perhaps we were designed by God for the purpose of living according to the divine will. If so, then happiness would consist in serving God and devoting oneself to a life of charity, piety, and hope. It is not surprising that medieval Christian theologians found a kindred philosophy in the ancient wisdom of the Greeks and that they used it to further develop religious understanding.

Alternatively, to say that humans have a purpose might suggest that we have a naturally given function as biological beings. For instance, we often talk as if ample sunlight and water serve the purpose of a plant's flourishing. This suggests that even though plants are not artifacts, they might have a purpose, and that their purpose might be, like ours, to flourish. So, we might similarly think that, as biological beings, our purpose is also open to such natural explanations. For example, evolutionary psychologist Daniel Nettle suggests that we, like plants and all other biological organisms, have a natural purpose: that of biological fitness. What it means for us to flourish is that we have those capacities that position us well to survive and procreate. We could then specify the virtues or excellences specific to our species that lead to a successful achievement of that end.[6] Nettle suggests that our psychological experiences, including those of pleasure, satisfaction, fear, and the like, serve these natural purposes.[7] However, such an evolutionary explanation leaves us wanting more. If our *telos* is wholly biological, it loses some of its luster. It ceases to have the pre-eminent value necessary for a final and complete end of life. Are we really supposed to believe that our happiness rests only on surviving long enough to successfully further the species? Is there no other end at which we might aim and call our purpose in living? Here, again, religious faith might offer a plausible response.

Yet perhaps there is another way to understand our "natural purpose" other than biologically. It does seem, after all, as if we have aims that go

---

6   While there is some controversy concerning whether biology needs to be understood in such ways, it seems plausible that teleology (i.e., explanations of things, processes, or actions based on their purpose) cannot be eliminated from biology.

7   Nettle (2005).

beyond what is merely biological. We are also creative, rational, political, and moral beings. Maybe something like this list of central capabilities could serve as a foundation for understanding what it means to flourish as a human person. The more capabilities we are able to successfully exercise, the more we flourish and, therefore, the happier we are. So, perhaps, when the ancient Greeks talk of human beings as having purposes, it is not as mysterious as it might first sound. Still, what does it mean to flourish in life? What does the very best life amount to?

The Transformative Power of Virtue

According to Plato, the very best life one can live is the life of virtue. In fact, the virtuous life just is the happy life, and vice versa. On this view, living virtuously is all it takes to be happy, and more than that, it is the *only* way to be happy. Again, though, to establish this claim he needs to show how it is that the man who is virtuous but crucified is happier than the man who is vicious but honored. That is a tall order, as Glaucon's set of examples seems to show the reverse, namely that injustice is more frequently the ally of happiness, and that the life of virtue is often undertaken at the expense of one's happiness. In this scenario, Glaucon has stripped away the instrumental benefits of virtue so that he may question whether the virtuous life would still stand on its own as the truly better life. Why does Plato believe that moral virtue is sufficient for happiness? Why does he think this is at all plausible?

The answer relies in part on the fact that when one acquires virtue, it transforms one's understanding of happiness. Plato explains that living virtuously leads one to think about happiness in the proper way: in a way that reveals that the man on the rack has everything of value, and the man with honor and power is missing it all. Plato identifies being virtuous with being just. *Being* just is much more important than *appearing* just, and being unjust is always an evil, even if one can get away with it. Simply by living virtuously, the virtuous person is happy. One could take all other things from her, and as long as she remained steadfastly virtuous, she would remain happy. The reason for this, as Annas explains, is that "the virtuous person is not tempted to identify happiness with something like having a lot of money, for virtue enables you to correct ordinary valuations and arrive at a true estimate of value."[8] Part of acquiring virtue entails that we come to see the proper value of things – we come to enjoy only those activities that exemplify virtue.

---

8   Annas (1998: 49).

The virtuous person realizes that all other conventional goods – such as health, wealth, and political power – only contribute to happiness as part of an overall virtuous life. They are of no value on their own; they contribute to happiness only if they are utilized properly. On the other hand, the unjust and vicious person who spends life pursuing conventional goods is mistaken with respect to what makes for a happy life. Because the vicious man lacks virtue, no amount of conventional goods can bring him happiness; more importantly, they will likely further entrench his unhappiness, as they will reinforce his false view. As a result, it is misleading to think that conventional goods are actually part of happiness, since virtue alone is sufficient.

Of course, one might at this point be rightfully skeptical. What promise do we have that if we take on this project of transformation we will actually find true and genuine happiness? Isn't it also possible for it to end in misery? As some reassuring evidence that the life of wisdom and virtue will lead to the happy life, consider the disposition commonly associated with wise sages. Do we think that they are happy or unhappy? Our intuition seems to associate wisdom with a sort of contentment and gaiety in life, even into old age, such that it is difficult to imagine an unhappy but truly wise person. So perhaps Plato's suggestions for how to live are not so far-fetched. Perhaps pursuing the life of virtue can indeed lead us toward a happier and more contented life. Yet this is a far cry from the type of man, described by Glaucon, who has suffered immensely. We will need to know more if we are to be convinced of Plato's position that a person in those circumstances can truly be happy.

Plato offers a series of arguments to meet this challenge. In order to see the connection between being virtuous and being truly happy, we must remember that happiness is a sort of flourishing. It results from our perfecting our nature. For Plato, flourishing consists in experiencing inner harmony by way of an attuned soul, and this sort of inner harmony can be achieved only through living virtuously. Plato explains:

> Instead of dealing with a man's outward performance of his own work, [justice] has to do with that inward performance of it which truly concerns the man himself, and his own interests; so that the just man will not permit the several principles within him to do any work but their own, nor allow the distinct classes in his soul to interfere with each other, but will really set his house in order; and having gained the mastery over himself, will so regulate his own character as to be on good terms with himself, and to set those three principles in

tune together, as if they were verily three chords of a harmony ... and
after he has bound all these together, and reduced the many elements
of his nature to a real unity, as a temperate and duly harmonized man,
he will then at length proceed to do whatever he may have to do.[9]

So to be happy is to have a harmonious soul: to be on good terms with
yourself and to experience inner harmony through self-control and character regulation. All of this results from living the life of virtue. To achieve
eudaimonia, or to become an excellent human being, we must attend to
the parts of our nature properly. When a person has properly ordered her
soul so that its parts are unified in accordance with nature, she will experience psychic harmony and a sense of being at peace with herself. Plato
believes we have a composite nature consisting of three essential parts: our
appetitive or desiring self; our spirited or emotional self; and our rational
self. Even if we are wary about believing we have a soul, Plato's position
is still insightful insofar as he is taken to be discussing different aspects or
principles at work in our psychology. In other words, we can put aside the
contentious metaphysics of the soul and instead apply what Plato says to our
conscious experience.

According to Plato, a soul that is in harmony will be one in which the
three parts work together properly, each performing its own unique function without interfering with the functions of the other parts. This, however, should not be taken to mean they all play an equal role. For Plato,
reason is the ruling principle of our soul, and it should be fully in charge
when we make decisions. It is our cognitive or "executive" self, and in a
well-ordered soul it regulates and governs the other two parts, integrating
and directing our activities toward furthering our well-being. Our spirited
principle is the part of us that is closely associated with shame, envy, and
anger, along with pride, courage, and honor. Spirit's job is to assist reason in
ruling over and regulating our appetites by causing us to feel shame when
we act in vicious and irrational ways, and to feel pride when we act virtuously. In other words, a well-functioning spirited principle is the source
of our moral conscience, the source of the internal sanctions we use to
motivate proper action and correct for vicious errors. Finally, our appetites
provide us with information about our wants and needs; however, because
we have so many appetites, they need to be held in check. Our appetites
seem boundless and directed at many different objects. They cannot be

---

9   Plato, *Republic* IV.443d–e.

trusted always to lead us toward what is most important in life; often, to the contrary, they lead us astray to pursue ends that are bad for us. So we must always subject the appetites to rational scrutiny, making sure that satisfying them now and in this way is proper and conducive to our happiness. To have a soul in which the three parts function well and in accord with their function is, according to Plato, the same as to be a just or virtuous person.

As an analogy for the well-ordered soul, we could describe reason as the "shepherd," appetites as the "sheep," and spirit as the "sheepdog" of the soul. The dog is beholden to the shepherd but is also capable of being trained so that it can exercise a degree of its own volition in performing its duties. When the shepherd and dog work in tandem it is easy to control the herd. The whole operation works smoothly, like a well-oiled machine. On the other hand, when the dog obstinately fails to follow commands, it is difficult to keep the herd under control and the results are tumultuous and disorderly. At still other times, if excited and riled up, the herd may even be able to overpower the shepherd and his dog, resulting in similar chaos. As with flocks of sheep, so too with souls: if our appetites overrun our reason and spirit, our lives become tumultuous and chaotic. But when reason reigns and, with the help of spirit, is able to corral our appetites, we experience inner harmony.

Unhappiness, by contrast, is a disharmony of the soul caused by its parts operating at odds with each other. When there is discord – when the parts of the soul are fighting against each other – we do not experience ourselves as a unified and harmonious person. Instead, we feel internally divided and suffer inwardly. Those of us who have ever been on a diet understand this phenomenon and can relate it to our own lives. We open the fridge late at night to grab some water and notice that last piece of chocolate cake staring back at us. Suddenly we have an urge to wolf it down. Of course, at the very same time, we know we are on a diet and we try to resist the temptation. There ensues an inner dialogue where we try to talk ourselves out of eating the delicious-looking cake. Some of us will succeed, some will not, and when we succeed we might feel pride, while when we don't we might feel guilt. Either way, we experience ourselves as internally divided; we experience inner discord. Additionally, we feel a separation in ourselves when we struggle over whether to keep or break our promises, to stick with our plan to quit smoking or give in and light up, to go to work or call in sick, or many other similar experiences. While we may not frequently experience this division, we at least sometimes have first-hand experience of what it is like to have a discordant and divided psychology.

Plato himself offers us a powerful illustration of a disharmonious soul: the story of Leontius, a young man who, while walking into town one day, witnesses some dead bodies lying on the ground next to an executioner. Plato continues:

> He immediately felt a desire to look at them, but at the same time loathing the thought he tried to divert himself from it. For some time he struggled with himself, and covered his eyes, until at length, over-mastered by the desire, he opened his eyes wide with his fingers, and running up to the bodies exclaimed, "There! You Wretches! Gaze your fill at the beautiful spectacle!"[10]

Though extreme, the story of Leontius illustrates a rather common experience: we can both desire something and yet feel ashamed or guilty of that desire and become angry with ourselves for giving in to it. The situation involving Leontius is one in which his disgust with himself runs counter to his morbid desires; he despises himself because he is overpowered by his appetites against the dictates of his reason. This illustrates the three parts. Reason suggests to Leontius that there is no good to come through satisfying his sick curiosity. Still, his appetites give rise to a compulsion to which he eventually succumbs. When thus overwhelmed by his desire, he immediately feels guilt, anger, and disgust at himself for giving in to what he knows is a morbid desire.

On the other hand, the virtuous person would realize from the outset that this kind of desire is irrational and inappropriate. The life of virtue consists in having a well-ordered soul in which reason is in full control of the person, organizing her pursuits and regulating her decisions. Having been duly transformed through the acquisition of virtue, she would view such a desire, not at all as pleasurable, but as disgusting. Yet this indicates that the acquisition of virtue will not only alter what we take to have value in life, but also change how we experience things emotionally. What we might have once thought pleasant will now strike us as banal, or perhaps even repulsive. Why? What is it about acquiring virtue that leads us to no longer take pleasure in satisfying certain of our appetites? And why is the gratification of certain desires bad for us? Why does giving in to such temptations lead to our unhappiness?

---

10 Ibid., IV.440a.

The King, the Tyrant, and the Democrat: The Role of Pleasure in the Life of Virtue

To illustrate the pernicious effects of allowing our appetites free reign, Plato uses a metaphor of three different people, each of whom represents a different type of life a person could lead. The kingly man is the just man whose reason is firmly in control and regulates his life; the tyrannical man is the unjust man whose appetites rule completely; and the democratic man is one in whom appetites are indulged but have yet to entirely control his course of conduct because he still adheres to law and morality. Plato then explains how and why the tyrannical or unjust man's soul is unsettled by pointing to his psychic disharmony. Further, Plato argues that the democratic man will eventually succumb to the same fate if he does not more fully commit to the life of virtue.

In order to get the full picture here, we need to know that, according to Plato, there are two types of desires in a person: necessary and unnecessary. Necessary desires are those that we cannot suppress or eliminate, as our nature compels us to satisfy them. Because they support our nature, satisfying them is beneficial to us. For example, eating is necessary for our continued existence, and satisfying this desire supports our health and strength. Unnecessary desires, on the other hand, are those that serve no real purpose in life and can be eliminated through discipline without causing any harm to the person. Satisfying these desires, though it may seem enjoyable, brings us no genuine good, and it can even be quite harmful to us. These desires are harmful not only to the body, but also to the soul in that they can interfere with our pursuit of wisdom and virtue. For instance, an exorbitant intake of alcohol or sugar will cause bodily disease and also impair certain rational abilities, such as reliable memory. Unnecessary desires can be further divided into two types: those that one can indulge in a lawful way and those that are expressly forbidden by the law. So while we have many gluttonous desires, some of them can be satisfied legally, as in ravaging an all-you-can-eat food buffet, while others are satisfied only illegally, such as satisfying a desire to eat meat through cannibalism.

These unlawful unnecessary desires are particularly nasty in their effects. Despite our finding them unsettling, it is hard to rid ourselves completely of their presence, as they tend to emerge in our dreams when we are sleeping and when reason does not have as tight a hold on the soul. As Plato explains, when asleep and dreaming, "the wild animal part ... becomes rampant.... You know that in such moments there is nothing that it dares not do, released and delivered as it is from any sense of shame [spirit] and reflection [reason]."[11] Similarly, when people are drunk, rational capacities are impaired such that drunks often become more violent, rash, and arrogant. We all recognize that we must be on guard against this side of ourselves – we must be sure to "cage the beast" within. What distinguishes the tyrannical man is his willingness to let the beast out and to allow it to rule his behavior.

The tyrannical man's life, asserts Plato, can never be a happy one, for he has lost control of himself and is, instead, overtaken by his appetitive soul. He has become, while awake, what most of us are only in sleep: he is a living nightmare. The tyrannical man is ruled by his unnecessary desires so much so that he is willing to engage in many immoral and vicious acts in order to satisfy them, even going to such great lengths as theft and murder to attain them. Plato describes the tyrannical man as one who lives only for parties, drink, and sex, who will squander all of his wealth in pursuit of them, and when his resources are exhausted will rob others, even those he loves, in order to continue to indulge his excessive appetites. Thus, states Plato:

> [The tyrant] cannot help being and ... becoming more and more envious, faithless, unjust, friendless, unhealthy, and the host and nurse of every vice; and, in consequence of all this, he must in the first place be unhappy in himself, and in the next place he must make those who are near him as unhappy as himself.... [H]e is the happiest man who is best and most just, that is, who is most kingly, and who rules over himself royally; whereas, he is the most wretched man who is worst and most unjust, that is, who is most tyrannical, and who plays the tyrant.[12]

The tyrant can never trust anyone and therefore has no true friends. He will be full of fear, grief, remorse, lamentation, and even madness. His soul will not be free, but instead enslaved by craving and confusion. He must suffer from loneliness, an unhealthy psychology, and a fractured identity. All of this has serious affects on his happiness.

This seems an apt description of Ted Bundy. His appetites were out of control, and there was no internal sanction in the form of a feeling of shame

---

11 Ibid., IX.571c.
12 Ibid., IX.580a–b.

or guilt to rein them in. In fact, Bundy asserted that in killing others he had released his "true uninhibited self." He was "uninhibited" because he did not feel guilt for his horrendous actions. Yet is being uninhibited in this sense a good thing? Bundy had a poorly functioning spirit (or none at all), and he felt no internal sanctions when he indulged his vicious appetites. Nothing aided reason to compel virtuous behavior. The purpose of guilt is to alert us when we are being vicious and to make us suffer inwardly, thus also correcting our future conduct. Yet, as Bundy himself notes, in the absence of a properly functioning conscience, the only thing left to guide his conduct was pursuit of pleasure. Perhaps, then, Plato offers us one way to interpret psychopathy: it is when one has an absent, diseased, or otherwise malfunctioning spirit. Of course, such a life is incapable of inner harmony. Bundy's lack of shame betrays an unhealthy and disorderly soul.

Unlike the tyrant, the virtuous person in pursuit of happiness knows what kind of person she has to be in order to achieve it. She is not tempted to identify happiness with the satisfaction of appetites, whether they are for money or titles or power, because she realizes that such pursuits are hollow. Instead, the wise person seeks happiness in virtue. She redirects her attention away from the shallow desires of the herd to what has true and ultimate value. Transformed by virtue, she realizes where she needs to look for happiness and understands the sort of person she needs to be in order to achieve it. Moreover, even her emotional experience of life is altered so that she takes great pleasure in living virtuously and views satisfying her base appetites with contempt.

So far, then, Plato has argued that the virtuous kingly person experiences happiness since he experiences inner harmony and is on good terms with himself. Moreover, the vicious tyrannical person is unhappy and wretched since he experiences inner discord as well as frustration and alienation from society. But why not be the democratic person? Isn't there a way to indulge our unnecessary appetites lawfully and so have the best of both worlds? Why is the virtuous person the only one who is happy, according to Plato?

Essentially, Plato argues that only the virtuous and wise man is competent to judge the nature of the happy life, as he has experienced many types of pleasures and has the knowledge to think clearly about different kinds of lives. This sounds similar to Mill's competent judge argument, discussed in Chapter Four: only one who has experienced all kinds of pleasures can truly judge which of them is superior. On the other hand, one who is concerned only to satiate bodily desires has no true experience with virtue or wisdom and so knows nothing of their importance. Plato puts this point boldly:

> Those, therefore, who are inexperienced with prudence and virtue, and who spend their time in perpetual banqueting and similar indulgences, are carried down, as it appears, and back again only as far as the midway point on the upward road; and between these limits they roam their life long, without ever overstepping them so as to look up towards, or be carried to, the true above – and they have never been really filled with what is real, or tasted sure and unmingled pleasure; but like cattle, they are always looking downwards, and hanging their heads to the ground, and poking them into their dining-tables, while they graze and get fat and propagate their species; and, to satiate their greedy desire for these enjoyments, they kick and butt with hoofs and horns of iron, till they kill one another under the influence of ravenous appetites – trying to fill their leaky part with things that are not.[13]

Thus, the person who lives a life of the appetites cannot be happy since he is in endless pursuit of money, bodily pleasures, and material possessions, rather than virtue. His ravenous appetites will lead to poor physical and mental health and require him to compete with others for more and more things for bodily enjoyment, eventually leading to strife and war. Hence even the democratic life is unhealthy, empty, and miserable. This is an eerily familiar description of contemporary life in the United States, where increasing consumerism has yielded unhealthy outcomes like higher rates of stress, anxiety, depression, obesity, diabetes, and heart disease, and has led to frequent violence both domestically and through foreign invasion.

Notice that, in the above passage, Plato states that people who pursue the life of the appetites only ever reach the "midway point on the upward road," and they have never "tasted sure and unmingled pleasure." This suggests that pleasures of the body (non-intellectual pleasures) are not really pleasures at all but are at best a neutral state – merely the absence of pain. As an example, Plato notes how often the sick and those in pain proclaim that nothing is more pleasant than health and absence of pain, but that before they were sick or in pain, they had not found out its "supreme pleasantness." This is an intriguing observation. If you think about being healthy and ask yourself whether you actually experience positive pleasure as a result, you might be shocked to notice that you do not. Instead, health seems to be one of those things you only notice in its absence. When you are unhealthy you suffer, yet when you are healthy you rarely take note. In fact, argues Plato,

---

13 Ibid., IX.586a.

this is true of many of the so-called pleasures of the body – they are a kind of release from pain. He writes, "Hence, the repose felt at the times we speak of is not really, but only appears to be, pleasant by the side of what is painful, and painful by the side of what is pleasant; and these appearances will in no instance stand the test of comparison with true pleasure, because they are only some kind of bewilderment."[14] So to satisfy a physical desire is just to quell a certain type of painful yearning or craving. At best, all we can accomplish in pursuit of physical pleasure is to escape from pain. To pursue them, then, at the expense of the pleasures of virtue seems foolish since they can never really make good on the promise of happiness.

To be sure, it is not always the case that enjoyable physical sensations are just the absence of pain. If we have no pre-existing desire, then there is no pre-existing pain to escape. As such, it is possible to experience a sensation as truly pleasurable, though it will likely be fleeting and have little to no impact on our happiness. For example, as Plato notes, catching the passing scent of a fragrant flower on a spring day does lead to a modicum of positive pleasure. It is not just the absence of pain, because we did not set out that day desiring or craving good-smelling flowers, so we had no appetite to satisfy. Even so, such cases of genuine physical pleasures are more the exception than the rule.

More typically, when we satisfy a desire or appetite, we get nothing positive out of it. We might temporarily satisfy a desire, of course, but another one soon crops up again. The body is never full. We are like a bucket with holes, or as Plato says, a "leaky part." No matter how much we put into it, it soon wants more. In addition, the more we indulge the desires of the appetitive soul, the more powerful they become. The more food we eat today, the hungrier we will feel tomorrow. The pursuit of bodily pleasures will result only in stronger desires in the future, which are themselves a kind of pain or suffering. In a twist of irony, then, pursuit of hedonic delights actually ends in increased suffering.

Chasing after non-intellectual pleasures also helps to reinforce the tyranny of one's appetites over reason. As our appetites grow stronger through repeated satiation, it becomes more and more difficult to ignore them. They eventually consume us. This is what has happened to the tyrant, and it will also happen to the democratic man if he continues on the path he is on. The more we cede control of our lives to the appetitive principle of our soul, the more ravenous our appetites become until they completely dominate our

---

14 Ibid., IX.583d.

being and we forsake everything that is of true value. Rather than spend our energies and efforts working on bettering our characters as persons, we instead concentrate only on filling our bodies. In this way, claims Plato, our bodies come to overmaster us, when it is we who should master them.

Pursuing such experiences, therefore, is inadvisable. One rarely gets beyond the absence of suffering – beyond the neutral point on the pleasure and pain scale. More than that, one would be willingly giving control of one's life over to its most base aspect. For these reasons, Plato contends that true lovers of wisdom are not concerned with satiating the desires of the body. They recognize that they get nothing from such activity. The lover of wisdom and reason, therefore, is contrasted with the lover of the body (the hedonist), and, Plato argues, the life of wisdom and virtue is superior in all respects.

In summary, Plato sources happiness entirely in our virtue. Acting virtuously consists in a properly functioning harmonious soul. We can consider harmonious souls as "healthy" and disharmonious souls as "diseased" in much the same way as we can speak of health and disease in our bodies. Health in the body occurs when the various organs function well and in accord with nature, allowing us to flourish physically. Likewise, a body is diseased when it fails to function naturally. The purpose of medicine is to restore the natural balance – the natural harmony – of all the various bodily forces. Just as the body fails to be healthy when its organs act in discord and against their natural purpose, so too is a soul unhealthy when its various principles conflict with one another and prevent the soul from achieving inner harmony. "Then virtue," Plato states, "will be a kind of health and beauty, and good habit of the soul; and vice will be a disease, and deformity, and sickness of it."[15] Only the life of virtue can be happy, and anyone who is vicious experiences deep psychological sickness and suffering. If the appetites overwhelm reason or spirited aggression usurps reason, such injustice and vice within the soul are as unnatural and as damaging as cancer is to the body.

Philosophy is the medicine of the soul, aiming at mental health in the same way as the medical arts aim at a healthy body: attempting to restore the natural functioning of the various parts. As a result, practicing philosophy has the practical effect of helping people live better lives by way of therapy – removing our false beliefs – and advice – offering instructions on how to live. To become fully virtuous we need to undergo rigorous

---

15 Ibid., IV.444e.

moral examination through reason, which involves understanding what is truly good and then deciding to act on that basis. No other conventional goods are necessary to be happy. Thus we can be happy as long as we are virtuous, and this holds true even if we are unjustly persecuted for a false reputation. But can this really be true? Surely, being virtuous can be one large part of a happy life, but wouldn't a life be even happier still if it also included things like honor, health, and wealth? Plato may have convinced us that virtue is essential to the happy life, but is it sufficient? Is it the only thing we need?

The Complete Life

Glaucon presented us with only two choices: the life of a thoroughly unjust man with the reputation for justice, and the life of a thoroughly just man with a false reputation for injustice. Perhaps Plato's arguments have convinced you that, in this particular case, because virtue is required for happiness, the crucified just man is the happier of the two. What if there was a third option, however? Suppose there is a thoroughly just woman who has the reputation she deserves. Being recognized as just, she therefore receives wealth, honor, loyalty, and friendship as a result. Further, she lives to a ripe old age and in good health. If you had to choose between the two lives described by Glaucon and this one, which is best? This third life clearly seems better and happier. So, although virtue might be necessary, perhaps it is not the only thing important to a happy life. Perhaps the virtuous life full of conventional goods is *happiest* and is what we are after when we seek an understanding of the truly complete and ideal life.

Aristotle takes issue with the claims of Plato that a man without conventional goods – such as the man who experiences great misfortune or the man who is racked and scourged – is happy so long as he is virtuous. In fact, he writes, "Those who say that the victim on the rack or the man who falls into great misfortunes is happy if he is good, are, whether they mean to or not, talking nonsense."[16] After all, not only does this person suffer immense pain and physical torment, but he also suffers unwarranted public shame, embarrassment, and an unjustified loss of honor. His name is tarnished, and even to a virtuous person this must sting. Thus, while his teacher Plato believed that a life of virtue was sufficient for happiness, Aristotle thinks that there is more to a happy life than living virtuously. To be clear, Aristotle

---

16 Aristotle, *Nicomachean Ethics* VII.13.

does think that living in a morally virtuous way is necessary to the happy life – we cannot be happy without being virtuous – but he also thinks there are other ingredients.

If we take seriously the idea that the happy life is complete and lacks nothing that could possibly make it better, then it seems that happiness cannot be narrowed down to just a single domain of human activity. Just as it is not the same as only feeling pleasure or only being satisfied, nor is it the same as only being morally virtuous. A truly fulfilled and complete life will contain all of these elements at least, and probably many more, since it is, after all, the *very best life* we are trying to describe. This also makes sense of philosopher Richard Kraut's claims in the previous chapter about what we are wishing when we wish a newborn baby a happy life. When we wish a child a happy life, we are wishing for her an *excellent* life. As noted, we hope that she may find success in attaining what she values, provided that her choices are not restricted by unfortunate circumstances. Therefore, wishes for happiness seem to include the idea of a life that excludes major misfortunes. We are wishing that she may live long and prosper!

So what is the "very best" life? Aristotle identifies happiness with flourishing in every way, with living an exemplary life. For Aristotle, an excellent life is one in which a person performs the function of humanity well. He states, "For just as for a flute-player, a sculptor, or any artist, and, in general, for all things that have a function or activity, the good and the 'well' is thought to reside in the function, so would it seem to be for man, if he has a function."[17] What, then, is the function of a human being? Aristotle dismisses the idea that our function is merely to live; we are more than a biological organism. After all, "Life seems to belong even to plants, but we are seeking what is peculiar to man."[18] Likewise, sentience, or the ability to consciously perceive and respond to one's environment, is shared with other animals and so cannot be our special function. What is left?

> There remains then, an active life of the elements that has a rational principle.... Now if the function of man is an activity of soul which follows or implies a rational principle ... human good turns out to be activity of the soul exhibiting excellence, and if there are more than one excellence, in accordance with the best and most complete. But we must add "in a complete life." For one swallow does not make a

---

17 Ibid., I.7.
18 Ibid.

summer, nor does one day; and so too one day, or a short time, does not make a man blessed and happy.[19]

So to live an excellent human life is to live an active life in a way that follows from reasoned deliberation about how best to live. It will require that we develop all of our distinctly human capacities for reason, creativity, and virtue, since each of these will help us to live better, more distinctly human lives. In other words, to develop these human capacities is to more fully perfect our nature. Moreover, the life must be complete in the sense that it cannot be cut unnaturally short, nor can you be happy if you only live this way for a brief period of time. To be happy, this must be a general feature of and throughout your entire life.

The insights about the active and complete nature of happiness also shed light on why Aristotle disagrees with Plato that the life of happiness is the life of virtue. Even a life that is fully dedicated to virtue "appears somewhat incomplete," states Aristotle, "for possession of virtue seems actually compatible with being asleep, or with lifelong inactivity, and further, with the greatest sufferings and misfortunes; but a man who was living so no one would call happy, unless he were maintaining a thesis at all costs."[20] In other words, we would not think a person happy and living a complete life if she were to spend her entire life in a vegetative state. Imagine, for instance, a woman in a coma for her entire natural life. True, this woman is not morally vicious, as she has committed no evil acts. In fact, she might even possess a morally virtuous character, though she is unable to exercise it. Actually, we might think that the person in a coma is much like one who would live inside Nozick's Experience Machine. Although the person in the machine may possess a virtuous character, and therefore may have chosen to experience things that display her nobility of taste, she is not active in reality. She is in a vegetative state; she is "an indeterminate blob."[21] A person in such a state cannot be actively virtuous; in fact, she really cannot be any way at all. Possession of virtue is thus insufficient to guarantee happiness.

According to Aristotle, virtuous *activity* is far more important than simply possessing virtue, for the reason that happiness refers to an active way of living rather than some condition of a person. Aristotle elaborates that it makes all the difference whether "we place the chief good in possession

---

19 Ibid.
20 Ibid., I.5.
21 Nozick (1974: 43).

or in use, in state of mind or in activity. For the state of mind may exist without producing any good result, as in a man who is asleep or in some other way quite inactive, but the activity cannot; for one who has the activity will of necessity be acting, and acting well."[22] Thus, insofar as happiness is a matter of living life well, it is an activity. And, to be happy, we must be actively engaged in the living of our life.

Beyond the active life of virtue and reasoned deliberation, what more might Aristotle include in the excellent life? So far, everything he has mentioned is something internal to the person. Things such as possessing and acting on a virtuous character, or using reason and practical wisdom to deliberate about how best to live, are things over which we can exercise some measure of control. Yet, unlike Plato, Aristotle takes the eudaimon life to possess conventional goods as well, since happiness is incompatible with the "greatest sufferings and misfortunes," which will also impede one's virtuous activity:

> Yet evidently, as we said, [happiness] needs the external goods as well; for it is impossible, or not easy, to do noble acts without the proper equipment. In many actions we use friends and riches and political power as instruments; and there are some things the lack of which takes the lustre from happiness – good birth, good children, beauty; for the man who is very ugly in appearance or ill-born or solitary and childless is not very likely to be happy, and perhaps a man would be . still less likely if he had thoroughly bad children or friends or had lost good children or friends by death. As we said, then, happiness seems to need this sort of prosperity in addition.[23]

Of course, given that many of these elements, such as honor, political power, wealth, good birth, and good looks, are outside of our willful control, this means that our happiness is partly a matter of chance and good fortune. Aristotle admits that in order to become fully happy, the world will have to cooperate. Happiness requires that we prosper not only in our characters, but also in other circumstances of life.

Consider wealth as an example. For Aristotle, being wealthy can facilitate happiness in a variety of ways. First, and perhaps most obviously, the wealthy person need not be concerned with the daily task of securing

---

22 Aristotle, *Nicomachean Ethics* I.8.
23 Ibid.

enough resources to survive. She has, therefore, more leisure time available in which to pursue her own development. Hence, she can more frequently engage in contemplation and can undertake virtuous activities more often and to a greater degree. Second, wealth allows her to share more resources with those in need. In so doing, she will garner more recognition as a great person. Honor and reputation attend great displays of wealth and virtue. This not only leads to advantages in life, but also secures to her a more robust and noble legacy. Some living examples of this might be Warren Buffett and Bill and Melinda Gates, who are not only among the richest people in history, but also renowned philanthropists. There may be others in the world who have sacrificed a greater proportion of their resources to good causes. Yet, on account of their bountiful monetary generosity, the world will remember Buffett and the Gateses as great persons of our time, while forgetting others who might well have had an equally deserving character but more meager means.

Beyond wealth, Aristotle worries that an otherwise blessed life can sometimes end in terrible tragedy. Is one who suffers some tragic event late in life, such as a loss of reputation, honor, or family and friends, still to be counted as happy? Aristotle answers that "one who has experienced such chances and has ended wretchedly no one calls happy."[24] Do we agree? Consider, for instance, the life of Joe Paterno. Paterno lived a long life, dying at the age of 85. For 46 years, he was head coach of the Penn State Nittany Lions, and he ended his career with more wins than any college coach in history. More than a football coach, he was a beloved figure in the college community, in part because of the emphasis that he placed on moral conduct. He donated more than $4 million to Penn State and funded the school's world-class research library that now bears his name. The community erected a statue of Paterno in order to memorialize and honor him for his significance to the town and university. He was a beloved public figure, seeming to possess everything required for a truly eudaimon life: honor, virtue, wealth, success, and a long life. However, two and a half months before his death, a scandal broke that exposed Paterno's former assistant coach of engaging in acts of pedophilia and child rape while coaching at Penn State, sometimes even using Penn State facilities. Many thought that Paterno clearly would have known and yet said nothing. His otherwise pristine reputation was tarnished, and he was severely sanctioned. Rather than allow him to retire at the end of the season, the Penn State Board of

---

24 Ibid., I.9.

Trustees immediately fired and dismissed him. After his death, the NCAA revoked all of Paterno's wins after 1998, dropping him from first down to twelfth among the winningest college football coaches, and school authorities removed his statue from Penn State's campus. Further, an investigation conducted after the scandal by former FBI director Louis Freeh concluded that Paterno concealed facts surrounding the abuses by his assistant coach.[25] So was Paterno's life a happy life? He spent 99.8 per cent of his time living a life of honor, prestige, and praise. But did that last 0.2 per cent ruin his happiness?[26]

According to Aristotle, when a life comes to such a tragic end, we cannot help but think that its happiness is ruined. Paterno's legacy is forever to be associated with this event, whether rightfully or not. Many would rather choose to die in anonymity than to always be remembered as being involved with such a vicious affair, and would not trade places with Paterno despite the overwhelming abundance of good throughout his life. Perhaps, then, Aristotle is correct: catastrophic events, if powerful enough, can destroy an otherwise happy life. If so, then our judgments about a person's happiness must always be made cautiously and with the knowledge that tomorrow might change everything. Aristotle concludes, "He is happy who is active in accordance with complete virtue and is sufficiently equipped with external goods, not for some chance period but throughout a complete life ... and who is destined to live thus and die as befits his life."[27] Thus, we cannot know a life to be happy until after we have seen it unfold in its entirety.

The Psychological Rewards of the Eudaimon Life

According to Aristotle, happiness is an excellent human life that has fulfilled its potential in *every* way and to the highest degree; it is a life possessed of all the goods that can make it better. These goods include both mental and physical health, wealth, moral and theoretical wisdom, friends, beauty,

---

25 Some of this information is taken from http://espn.go.com/college-football/story/_/id/8191027/penn-state-hit-60-million-fine-4-year-bowl-ban-wins-dating-1998.

26 In fact, to the extent that we think certain events after his death – such as the removal of his statue, or the revision of his win-loss record – affect our judgment of whether Paterno's life was happy, we see that an intuitive way of thinking about happiness is that it is not purely psychological. In other words, the question of whether we lived happily can be affected by things of which we are unaware, and even by some things that may happen after our death. This supports Aristotle's claim that at least for some time, events that happen even after death could have at least some effect on a person's happiness. See *Nicomachean Ethics* I.10.

27 Ibid., I.12.

and a long life. A life is enriched and made more perfect by possessing such things. Yet a life blessed in these ways but lacking in pleasure and satisfaction also seems to be deficient in some way. Accordingly, Aristotle maintains that one who is in successful pursuit of the happy life will, in fact, take great satisfaction in his life and will also enjoy many pleasures throughout. Kraut elaborates: "*Eudaimonia* involves the recognition that one's desire for the good is being fulfilled, and therefore one who attains *eudaimonia* is necessarily happy with his life. His deepest desires are being satisfied, where those desires are directed at worthwhile goals, and realizing this, he has an especially affirmative attitude towards himself and his life."[28] A person who has achieved eudaimonia will be one who regularly exercises intellectual and moral capacities (among others) and enjoys doing so. Furthermore, he will realize that happiness is the greatest good and know that he possesses this good and all that it includes. Accordingly, he will greatly enjoy his life on account of its desirability and will hold himself in high regard.

The psychological states of satisfaction and pleasure attend the happy life, according to Aristotle. The difference between Aristotle's eudaimonism and our other theories of happiness is that the mere experience of pleasure or satisfaction is not what matters to happiness. Something beyond our first-hand experience matters: namely, the active process by which these mental states are achieved is central to their value to the happy life. One who is simply pleased or satisfied may not be happy if she has improper goals or disproportionately strong desires for external goods. This leads us to another question: In what ways does pleasure appropriately arise from our activities?

Aristotle claims that pleasure typically attends activity done well. This is an astute insight into a rather common experience in life. Take, as a simple example, the game of golf. Golf is notoriously vexing. When one plays poorly, there is no end to the cursing or the throwing of clubs out of frustration. On the other hand, when played with skill, the very same activity can be quite enjoyable. This is true of most skills we can acquire. When we are beginners or novices at some task, often we experience annoyance, anger, and impatience at our lack of ability. Yet when we persist and further master the skill, we find that the activity has been transformed into a pleasurable one. Additionally, the better we get at it, and the easier it becomes for us to perform the action, the more pleasurable is the experience. This is one of the ways in which gaining virtue can transform our experience

---

28 Kraut (1979: 174).

of life: it can lead to our taking pleasure and enjoyment from activities that once seemed painful or boring. The lesson, it seems, is that to receive pleasure from our activities, we first have to suffer through the frustration of becoming proficient. Only after some amount of effort and training will we finally reap the rewards of enjoyment.

Moreover, for each activity, there is a proper pleasure that completes it. For that pleasure to arise, the activity must be done well, which involves matching our activities to the appropriate objects. Using the example of pleasant sensations, Aristotle explains:

> Since every sense is active in relation to its object, and a sense which is in good condition acts perfectly in relation to the most beautiful of its objects ... it follows that in the case of each sense the best activity is that of the best-conditioned organ in relation to the finest of its objects. And this activity will be the most complete and pleasant.[29]

So the feeling of pleasure arises when a well-functioning organ is taking in one of its most beautiful objects. This can be illustrated more fully using the sense of sight. Suppose Alvin has poorly functioning eyes; perhaps as a result of old age and cataracts he can no longer see crisply even with the aid of glasses. If Alvin is presented with a beautiful object to look at, will he get the entire pleasure out of it? Presumably not, because he is unable to fully appreciate the beauty of the object due to his poor eyesight. Likewise, suppose Jon has perfectly functioning eyes but is presented with an ugly object, say a pile of dead corpses, as was the case for Leontius. Will he get pleasure here? No, because although his eyes are functioning well, the sight is ghastly and hence painful to see. Putting these examples together, we will experience pleasure in the activity of sight only when our eyes are functioning properly and are interacting with a beautiful object.

In order to experience the full range of pleasures we must cultivate our virtues, skills, and character so that we are transformed into the type of person who can take pleasure in appropriately beautiful objects and activities. Martha Nussbaum summarizes the point nicely:

> Here is what Aristotle thought: that activity is far and away the main thing and that pleasure will normally crop up in connection with doing good activities without struggle, the way a virtuous person

---

29 Aristotle, *Nicomachean Ethics* X.4.

does them. Pleasure accompanies activity and completes it, like, he says, the bloom on the cheek of a healthy young person. That example implies too, that it would be totally mistaken to pry the pleasure apart from the activity and seek it on its own: for it would then not be the bloom on the cheek of a healthy person, it would be the rouge on the cheek of a person who has not bothered to cultivate health.[30]

For Aristotle, pleasure attends activity done well; it occurs when we act with skilled proficiency and direct our activities toward the appropriate ends. But this means that hedonists are mistaken insofar as they separate the pleasure from the activity and hold it up as the ultimate goal. That misses the point: the activity is what matters, claims Aristotle. It is only by focusing our efforts on excellent activity that the pleasure will ever arise. To do otherwise, to pursue the sensation of pleasure for its own sake, would never yield true enjoyment, just as putting makeup on a cheek does not make for true beauty or health.

The above relationship between pleasure and activity highlights a theme discussed throughout the book, namely that some pleasures are good for us, and some are bad. Just as Plato thinks that some pleasures can distract us from the life of virtue and therefore prevent us from achieving a happy life, Aristotle thinks that some pleasures are harmful. He writes, "The pleasure proper to a worthy activity is good and that proper to an unworthy activity bad; just as the appetites for noble objects are laudable, those for base objects culpable."[31] So Aristotle thinks it possible to rank pleasures from best to worst according to what activities they follow from. Those activities that help us to more fully realize our nature and come closer to achieving our purpose are better than those that do not.

Because excellent activity is the main value, and also because the full flourishing of our nature is the purpose at which we aim in everything we do, it seems rather trite to think of pleasant amusements as deeply important to the happy life. "Happiness, therefore," reasons Aristotle, "does not lie in amusement; it would, indeed, be strange if the end were amusement, and one were to take trouble and suffer hardship all one's life in order to amuse oneself.... Now, to exert oneself and work for the sake of amusement seems silly and utterly childish."[32] Even though we can in fact enjoy simple pleasures, they

---

30 Nussbaum (2012: 341).

31 Aristotle, *Nicomachean Ethics* X.5.

32 Ibid., X.6.

cannot really matter to happiness. They lack the normative power necessary to be the unifying and complete end at which our lives aim. Furthermore, even a person suffering serious misfortune can experience them in passing; yet in such a case we would not thereby argue that the person is happy as a result. Still, claims Aristotle, pleasant amusements can help us achieve happiness insofar as they help us to unwind or relax after a hard day of pursuing the good. One cannot unceasingly pursue the life of reasoned contemplation and moral virtue. After all, philosophical activity requires immense concentration and one cannot continue to focus with such care and power indefinitely. Eventually we need to rest, and pleasant amusements offer a nice respite. So it seems non-intellectual pleasures have some instrumental value in that they refresh our energies so that we might continue the hard work of fashioning ourselves after the ideal of the eudaimon life.

In the end, however, we cannot take seriously the idea that the whole point of life is to pursue amusement. To do so seems to actively choose a life wherein we deny our true nature. Rather, we ought to "strain every nerve to live in accordance with the best thing in us," which is our rational capacity, according to Aristotle. In fact, he continues:

> Even if [reason] be small in bulk, much more does it in power and worth surpass everything. And this would seem actually to *be* each man, since it is the authoritative and better part of him. It would be strange, then, if he were to choose not the life of himself but that of something else.... [F]or man therefore, the life according to reason is best and pleasantest, since reason more than anything else is man. This life therefore is also the happiest.[33]

The pleasures of rational contemplation are renowned for their purity and their enduring nature. Thinking is something we can do more continuously than anything else. Moreover, the rational part of our soul is what defines our individual identity, and it is also the mark of our species. As far as we know, we possess this ability to a greater degree than any other being. Our rational capacity, therefore, is most central to our nature, and we will find activities that engage this aspect of our being to be most pleasant and to contribute most to our happiness.

To summarize, according to Aristotle, happiness is the full flourishing of our entire nature as human persons. As a complete and final end, a life of

---

33 Ibid., X.7.

eudaimonia can contain no major deficiency. Happiness requires that we deliberate about what the very best life would be, and then set about trying to achieve it. When we begin to think about the very best life – the complete life – we quickly realize just how much contributes to it. Happiness requires far more than virtue, as Plato thought. We need to be not only virtuous, but also actively engaged in the living of our life. One who has achieved eudaimonia will be one who regularly exercises virtue and enjoys doing so. Further, she will realize that this is the greatest good and know that she possesses this good. This means that the happy person will experience much pleasure and satisfaction. Additionally, she will have moderate desires for external goods and will achieve all of her major goals. Her life cannot be one that is subject to severe misfortune. Happiness is thus best seen as a lifelong pursuit that takes much time and effort, and even some luck, to secure. The truly complete and happy life is an exemplary achievement indeed!

However, Aristotle's all-inclusive conception puts happiness out of reach for all but the luckiest. The expansive feature of his conception that recommends it as a compelling theory of the best life imaginable also suggests that it is too demanding as a theory of happiness. Do we really think that only a select group of people can be happy? That seems a rather stark assessment.

A Theory of Capabilities

Everything that Plato and Aristotle have argued seems to depend on assuming that we have a *telos*, a final end or purpose at which our life aims. To flourish as a human person is to live well according to our *telos*. Yet, as we expressed earlier, we might be unconvinced that our lives have a final end, or that we have some singular function as a result of our nature. Nevertheless, it is possible to offer accounts of flourishing that do not rely on the Greek idea of a *telos*. Instead, to flourish as a human being is to have the skills and tools necessary to respond to the challenges we face in life. As humans, we are a particular kind of being, living in a particular kind of environment. This means that we will face very similar kinds of problems and issues as we navigate our way through life. There are certain common and ubiquitous practical concerns we all encounter, such as how to deal with our bodily desires, limited resources, social and communal living, the future, and our mortality, among other things. To flourish is to have the capacity to excel in the face of such challenges. We can respond better or worse to these circumstances, and so maybe what it means to be happy and live well is that we are capable of responding in excellent ways to common human concerns. Virtues or capabilities arise in line with these common spheres of experience. Such an account is both richer than the pure biological account of flourishing (though because we are biological beings, this will be one element in our flourishing) and also more naturalistic than a Greek teleological account of flourishing.

In fact, this approach characterizes Nussbaum's list of central human *capabilities* that form the basis of her *capabilities theory*. Capabilities are essential to living well; they are capacities to do and be certain things that are central to human happiness and well-being. Fully understanding what a capability is goes hand in hand with understanding the notion of a *functioning*. Economist and philosopher Amartya Sen, also a proponent of an objective list theory of happiness based on capabilities, explains that functionings "represent parts of the state of a person – in particular the various things that he or she manages to do or be in leading a life. The *capability* of a person reflects the alternative combinations of functionings that the person can achieve, and from which he or she can choose one collection."[34] A functioning, then, is a particular actualization of a capability. For example, as we will soon see, one of the capabilities that Nussbaum identifies is that of play. She states that in order to live a happy life it is important for people to have the ability to laugh, to play, and to enjoy recreational activities. Yet there are various forms this could take – various particular functionings of this capability. Some will choose to head to the state park and kayak on the river, while others will hit the golf course for a round. Each is a particular functioning that falls under the capability of play.

The capabilities theory seeks to promote a complex and multidimensional account of happiness. It does not reduce human happiness to the single domain of positive psychology, virtuous conduct, or biological fitness. Rather, it accounts for other significant and valuable elements of a happy life. So what are the central capabilities identified by Nussbaum? She offers a list of ten, each of which is an essential dimension along which we can fare better or poorly, and so be more or less happy as a result:

1. *Life*: Being able to live to the end of a human life of normal length; not dying prematurely, or before one's life is so reduced as to be not worth living.
2. *Bodily Health*: Being able to have good health, including reproductive health; to be adequately nourished; to have adequate shelter.

---

34 Sen (1993: 31).

3. *Bodily Integrity*: Being able to move freely from place to place; to be secure against violent assault, including sexual assault and domestic violence; having opportunities for sexual satisfaction and for choice in matters of reproduction.

4. *Senses, Imagination, and Thought*: Being able to use the senses; being able to imagine, to think, and to reason – and to do these things in a "truly human" way, a way informed and cultivated by an adequate education ... Being able to have pleasurable experiences and to avoid non-beneficial pain.

5. *Emotions*: Being able to have attachments to things and people outside ourselves ... in general, to love, to grieve, to experience longing, gratitude, and justified anger....

6. *Practical Reason*: Being able to form a conception of the good and to engage in critical reflection about the planning of one's life. This entails protection for the liberty of conscience and religious observance.

7. *Affiliation*
   A. *Friendship*: Being able to live for and to others, to recognize and show concern for other human beings, to engage in various forms of social interaction....
   B. *Respect*: Having the social bases of self-respect and non-humiliation.... This entails provisions of non-discrimination on the basis of race, sex, ethnicity, caste, religion, and national origin.

8. *Other Species*: Being able to live with concern for and in relation to animals, plants, and the world of nature.

9. *Play*: Being able to laugh, to play, and to enjoy recreational activities.

10. *Control over One's Environment*
    A. *Political*: Being able to participate effectively in political choices that govern one's life; having the right of political participation, protections of free speech and association.
    B. *Material*: Being able to hold property (both land and movable goods); having the right to employment; having freedom from unwarranted search and seizure.[35]

Nussbaum argues that the list of capabilities achieves a sort of consensus value insofar as it captures widely agreed upon valuable ways of living.

---

35 Nussbaum (1997: 288–89).

Additionally, the list of capabilities is broadly applicable. It holds cross-culturally to societies with diverse views about the good.

In fact, each capability corresponds to a universal and concrete sphere of human experience: an arena of activity within which all human beings must make some choice or other, and respond in some way.[36] In responding in some ways rather than others, in living life in certain ways, we enhance or diminish our happiness. For example, as humans we must confront our temporary earthly existence. We hope to be able to live a long life of high quality, but we also know that sickness and death are part of the human condition. This is a universal human experience and it grounds the capabilities of life and bodily health. Yet some will react to this fact in less effective ways than others. Some, for example, will respond by suffering severe existential crises. They throw themselves into despair, believing nihilistically that life is meaningless. Others, to the contrary, will see the temporary nature of life as a reminder of the precious nature of each moment and so urgently seek to live in ways that do not take life for granted. One of these responses is better than the other; one will lead to more happiness and a better life.

Likewise, concerning the capability of control over our environment, there are better and worse ways to respond. Especially in regards to political aspects of social and communal living, there are important capabilities that we can guarantee to each other and that make living life better. For instance, encouraging and facilitating political participation is better than tyrannical rule; protecting basic liberties and rights such as those of free speech and association will enhance human well-being over silencing opinions and preventing people from pursuing relationships with others that they find meaningful and significant. Our concern with the conditions of justice, therefore, seems to apply to us no matter what social setting we find ourselves in. It seems universal to the species. Capabilities reflect central aspects of the human condition. Because they are connected with our humanity, their exercise makes life more fully human. Capabilities therefore serve as the foundation of a theory of human happiness and well-being.

How Much Is Enough?

Aristotle holds that an individual's happiness depends on leading the best life she is capable of, whether or not she realizes what the standards for such

---

36 This is similar to the ways in which Nussbaum interprets how Aristotle arrives at his list of virtues; see Nussbaum (1993: 245–50).

a life are. Moreover, the happy life and the standards according to which it is assessed are fixed by her nature as a human being; part of her pursuit of happiness consists in discovering this full nature. Each person has certain human capacities and talents that can be developed, and if someone is very far from developing her capacities, then she is not happy. This is so even if she is satisfied with her life as a result of much lower standards or a lack of knowledge about her capacities. Likewise, Nussbaum argues that for a person to achieve happiness, she must have developed all of her capabilities. Nussbaum further asserts there is something bad about not having something on the list, and so we should seek a life in which each and every one of our capabilities is exercised.[37]

Kraut criticizes such eudaimonist theories of happiness in two ways. First, he claims, Aristotle's account is too rigid. Second, he says that the theory makes it tough to figure out how far we are from ideal happiness. It is important to note that these criticisms of Aristotle can apply more broadly to other eudaimonist accounts. With respect to rigidity, for instance, Plato, Aristotle, and even Nussbaum argue that happiness is the same for everyone: the standards for appraising whether a person is happy are universal to the species. They do not allow for individual differences, and in so doing their theories preclude certain people from achieving happiness. In particular, children are incapable of being happy, according to Aristotle, as they have yet to live enough of their lives and in the right way to be considered so. So too, are people who have diminished capacities, whether that be through their own laziness or through natural causes. A person born with a severe learning disability, for example, will be barred from achieving happiness, given the essential role that reason plays in happiness and virtue for both Aristotle and Plato. Likewise with our other capacities: we are not all born with the same talents for creative expression or practical wisdom, for instance. Thus, if we are very far from the complete human life, then we are not happy because we could be leading a much better life; we are not yet flourishing as a human person. This, however, means that very few of us will achieve happiness in our lifetime. This is especially true on Aristotle's account, given the enormous number of things that need to go right in order for us to be happy, some of which are matters of pure chance.

However, Kraut argues that we cannot require that a happy life be a truly complete life, since this would make happiness an impossible ideal. Instead, one should formulate an account of happiness that requires each

---

37 Nussbaum (1997: 300).

of us to flourish with what we are given. Because each of us has different capacities, what is ideal for one might not be ideal for another. Rather than appeal to some ideal human standard, we could instead define a person's potential according to her particular talents and traits so that her potential is uniquely tied to her individual nature, not her nature as a member of our species. In other words, each person's natural aptitudes and particular activities could set the limits of what it means for her to flourish and thereby achieve happiness. A person will be happy to the extent that she comes close to meeting the standards set by her particular capacities. In this way, a child born with Down's Syndrome, for example, would still be capable of being happy, since what it means for her to flourish would be individually defined according to her potentialities.

Of course, Kraut still notes problems with this approach. Even on the understanding that there might not be one ideal life, but rather each person's ideal is set by his own capacities, we still need to answer the question of how close we have to come to reaching our ideal. How close is close enough? Surely, if we have failed to be the best possible person we can be with our given talents, then we have not lived the *happiest* life possible; but are we then *unhappy*? As Kraut explains, "Of course, all of our lives, or nearly all, could be somewhat better – but could they be significantly better? To answer this question, the objectivist will have to say what the best attainable life is for each of us, and he must provide some reasonable way of measuring our distance from this reachable ideal."[38] We will need some carefully articulated way of figuring out how far we have yet to go and what counts as far enough. Perhaps we could specify some threshold level beyond which a person counts as being happy. As long as one develops a certain number of their capacities to a high degree, he is close enough to the ideal to be considered happy. But just how many capacities, and to what degree, do we need to develop in order to be considered happy?

For example, Kraut asks, "might someone make a poor use of his reasoning abilities, but make such excellent use of other capacities and talents that he comes reasonably close to leading one of the lives that could be ideal for him?"[39] Or, what about an individual who has no interest at all in Nussbaum's capability of play? Perhaps the person finds recreation and leisure a trivial and frivolous amusement not worthy of a life of greatness. Does this really mean that his life is worse off because he falls short of one

---

38 Kraut (1979: 196).
39 Ibid., 191.

of the capabilities? Or what about an accomplished athlete who devotes his life to a sport to the exclusion of all other pursuits, whether these are intellectual, creative, practical, political, or something else? In fact, is it not required, in order to develop a skill to such a high level, that we neglect other pursuits and talents? An athlete who has reached the ultimate level in his sport will have had to devote an inordinate degree of his attention and energies on developing just this one talent. When he does so he is often lauded as a modern-day hero. Are we willing to say of this man that he cannot be well-off because he doesn't exercise all of the capabilities on Nussbaum's list? Why should we even think some of these capabilities are essential? And why wouldn't it be sufficient for happiness to develop one of our capacities to the point of perfection?

Take for example the lead character in Johnny Cash's song "The Legend of John Henry's Hammer."[40] John Henry set about early in life to develop skills that would allow him to earn a living. He was so good at one skill in particular – driving steel – that he earned legendary status. But his line boss taunts him by claiming that a new steam drill will do the same work, and faster at that. Henry's response is to ask, "Did the Lord say that machines oughtta take the place of livin?" He then challenges the steam drill to a race. The battle is epic. The steam drill cannot keep up, and it works so hard that it eventually explodes, scattering itself across the hills. Although Henry wins the contest, he dies from exhaustion with his hammer in his hand. So what do we make of this? Was Henry happy? Was he even close to happiness? On the one hand, it is clear that Henry did not develop his rational capacities to the degree Aristotle advises. After all, he spent his entire life working to perfect only one skill: to "make the cold steel ring."[41] It is also true that because of his determination to best a machine, he dies prematurely. Yet, on the other hand, Cash portrays Henry's life as epic – as a laudable testament to the best our nature is capable of, the best of the human spirit. His life is the stuff of legends, literally. So which is it? Is Henry's life exemplary, or is it the opposite?

There seems to be no clear answer on offer from the eudaimonist accounts of happiness we have considered so far. If we just stipulate how many of our capacities and to what degree we need to develop them in order to be counted as happy, we risk being arbitrary. On the other hand, requiring excellence in all domains, as Aristotle's view of happiness does,

---

40 Cash and Carter (1962).
41 Ibid.

is far too restrictive and exclusionary. We should be cautious of setting our standard so high that it renders a view of happiness too restrictive.

Kraut's own view of happiness is a subjectivist account, according to which a person is happy as long as he actually lives up to the standards he places on his life. This requires that a person think about what he values in life and then set about pursuing it in order to be happy. Kraut is careful to point out, however, that he is not an "extreme subjectivist," or one who asserts that a person is happy just so long as he thinks he is. Rather, his view is that one's life has to come reasonably close to meeting one's chosen standards in order to count as happy. In this way, it is possible for a person to mistakenly believe he is happy, as he could erroneously judge that his life has met his standards when it has not (such as in the cases of deception discussed in the previous chapter). Even so, it is up to each person to decide whether he has come reasonably close to meeting his standards: "when a person has a good idea of how close he is to meeting his goals, then it is up to him to determine whether his distance from these goals is so large as to make him unhappy. What one person considers close another may not...."[42] Thus, according to Kraut, our happiness does not require that we come close to fulfilling our universal human potential or even our individual potential. Nevertheless, he does admit that the closer we are to flourishing with our given individual talents and capacities, the happier we will be. At the same time, it is enough to be happy that we live a life that meets our standards, even if we set our standards low relative to our latent abilities.

Were he to consider the case of John Henry, Kraut might plausibly conclude that he was happy. As long as Henry set and met the standards he had for himself, including being the best at driving steel and having a good woman by his side, he lived a happy life. Of course, Kraut might add, Henry could have been *happier* still if he had capitalized on some of his other abilities. Perhaps, for example, he could have pursued a better education. Or maybe he had a hidden musical talent, which, if developed, would have brought great happiness to his life. Still, since Henry did not value these potentialities we cannot count him unhappy for not having exercised them. If, on the other hand, there were standards that Henry placed on himself that he failed to meet, then he *was* unhappy. Perhaps, for instance, dying young while besting a machine met his standard to be the best at his work but precluded his becoming a good father, another of the goals he may have had in life.

---

42 Kraut (1979: 190, n. 32).

Whatever else may be true, it is clear that with enough resources, and coupled with the right wisdom and moral character, a person can make significant and meaningful contributions to the world. Yet what if we do not have access to the resources and talents that eudaimonists say the happy life requires? Does this mean we are destined to a life of unhappiness? If we suffer from poverty, or mental disability, or lack of education, is there any way for us to be happy? Or are we destined to be miserable? Few possess the extensive number of material and intellectual resources required for a truly eudaimon life. In fact, many live lives that are full of suffering. Is there any way at all for us to make sense of the idea that we can, even in such circumstances, achieve some level of happiness and well-being? It is to these questions that we turn next.

Chapter 10:   Finding Equanimity in the Face of Suffering

EPICTETUS WAS BORN AROUND 50 CE in Hierapolis, Phrygia, as a slave, and then was sent to Rome to study under the Stoic teacher Musonius Rufus. He was eventually freed later in life and became a teacher, establishing his own school of Stoic philosophy. His most famous pupil was the future ruler of the Roman Empire, Marcus Aurelius Antoninus. Epictetus was noted to have a permanent physical disability, which some speculate was due to abuse he suffered during his servitude. He also lived very modestly, rejecting the pursuit of conventional goods such as wealth and power. Later in life, Epictetus was banished from Rome by the emperor Domitian and lived the rest of his life in exile in Nicopolis.[1] To be sure, Epictetus achieved a tremendous level of success in his life, establishing a school that continues to have followers even to this day. Still, he had to live much of his life either as a slave or in exile. In spite of this, Epictetus avowed his happiness throughout all of the tumult, asserting that one's happiness is completely dependent on one's own thoughts and actions, and not on anything external to oneself.

Tenzin Gyatso, the fourteenth Dalai Lama and the spiritual and political leader of the Tibetan people, was born in 1935 in the small village of Takster in northeastern Tibet. However, in 1959 at the age of 23, he was exiled to India during the Chinese occupation of Tibet, and he has lived in Dharamsala since that time, continuing to fight for the political rights of

---

1   Biographical material taken from Long (2004).

Tibet and its citizens, as well as advocating for the preservation of Tibet's rich cultural and religious heritage.[2] Relations between China and Tibet have continued to worsen, with hundreds of thousands of Tibetans, if not more, losing their lives.[3] Undeniably, the Dalai Lama has also had his share of positive experiences, being able to travel around the world and engage in conversations with the greatest scientists and political leaders. Even so, he has experienced much adversity throughout his life, having had to witness the destruction of his homeland and the loss of Tibetan lives. Yet through all of it, the Dalai Lama maintains that he is happy. He asserts that happiness rests on a calm and stable mind that comes about through inner discipline. As long as one has the right state of mind, then nothing external to oneself can interfere with one's happiness.

That each man claims he is happy is very powerful, given the degree to which each experienced suffering in his lifetime. It seems that regardless of the events around them, both Epictetus and the Dalai Lama managed to retain their happiness. Further, they have each lived their life in a way consistent with their philosophical outlook. Stoic and Buddhist philosophies represent versions of eudaimonism, the theory according to which happiness consists in a life well lived, in flourishing and fulfilling our positive human potential. Our potential is best achieved when we are living according to our nature rather than against it. According to both Epictetus and the Dalai Lama, flourishing is primarily internal and under our willful control. This then suggests that happiness is something that does not so much happen to us; rather, it is something we can create in ourselves.[4] In contrast with Aristotle, then, both maintain that one does not have to fully prosper in order to be happy; one can be happy even in the face of misfortune. We could consider Epictetus and the Dalai Lama as exemplars of their respective philosophies. Each seemed to overcome great obstacles in life, all while maintaining their individual happiness. How were they able to do so? How can one be happy in the face of such suffering?

The need to address suffering in a book primarily focused on happiness is a result of the recognition that for many people in the world, suffering is a regular occurrence in their daily lives. The topic of happiness might

---

2   http://www.dalailama.com/biography/chronology-of-events.

3   http://tibetoffice.org/tibet-info/invasion-after.

4   While the advice that Epictetus and the Dalai Lama offer is informed by their eudaimonist views of happiness, their advice is also consistent in many places with much of what hedonism and desire satisfactionism would say, especially insofar as those views draw a tight connection between happiness and well-being.

well strike them as platitudinous and empty. Yet perhaps happiness is not some bright and cheery emotion in the "smiley face" sense. Maybe happiness is our ability to find meaning or equanimity in the face of suffering. Exploring in what ways one can achieve contentment, serenity, or equanimity even in the face of objectively poor life circumstances is a valuable element in practical wisdom that should not be ignored. After all, flourishing requires not only that we focus on our strengths and on enhancing our positive psychology, but also that we seek to remedy our weaknesses and overcome negative emotions. Therefore, to paint a full picture of happiness seems to require that we say something about how to respond in the face of suffering. Doing so also accords well with our knowledge of the brain. Positive and negative emotionality run on separate systems, so we cannot generate cheer by eliminating anger, and we cannot remove depression by focusing on joy. It is a two-fold strategy where we must cultivate the positive states of mind *and* eliminate the negative states of mind. Thus it makes sense to say something on suffering even in a book on happiness.

This chapter will focus on the idea that happiness involves living in a mindful way, accompanied by a sense of contentment, serenity, or mental calm. When we live in such ways we can maintain our happiness regardless of what challenges we may face. We will explore much of the advice offered by the Stoic and Buddhist traditions, bringing in contemporary research as support along the way. In particular, we might be able to eliminate our suffering completely, or at least minimize it, through changing our reactions so that suffering does not occur. Or we might be able to cope with our suffering by finding meaning or value in it, including realizing that we have an opportunity to grow from the experience. It is important to realize that while suffering is natural, much of our suffering is self-created. In one way, this makes it easier to eliminate it, since it is unnecessary. In another way, however, it makes it more difficult because it requires much self-knowledge and inner discipline.

Equanimity as the Goal

The Stoics characterize eudaimonia as involving a steady state of tranquility or equanimity, where one is free from disturbances of the mind.[5] It is often characterized as a kind of serenity or composure, even under the most

---

5   In this they clearly disagree with Aristotle, who maintained that happiness was an activity. The Stoics, on the other hand, thought of it as a state of the soul caused by virtuous activity,

trying of circumstances. The goal is to calm the turbulent waters of the mind. Buddhists suggest a similar understanding. A happy life, according to the Dalai Lama, is built on a calm and stable state of mind, so that the greater our calmness and peace of mind, the greater our ability to enjoy life. According to the Dalai Lama, inner discipline is key. Elaborating, he writes:

> As long as there is a lack of the inner discipline that brings calmness of mind, no matter what external facilities or conditions you have, they will never give you the feeling of joy and happiness that you are seeking. On the other hand, if you possess this inner quality, a calmness of mind, a degree of stability within, then even if you lack various external facilities that you would normally consider necessary for happiness, it is still possible to live a happy and joyful life.[6]

Happiness is a calm, tranquil, stable psychological state. It is resilient and remains unperturbed even in the face of outward difficulty. The goal is equanimity – an evenness of mind.

It is crucial to understand that achieving equanimity requires *discipline*. After all, changing how one thinks and one's outlook on life takes practice and time; it is not something we can achieve in a few days. Among the benefits of inner discipline is that it positions us to more clearly detect and therefore disarm irrational thoughts, which happen to be the cause of much of our suffering. Nevertheless, the Dalai Lama points out that we should not be misled into thinking that there is one magic secret that, once discovered, will immediately bestow upon us a lasting happiness. In fact, shaping the mind for happiness requires attending carefully to many factors. Drawing an analogy with physical health, the Dalai Lama notes that the body does not need only one kind of nutrient, but instead needs many different nutrients from many different sources in order to be healthy. Likewise, in order to achieve mental health we will need to focus on various aspects of our psychology. Also, just as changing or shaping the physical body requires time and dedicated daily effort, the same is true if we want to transform our mind to achieve equanimity.

At the same time, to state that our goal is to achieve equanimity is not to assert that we ought to become unfeeling Vulcans. Epictetus explains,

---

rather than an activity of the soul typically attended by certain psychological states. See Bok (2010: 183, n. 8).

6   Dalai Lama and Cutler (1998: 26).

"For I must not be without feeling like a statue, but must maintain my natural and acquired relations, as a religious man, as son, brother, father, citizen."[7] Some feelings are appropriate in certain circumstances. Indeed, the wise sage is thought to possess good feelings such as joy and cheer when considering what is good, or to feel caution when considering bad choices. In the Buddhist tradition, the emotion of compassion is central. To feel compassion connects us to other sentient beings and compels us to work to overcome suffering in all its forms. However, these special kinds of emotions are clearly distinguished from ordinary emotions – what are called passions or mental afflictions – such as anger, regret, fear, grief, hatred, and jealousy. These passions are irrational and disruptive to the mind and need to be removed in order to achieve inner tranquility. Anger and hatred are especially harmful: not only do they impede our development of compassion, but they also interfere with our calmness of mind, faculty of judgment, and even our physical health.[8] In fact, according to the Dalai Lama, hatred is our ultimate inner enemy, as its only function is to destroy us. While persons whom we regard as enemies have other projects and aims, such as eating and sleeping, our hatred serves no other purpose than to cause us harm. We must be on guard, then, against letting ourselves be overcome by such afflictive emotions, as they will have lasting impacts on our ability to achieve happiness.

On the other hand, you might think that negative emotionality is an important part of our nature. For example, anger or hatred might provide an evolutionary advantage insofar as it compels us to protect our loved ones against enemies and can serve as a vehicle for social cohesion among groups. At least sometimes this must lead to positive change. Of course, even the Dalai Lama acknowledges that anger can sometimes be good for us, such as when we are angry at a serious injustice. Yet it seems obvious that it can also be quite bad for us, such as when we get angry at a person who is driving too slowly in front of us and then drive with "road rage" in response. We therefore need to learn the specific causal conditions that give rise to our anger in a particular situation so that we can ensure that it

---

7 Epictetus, *Discourses* III.2.

8 See, for example, Williams and Williams (1993). Stress and anger are archetypal examples of emotions that do not function properly. Not only do they feel bad, which is a disvalue, but they are often crippling and debilitating. Sometimes an emotion that feels bad can be positive if it compels behavior that is good for you in the long run. But stress and anger often serve no purpose and so are not good for anything. These emotions are "afflictive" in part because their feel-bad character does not compel appropriate behavior.

is an appropriate reaction; if it is not, we should seek to eliminate it. What distinguishes an emotional response as afflictive and therefore disturbing to our tranquility is that it is rooted in a misperception of reality. When an emotion is based on a correct understanding of the world and the particular circumstances we face within it, it functions properly and so serves our happiness. As a result, combating afflictive emotionality requires gaining knowledge concerning the world and our place in it.

The Determined Universe: A Lesson in What Lies within and beyond Our Control

Stoics believe in an ordered universe where things happen as they were designed to happen according to nature. Epictetus, for example, views the universe as a perfectly organized whole governed by determinism, where all events that occur could not have been different. Likewise, the Dalai Lama and other Buddhists also have a deterministic view of the universe based on the principle of causality. According to Buddhist philosophy, everything that arises or ceases in this world depends on certain prior conditions. As the Buddha notes, "when this is, that is; this arising, that arises; when this is not, that is not; this ceasing, that ceases."[9] In other words, something only exists dependent on conditions that came before it. Only because of certain conditions can something exist, and when these conditions do not exist, then that something will not exist.

Given that the cosmos is determined to be just as it is, in order to achieve equanimity it seems we will need to learn how to desire things to be exactly as they already are. "Do not seek to have events happen as you want them to," advises Epictetus. "Instead want them to happen as they do happen, and your life will go well."[10] The Dalai Lama offers similar advice when he recommends that the best method for achieving inner contentment is "not to have what we want but rather to want and appreciate what we have."[11] We will be happiest when we learn to want our lives to be as they already are, and unhappy if we want our lives to be other than they are. Adopting this attitude is essential to being in accord with nature. Further, once we see that the entire cosmos is determined to be just as it is, then we will regard any desire to change it as utterly unintelligible, since it is impossible for

---

9 *Samyutta Nikaya* (The Connected Discourses of the Buddha), 2.28.
10 Epictetus, *Enchiridion* c. 8.
11 Dalai Lama and Cutler (1998: 29).

things to be other than they are. Seeking to change the world to be other than it is will only yield frustration when we cannot transform the world into the way we want it to be. For example, complaining about the weather seems a rather futile exercise. Whether it is excessively hot and humid or extremely cold, both are facts over which we can exercise no control. To allow the weather to get to us means we are causing ourselves to suffer. Instead, we can learn to judge the weather indifferently. Sure, it is nice to know if it might rain, because that may well influence whether I carry an umbrella with me today. But I do not also need to be upset by the rain.

Of course, one need not accept a rigid determinism to see the truth that *many* things that happen in life are beyond our control and simply not up to us. We cannot control how others think and feel about us, and we cannot control the unfolding of events. For example, we all know that we cannot control the fact that we will die, or when it will happen (save for those who choose suicide). We can, however, control how we choose to react to our mortality. If we desire to avoid death, we are going to be made miserable by the natural fact that all humans die. To be averse to it will cause us suffering, but to accept it and not desire it to be other than it is will lead to happiness. It may well even bring out a beauty and urgency in the way we live life as a result of fully appreciating its temporary nature. If our plan for happiness depends on shaping the world according to our will, then we are bound to be frustrated, especially when we learn just how little of the world we can actually control.

In accord with this deterministic view, both the Stoics and the Buddhists understand suffering to be a natural part of the universe. To live is to experience at least some suffering, as none of us can escape grief, sorrow, sickness, death, and many other negative experiences. In fact, the first of the four noble truths – the pillars of Buddhist philosophy – is that there is suffering.[12] However, the second and third noble truths assert that because suffering is caused by antecedent conditions, it can also be overcome. As long as the conditions of suffering are absent, so too will the suffering cease to be. The fourth truth asserts that there is a way to eliminate the conditions of suffering, which involves the cultivation of wisdom, moral conduct, and mental discipline.[13]

---

12 Buddhists further explain that there are three different levels of suffering: suffering due to pain, suffering due to impermanence, and suffering due to the conditions responsible for rebirth. See, for example, Siderits (2007), ch. 2.

13 More specifically, the Noble Eightfold Path spells out the eight practices of wisdom (right view, right intention); moral conduct (right speech, right action, right livelihood); and mental

So in order to successfully root out the conditions of suffering, we need to understand the complex nature of causation.

We might initially be tempted to think of causation as a simple process whereby one cause leads to an effect, which in turn causes another effect, and so on, as if causes and effects are links in a chain, with each link connected only to one before and one after. Of course, upon even the slightest bit of reflection we realize that this understanding of causation is far too naïve. Instead, all things and events come to be as a result of a complex set of interrelated causes and conditions. Nothing exists separately or is the effect of any one cause, but rather all things arise dependently from a whole host of prior and simultaneous conditions. Some of these conditions we find we are able to change, while others we cannot.

As an illustration, in order to grow a plant so that it will flourish, it needs nutrient-rich soil, air, water, and sun. Each of these must be balanced in a way proper to the particular plant: a cactus requires less water than a tomato plant and can survive in much sunnier environments. We can exercise influence over some of these conditions, if we desire. If we are trying to grow a tomato plant, for example, we can oversee the soil in which we plant it, as well as how much water it receives. Yet a sudden freeze is beyond our individual control. But even this picture is still too simple. There are many other causal conditions, such as the chemical makeup of the atmosphere, the role of other living organisms in the soil, or the exact distance of the Earth from the Sun, without any one of which we could not successfully grow something as simple as a tomato plant. All we can do is our best with respect to what is within our power; and when we do so, we sow the seeds of success to the degree that we are able.

What this implies regarding the cessation of suffering is that we should seek to understand its causes and conditions and then do what we can to eliminate those that we can change. Certainly, even though we all suffer, there are better and worse ways to deal with our suffering. In the place of masking our symptoms with drugs or alcohol, or denial or repression, Stoic and Buddhist teachings suggest some strategies for coping with suffering and achieving a sort of psychological health. This involves eliminating those alterable conditions that cause suffering and creating those conditions under which happiness arises.

---

discipline (right exertion, right self-possession, and right concentration). See ibid. Insofar as the Noble Eightfold Path represents a guide to living well, we might think of it as offering an objective list of the necessary elements of a life well lived.

To begin, as noted already, we need to accept that suffering is a natural part of life. If we think of it as something unnatural, we are more likely to blame others and view ourselves as a victim. And when we start to think of ourselves as a victim, we create two problems instead of one: our initial suffering, and now the thought that our suffering is unfair. In fact, when we view ourselves as victims, this often also leads to feelings of fear and anger. "How can this happen to *me*?" we exclaim. Fear results from our experienced loss of control over our situation, and anger follows from thinking our suffering is unfair, a cosmic injustice. When this happens, we too often tend to hold on to these emotions, dwelling on them and reinforcing them, making their hold on us more powerful. This in turn makes our suffering worse. It becomes a self-feeding cycle of suffering, fear, anger, and more suffering.

Our energies and efforts should be focused instead on finding ways to mitigate the effect of suffering on our lives. Rather than despair and give in to self-pity, we should do what is in our power and search for solutions. As the Stoic Marcus Aurelius advises in his *Meditations*, "A cucumber is bitter. Throw it away. There are briars in the road. Turn aside from them. This is enough. Do not add, 'And why were such things made in the world?'"[14] When we suffer, we should focus on finding the causes of our suffering so that we can seek to eliminate them. If there is a solution to our problem, then there is no need to worry, as it is in our power to overcome; but if there is no solution, then worrying doesn't do us much good anyway. The Dalai Lama elaborates:

> It is more sensible to spend the energy focusing on the solution rather than worrying about the problem. *Alternatively, if there is no way out, no solution, no possibility of resolution, then there is also no point in being worried about it, because you can't do anything about it anyway.* In that case, the sooner you accept this fact, the easier it will be on you. This formula, of course, implies directly confronting the problem. Otherwise, you won't be able to find out whether or not there is a resolution to the problem.[15]

When we persist in worrying over what we cannot control, we cause ourselves to be miserable – our suffering becomes self-created. Many people,

---

14 Marcus Aurelius, *Meditations* 8.48.
15 Dalai Lama and Cutler (1998: 268); emphasis in original.

for example, find themselves stressing about how much stress is in their life. But worrying over the stress does nothing to solve the problem. Instead of stressing about stress, we would do better to eliminate the causes of it in our lives. If there is nothing we can do to prevent the stress, then there is no further reason to concern ourselves with it.

Key to overcoming suffering, then, is coming to understand the world for what it is. We need to have the right view of the world and our abilities to effect change within it, so that we can concentrate our efforts only on those things where we have some measure of influence. Importantly, this will include gaining knowledge about what is and what is not up to us, which, according to Epictetus, is the very first lesson one must learn on the path to equanimity:

> Some things are up to us and some are not up to us. Our opinions are up to us, and our impulses, desires, aversions — in short, whatever is our own doing. Our bodies are not up to us, nor are our possessions, our reputations, or our public offices, or, that is, whatever is not our own doing.[16]

Learning what is and is not up to us is essential because, claims Epictetus, our happiness depends only on those things over which we can exercise unrestricted control. He suggests that we learn not to concern ourselves with those things and events in our life over which we have no influence; instead, we should respond with contentment or equanimity, rather than with strong negative (or positive) emotions. In other words, if we want only what is in our power to secure, then we will always remain content, but to want things that are out of our power is to set ourselves up for emotional distress.

What is up to us, according to Epictetus, is our faculty of choice. In fact, our will is our essential feature. It defines who we are as individuals. We are fundamentally rational creatures, notes Epictetus, with the capacity to use our impressions of the world in a reflective manner. Like humans, other animals use their sense impressions of the world to guide their actions and behavior. However, unlike other animals, humans do more: they examine the content of their impressions to question both their truth and their value. An impression is a way of perceiving something in the world, which may or may not be accurate. For example, I may have an impression of an oasis

---

16 Epictetus, *Enchiridion* c. 1.

on the horizon, when it is in fact just a mirage, or I may have an impression that someone is annoyed with me when they are instead suffering from indigestion. What is important is to make sure that we do not willfully assent to our impressions until we can confirm that they are correct representations of the way things are.

While most of what happens in the world is actually out of our control, our will is entirely free. Because of this, we have complete authority over our thoughts, judgments, values, and desires – over whether we assent to our impressions, over how we interpret and react to events, over our intentions and actions, and over what we value and desire. This also means that no one can prevent a person from being virtuous, nor can a person be forced to be vicious. This is always up to the individual. As Epictetus writes in the *Discourses*, "No one then has power to procure me good or to involve me in evil, but I myself alone have authority over myself in these matters. So, when I have made these secure, what need have I to be disturbed about outward things? What need have I to fear tyrant, or disease, or poverty, or disaster?"[17] Acting from the motive of virtue is always within our power, and the virtuous person will thus never be frustrated, regardless of external circumstances. As a result, our happiness rests fully within the power of our will.

Understanding what is and is not up to us leads to the realization that although the universe may be beyond our willful manipulation, our reactions to it are not. In other words, although the outer world is determined, our inner world is free. Freedom, Epictetus maintains, consists in self-mastery, in controlling what we do and do not desire, and a person is master over herself when she can determine her own desires. Epictetus rejects the idea that emotions happen to us – that they are imposed on us by our circumstances or anything else external to the self. Instead, he believes our feelings are under our rule; they are an expression of what seems right or wrong to us based on our judgments of what has value in life. Accordingly, Epictetus argues that when we are distressed or disturbed about something, we should not blame the world or others, but instead place the responsibility for our reaction squarely on ourselves. Our *judgments* upset us, not the world. Hence, if we despair, it is the result of our judgment and not the thing as it happened, and we are then the source of our own misery. But if we are the source of our own suffering, then we can also be the ones to eliminate that suffering. It is within our ability to judge something as

---

17 Epictetus, *Discourses* IV.12.

indifferent rather than as good or bad, and thereby to avoid suffering. The Dalai Lama expresses a similar sentiment: whether and how much we suffer depends on how we *respond* to a situation, what *attitude* we adopt.

As an illustration, many of us have had the experience where a stranger or acquaintance has been rude, slinging insults and derogatory remarks our way. But it is always up to us to allow ourselves to be upset by these actions. And in those cases where we, too, lose our temper or let the provocation ruin the next several hours in our day, we lose. *We ourselves* destroy our peace of mind and cause ourselves suffering. Nobody can force us to react in one way rather than another. The Dalai Lama recommends that in the case where you hear of someone insulting you or otherwise talking poorly of you, you should "let the slander pass by you as if it were a silent wind passing behind your ears."[18] Epictetus goes even further, suggesting that you should respond, "Obviously he didn't know my other bad characteristics, since otherwise he wouldn't just have mentioned these."[19] Responding this way will disarm the insult and will allow you to retain authority over your will – to keep control of yourself. Naturally, it might be more difficult to respond in such a way rather than to allow yourself to get worked up by such a state of affairs, but it is within your power nonetheless, with the right practice and effort.

In contrast, our body, our relationships with others, our possessions, our status or power, the way our actions turn out – all of these things are independent from our will. We cannot will our body from illness to health, we cannot will others to treat us the way we treat them, we cannot will our objects not to be lost or stolen, we cannot will how others regard us, and we cannot will the success or failure of our activities. In fact, according to Epictetus, the pursuit of these things outside of our power will make us miserable because we will spend our energies wanting and trying to get things that are not up to us. For those things that are not up to us, we should learn to detach ourselves from desiring them to be otherwise.

Most importantly, then, we must be careful not to give over our will to others. We must take care not to let others interfere with our tranquility. Epictetus writes, "If someone turned your body over to just any person who happened to meet you, you would be angry. But are you not ashamed that you turn over your own faculty of judgment to whoever happens along, so that if he abuses you it is upset and confused?"[20] If a person were to sell you

---

18 Dalai Lama and Cutler (1998: 151–52).

19 Epictetus, *Enchiridion* c. 33.

20 Ibid., c. 28.

into slavery, you would rightly be angered. What right does that person have to command your body? And this is true even though your body is not your essential feature. Yet your will is most intimately connected with who you are. Epictetus marvels at the fact, then, that we sometimes willingly give over our will to others: we allow others to dictate our attitudes and control our minds. For example, the average American watches television for 2.8 hours a day.[21] When we watch certain programs on television we often become passive consumers of media; we allow advertisers and entertainers unfettered access to our mind in order to manufacture wants and cravings. This has measurable effects on our attitudes and values. Why do we willingly give over to such mind control? It seems much more pernicious and dangerous than giving over control of our body.

To achieve happiness, Epictetus recommends that we continually focus our attention on being rational in our thoughts and actions, making sure each day to undergo rigorous self-examination. Our goal is to replace our irrational beliefs, which cause afflictive passions, with rational judgments. This fundamentally involves making a proper use of our impressions. If we do not, then we are likely to be carried away by our mistaken desires and passions, resulting in unwise actions and unhappiness. Indeed, the sage is a person who does not readily assent to an afflictive emotion such as fear, but instead examines its foundation to see if it is fitting. If not, the sage replaces his fear with a more suitable response. As Epictetus explains, "do not be hurried away by the suddenness of the shock, but say, Wait for me a little, impression. Let me see what you are, and what is at stake: let me test you."[22] In this way, the sage corrects his impressions and attitudes by conscious reflection.

All this suggests, as the Dalai Lama states, that "right now, at this very moment, we have a mind, which is all the basic equipment we need to achieve complete happiness."[23] It is important to note that, by "mind," the Dalai Lama is referring to something broader than just cognitive ability or intellect; rather, it is more in line with the Tibetan word "*sem*." As he explains, *sem* "has a much broader meaning, closer to 'psyche' or 'spirit'; it includes intellect and feeling, heart and mind."[24] In this way we see a slight difference between Epictetus, who thinks our nature is exhausted by our rational will, and the Dalai Lama, who includes more than rationality

---

21 Bureau of Labor Statistics (http://www.bls.gov/news.release/atus.to1.htm).
22 Epictetus, *Discourses* II.18.
23 Dalai Lama and Cutler (1998: 37).
24 Ibid., 15.

as central to our identity. Nevertheless, it remains true for both that the sources of happiness are found within our own minds and not in external objects; and this means that no matter our situation, we have all the equipment we need to be happy: we have a mind.

If happiness depends solely on our minds, then how we interpret and react to the world is the only thing of importance. Whatever conditions we might encounter, it is up to us to decide how to respond and with what attitude. Recognizing the orderliness of the universe and acting correctly on the basis of that knowledge, we realize we have no need for anything beyond our mind since we cannot be made any better or worse off by things outside of our power. Our health might be poor, our finances tight, our job tiring or boring, our living situation unstable, our circle of friends small, our family deceased, and our political freedoms curtailed, but in spite of all of this, we might be able still to enjoy a lasting and stable happiness. To be sure, in the face of such formidable obstacles, it will not be an easy task. Thank goodness many of us do not face such terrible circumstances, so cultivating our happiness should be easier. Nevertheless, we can choose to view any challenge as an opportunity for growth. An enemy can serve as an occasion to practice tolerance, a misfortune as a chance for exploring new avenues and developing perseverance.

The Science of Mindfulness

Given that our essential feature is our capacity for rational choice, Epictetus claims that anything that does not aid or interfere with the operation of this faculty has no effect on our happiness unless we allow it. He states, "Illness interferes with the body, not with one's faculty of choice, unless that faculty of choice wishes it to. Lameness interferes with the limb, not with one's faculty of choice. Say this at each thing that happens to you, since you will find that it interferes with something else, not with you."[25] According to Epictetus, insofar as we have successfully learned the proper value of things, realizing that anything external to our minds is ultimately of no value, we should see that anything happening to our body has no effect on our will, and therefore it cannot affect our equanimity unless we allow it.

This, though, is an incredibly bold statement that seems to run counter to experience. After all, even something as simple as a hangover headache seems to affect our ability to concentrate or think carefully about things. In

---

25 Epictetus, *Enchiridion* c. 9.

such cases, therefore, it seems that pains in the body certainly do affect our ability to reason. Even more, we know that certain diseases like dementia or Alzheimer's directly affect our abilities to remember and reason well. And those who suffer from schizophrenia also exemplify the ways in which our body quite obviously has a real and significant impact upon our mind. So how much control over our minds do we really have? Are we as capable as Epictetus and the Dalai Lama suggest we are at gaining mastery over our desires and impressions so as to maintain our equanimity?

Perhaps Epictetus and the Dalai Lama overemphasize the amount of change we can bring about in our thoughts and actions. Doesn't at least some of how we experience and think about life rest on our genetics? That some of our happiness is genetically based is backed by scientific research suggesting that each of us has, as discussed in Chapter Two, a certain "set point," or a default level of happiness to which we tend to return naturally after positive or negative events.[26] Then again, some studies suggest that we can alter our resting set point.[27] Even so, it also seems apparent that our brain chemistry can have a large effect on our outlook and on our ability to use inner discipline to influence our reactions to life events. We also have deeply ingrained personality traits, such as neuroticism or extroversion, that can have large impacts on our happiness as well.[28] But these things need not completely preclude our having some power over our happiness. After all, therapeutic interventions such as cognitive behavioral therapy can help to ameliorate the symptoms of irrational afflictive emotions. Likewise, drugs such as MAOIs and SSRIs can be used to influence the level of brain chemicals responsible for abnormal levels of stress, anxiety, and depression. Therapy, when used in combination with medication, might therefore be able to increase our control over our ways of thinking.

But perhaps the most important factor that underpins our ability to train our mind is the *plasticity* of our brain. Plasticity refers to the brain's ability to change. As psychiatrist Howard Cutler notes, while it is true that our brains come hardwired with certain instructions encoded in nerve-cell activation patterns, our brains can be rewired to grow new connections in response to new input, in turn establishing new patterns among our cells. We can adopt new ways of thinking that will then take shape as new connections in the brain. We can replace negative ways of thinking (our old neural circuits)

---

26 Lykken and Tellegen (1996); Nettle (2005: 110–11).

27 Diener, Lucas, and Scollon (2006). Perhaps, however, one's set point can be altered within only a limited range.

28 Nettle (2005: 102–03); see also Diener and Biswas-Diener (2008: 148–49).

with positive ways of thinking (creating new neural circuits). This gives a tangible scientific basis to the idea that we can transform our minds and make our own happiness.[29]

In fact, there is now ample evidence to suggest that through practice we can come to transform our mental lives. The evidence comes from detailed studies of meditating Buddhist monks by Richard Davidson and his team.[30] In these studies, experienced meditators were asked to alternate between neutral periods and meditative periods. They were carefully monitored throughout, being connected to over 256 sensors measuring changes in the brain's electrical activity and changes in blood flow to the brain. The results were startling. Expert meditators were able to willfully increase cerebral activity in ways never before seen in the study of neuroscience. Furthermore, their brain activity was much more synchronized than that of the people in the control group, whose brain activity increased only slightly. The results suggest that the meditators were able to deliberately regulate their brain activity, showing that "the brain is capable of being trained and physically modified in ways few people can imagine."[31] The effects became more pronounced the more years a monk had been practicing meditation, leading Davidson to hypothesize that the changes in the brain not only were due to mental training, but also might be permanent.[32]

Of course, becoming an expert meditator takes years of dedicated practice. The studies cited above also showed that those inexperienced in meditation were unable to generate the same degree of coordinated control. For example, if asked to focus on a single object, or visualize a particular image, they were unable to limit their brain activity to just that one task for more than a few moments. Rewiring our brain takes a lot of concentrated effort and repetition. As a result, although our brains are plastic, this does not necessarily make achieving happiness easy – it will be challenging because it requires inner discipline and practice. Indeed, as psychologist Mihaly Csikszentmihalyi remarks, "Happiness, in fact, is a condition that must be prepared for, cultivated, and defended privately by each person."[33] In other words, there is no "easy fix" for happiness, or most of us would already be completely happy. Therefore, even though we can train our minds for happiness, it will still require much effort, discipline, and perseverance to achieve it.

---

29 Dalai Lama and Cutler (1998: 44–46).
30 Descriptions of the studies can be found in Ricard (2003: 188–91).
31 Ibid., 191.
32 Ibid., 192.
33 Csikszentmihalyi (1990: 2).

Practice is essential for developing habits in all facets of life, and this holds in the case of our habits for happiness as well. As with any skilled activity, if we want to develop it we will have to put in the time to do so. We can develop inner discipline, but it requires a schedule of continued training each day. However, as the monk studies show, the more we practice, the more capable we become; the more we practice, the more familiar we become with methods to eliminate negative states, and the easier it becomes to continue on our path to a calm state of mind. When we do encounter some disturbance in the mind, it will continue to affect us less and less, with the negative effects remaining only on the surface of our mind rather than affecting us deeply. We can thus more easily overcome negative states of mind, allowing them to pass quickly.

Epictetus and the Dalai Lama argue that we can train our mind to overcome our suffering, since much of our suffering is a result of our attitudes and not the circumstances we face. We therefore need to develop habits of mind that will mitigate our suffering. By replacing our current attitudes with those that more appropriately reflect the situation, we can combat afflictive emotions and achieve equanimity. Evidence from the monk studies seems to suggest that they might be right: we appear capable of rewiring our brains and training our minds in willfully directed ways. Of course, while it may be true that Buddhist monks are able to willfully direct their minds, how realistic is it to believe that *we* can do the same? In fact, there are many studies that show even a minimal amount of mindfulness practice, like meditation, can positively affect our emotions, level of stress, cognitive abilities, and physical health. Furthermore, practicing mindfulness can promote greater calmness and relaxation, physiological rest, and a stronger immune system, and can also assist in the treatment of illnesses such as heart disease and chronic pain, as well as mental health conditions such as depression, anxiety, stress, and insomnia. Mindfulness also improves the mind's ability to pay attention, resulting in possible benefits in intelligence, memory, and creativity. Moreover, many of these changes begin to accrue in as little as six weeks.[34] One need not isolate oneself at a mountain refuge for years of isolated training in order to begin to experience the benefits of mindfulness practice.

"Mindfulness" refers to a set of activities, all of which share a common aim: to increase our skill of concentration. Concentration is essential to the practice of inner discipline, which involves a focused awareness of our

---

34 Lyubomirsky (2007: 241–42).

consciousness. Mindfulness practices teach us how to focus our attention, and one way to increase mindfulness is to engage in some form of meditation. There are various methods of meditation, which can be practiced alone or in groups. Many of them instruct us to direct our concentration on some object or other, such as our breath, a single word, a mental image, a saying or a prayer, or some quality we wish to develop, such as compassion or forgiveness. Others simply ask us to keep our mind at ease, observing our thoughts in a nonjudgmental way. A key component of meditation is acknowledging what goes on in the mind and letting it go. When we notice that other distracting thoughts enter our mind, we should just accept these thoughts and not fight them; then we simply direct our focus back to the object of our concentration.

Some forms of mindfulness involve fully living in the present moment without being distracted by thoughts of the future or the past and without being preoccupied with worries or frustrations. Zen Buddhist Thich Nhat Hanh describes mindfulness as "the energy of being aware and awake to the present"[35] and as bringing "our full attention to what is within and around us."[36] Mindfulness thus can actually be practiced even while we engage in the most mundane of activities. We don't need to go away to a special retreat or set aside chunks of time in our day. We can implement mindfulness exercises immediately into nearly any facet of our ordinary lives. We can practice mindfulness while driving, eating, cooking, walking, and even just breathing. In a way, mindfulness allows us to turn off the automatic pilot that drives most of us throughout the day. How many of us really notice all the things that are going on around us or within our own minds? The idea is to fully engage our living at every moment.

One excellent mindfulness exercise involves reciting a *gatha*, which is a short mindfulness verse that helps us to heighten our awareness and thereby deepen our experience of whatever it is that we are doing. You could use some standard verses or even make your own. Here is a common verse recited in the morning as we wake up:

> *Waking up this morning, I smile.*
> *Twenty-four brand-new hours are before me.*
> *I vow to live fully in each moment*
> *and to look at all beings with eyes of compassion.*[37]

---

35 Thich Nhat Hanh (2009: ix).
36 Ibid., 9.
37 Ibid., 18.

This gatha is used in order to remind ourselves that we have precious hours to live and that we should focus on developing our compassion for others.

Again, one major benefit of engaging in mindfulness training is that it improves our inner discipline. The more we practice self-regulation, the more we attempt to exercise executive control over our minds, the better we get at it. This in turn means that when we face trying circumstances in the future, our thoughts will not run away with us. Rather, we will be able to take the time to examine our impressions, as Epictetus advises, and not to allow irrational reactions to disturb our equanimity. Practicing mindfulness, therefore, allows us to more capably overcome irrationality, a critical source of suffering in our lives.

Overcoming Irrationality and Dealing with Loss

According to psychologist Daniel Kahneman, there are two systems operating in our brains. "System 1," as he calls it, "operates automatically and quickly, with little or no effort and no sense of voluntary control." "System 2," on the other hand, "allocates attention to the effortful mental activities that demand it" and is "often associated with the subjective experience of agency, choice, and concentration."[38] Many of us make use of System 1 far too much of the time. In other words, we rest content with snap judgments and do not take the time to think through events in our lives from a rational perspective. To the degree that System 1 is involuntary, resting on it means we are not in control of our own minds. In fact, many of us do not even realize that this system is operative in our brains. We are thus not even aware or mindful of the judgments we make and the impressions we assent to as a result of System 1's maneuvers. Kahneman thinks we would do well to make more use of System 2; we would fare better in life if we engaged the rational system more.[39] As we have already seen, exercises aimed at increasing our mindfulness can enhance the power of our rational mind to influence our emotions and attitudes. In other words, techniques like meditation can strengthen System 2 and increase our propensity to rely on

---

38 Kahneman (2011: 20–21); italics removed from original.

39 For an interesting application of this sort of reasoning, see Greene (2013). Greene argues for what he calls the "bicameral mind," or a dual-process system of moral reasoning. One process, analogous to Kahneman's System 1, is automatic and leads to gut reactions to moral situations based mostly on emotional salience. The other system is more reflective and relies on reasoned cognition to reach moral conclusions. Like Kahneman, Greene argues that learning to rely on the reflective system would lead to more virtuous conduct.

it, rather than the unreflective System 1. But are there other methods for overcoming irrationality in our lives? Are there other ways to increase our use of System 2?

One method for overcoming irrational and dysfunctional mental reactions is through cognitive behavioral therapy. Cognitive behavioral therapy is a contemporary psychological approach that rests on the belief that our thoughts cause our emotions, and not the other way around. In other words, the way we think about something determines how we feel about it. Hence, if we can learn to transform our thinking, we can learn to overcome our negative and irrational emotional responses. Cognitive behavioral therapy encourages us to monitor when our excessively negative thoughts arise and then work to actively dispute these thoughts by gathering evidence that disproves them. For instance, are there other ways to look at this particular event? Is having this belief useful to you? What is the most likely consequence? Learning to routinely ask these sorts of questions is a form of training our mind to think differently so that we can more willfully regulate our future thoughts and emotions.

Cognitive behavioral therapy thus helps us to examine our thoughts to make sure they are appropriate for the situation. Some more specific advice includes avoiding viewing events in all-or-nothing terms, avoiding overgeneralizing, and avoiding selective perception.[40] For instance, after a painful breakup, you may think that you will be alone forever, but to think this way is to be lured by the trap of all-or-nothing thinking. You have many other relationships that provide you with meaningful connections, not to mention that there are countless potential future companions. As another example, while it might be easy to think that you are a total failure because you failed one exam, this would be to overgeneralize the actual situation. One exam does not make an entire course, nor does a single college course make an entire college career. Even more than that, academics is just one facet of your life, and you may be succeeding in many others. You should also be careful not to see only the bad and ignore the good. While something bad may have happened to you today, such as losing your wallet, you may have also made a new friend or acquired some interesting knowledge. All too often it is easy to focus only on the bad; but this would be to have an inaccurate perception of reality. Cognitive behavioral therapy thus encourages us to carefully examine our thoughts to make sure that we are not getting carried away into irrational thinking.

---

40 Dalai Lama and Cutler (1998: 244).

In fact, the ancient Stoics seemed to advocate for a version of cognitive behavioral therapy thousands of years ago. For example, Epictetus notes that when we are guests at another's house and someone (perhaps another guest or a child) breaks a dish, we often respond with something like, "It's just a dish. These things just happen." Remembering this should help to disarm the anger you might feel when something of yours is broken. That we invest more value in material objects when they belong to us than when they belong to others seems rather irrational.[41] The accidental breaking of a dish certainly does not warrant anger, though many of us are quickly carried over the edge by it.

The above is an example of what the Stoics refer to as the "premeditation of evils" or "negative visualization." The idea of negative visualization is that one way to better prepare ourselves for challenges is to think about the kinds of suffering that we might experience before they happen.[42] When we do so, we often discover that while the event may be bad, it is not nearly as bad as we had feared, and there are specific steps we could take to resolve it. Thus, as Seneca states, "He robs present ills of their power who has perceived their coming beforehand."[43] The fact that the universe is so fickle forces us to grapple with loss. Premeditating on the evil of loss can help us to overcome irrational fear, anger, and suffering when a negative situation occurs. As psychologist Albert Ellis explains, judging something as very bad rather than as absolutely terrible makes all the difference to our experience of suffering: "It is only to the absolutely horrific that we respond with blind terror; all other fears are finite, and thus susceptible to being coped with."[44]

Many might worry that the advice to premeditate upon the evils gets it wrong. Instead, the key to a happy mind is always to think positively, and so we seek assurances from our friends and loved ones that the things we fear will not actually come to pass. Yet it seems that thinking positively might not always be advantageous. According to studies conducted by psychologist Gabriele Oettingen, when we engage in positive visualization – imagining we have already accomplished some major task or received

---

41 This is related to what psychologists refer to as the "endowment effect" or "loss aversion." Essentially, we weigh losses more heavily than gains, and we demand much more to give up an item we already have than we do to newly purchase that very same item. See, for example, Kahneman, Knetsch, and Thaler (1991).

42 For an excellent discussion of negative visualization, see Irvine (2009), ch. 4.

43 Seneca, *De Consolatione ad Marciam* IX.5.

44 Burkeman (2012: 48).

some desired good – we trick our brains into thinking we have already suc-ceeded, thereby short-circuiting our motivation to pursue it.[45] Moreover, when our friends offer us reassurance that what we fear will not happen, they do nothing to combat the irrational thought that it would be unimag-inably terrible if it did. Hence, reassurance often has the unforeseen effect of tightening the coils of our anxiety rather than loosening them.[46] It also reinforces the illusion of control; it suggests that we will be able to prevent suffering. However, we don't have the ability to prevent many future events from happening, so when the feared event does happen, we will be caught totally off-guard. Not only will we be stunned and overwhelmed when we experience a perceived lack of control over our situation, but we will also experience our fear in its full force because we have not realized its irrationality.

On the other hand, if we engage in the premeditation of evils, we will not be so shocked by the occurrence of the negative event and we will also have readied ourselves to deal with it. In fact, through negative visualiza-tion we come to realize that when things go wrong, as they most surely will, they are almost always nowhere nearly as bad as we imagined them to be. Our fears are often exaggerated to the point of being utterly unfounded. It is for this reason that Seneca even advises that we do more than just engage in negative visualization; we should also engage in negative experi-ence. To that end, he suggests the following:

> Set aside a certain number of days, during which you shall be content
> with the scantiest and cheapest fare, with coarse and rough dress, say-
> ing to yourself the while: "Is this the condition that I feared?" It is
> precisely in times of immunity from care that the soul should toughen
> itself beforehand for occasions of greater stress, and it is while Fortune
> is kind that it should fortify itself against her violence.[47]

Like a soldier who in a time of peace runs drills to prepare for war, so too, instructs Seneca, should we ready ourselves for a bad future. We should actively engage in activities that challenge us. For example, we could fast for some period of time, or live without electricity for several days, or even try to live without shelter. By so doing, we disarm our anxiety and fortify

---

45 Ibid., 27.
46 Ibid., 34.
47 Seneca, *Moral Letters to Lucilius* 119.

our equanimity, since in going through the experience we realize it is not nearly as bad as we imagined it would be, and we find that we have within us what it takes to deal with the situation.

Engaging in negative visualization can also help us is in dealing with loss. Epictetus claims that when some misfortune happens to us, such as when we lose something of value, as in a material possession or a loved one, our impression that this loss is a completely horrible disaster is unfounded. Instead, while of course we would prefer such a situation not to occur, the loss of our valuables is in itself neither good nor bad. The accurate impression is merely that this loss occurred, which is a part of the natural order of things. It is not appropriate to add to that impression some extra notion that this loss is bad and harmful to oneself, for the loss itself is indifferent. Thus, to claim that you have been wrongfully harmed by the loss of something valuable to you is to assent to the wrong impression, which only serves to create needless suffering.

In training our mind for happiness, then, we should always remind ourselves of the nature of things:

> In the case of everything attractive or useful or that you are fond of, remember to say just what sort of thing it is, beginning with the least little things. If you are fond of a jug, say "I am fond of a jug!" For then when it is broken you will not be upset. If you kiss your child or your wife, say that you are kissing a human being; for when it dies you will not be upset.[48]

If we really enjoy a jug for what it is in itself, then we will recognize that it is in the nature of physical objects to decay, break, and die. The same is true with those we love. To love a thing as it is or a person for who they are is to recognize their natural impermanence. Buddhists maintain that everything is constantly changing and that nothing is permanent. As the Dalai Lama explains, "All things, events, and phenomena are dynamic, changing every moment; nothing remains static.... And since it is the nature of all phenomena to change every moment, this indicates to us that all things lack the ability to endure; lack the ability to remain the same. And since all things are subject to change, nothing exists in a permanent condition...."[49] And because things are impermanent, we should not desperately cling to them.

---

48 Epictetus, *Enchiridion* c. 3.
49 Dalai Lama and Cutler (1998: 163).

Otherwise, if we become attached to things, then we will be made to suffer when they inevitably cease to exist.

In fact, perhaps the best way to deal with the pain of loss is to learn not to see it as a loss in the first place. How can we do that? The advice of the Stoics is to treat everything as if it were on loan from the cosmos. We might call it our own, but it is not. Epictetus advises that we should treat the world "as travelers treat an inn."[50] Therefore, it is foolish to revel in good fortune as it is a matter of luck. You do not truly possess anything; instead, as easily as anything has been given, it can be taken from us. Seneca writes:

Never have I trusted Fortune, even when she seemed to be offering peace; the blessings she most fondly bestowed upon me – money, office, and influence – I stored all of them in a place from which she could take them back without disturbing me. Between them and me I have kept a wide space; and so she has merely taken them, not torn them, from me. No man is crushed by hostile Fortune who is not first deceived by her smiles. Those who love her gifts as if they were their very own and lasting, who desire to be esteemed on account of them, grovel and mourn when the false and fickle delights forsake their empty, childish minds, that are ignorant of every stable pleasure; but he who is not puffed up by happy fortune does not collapse when it is reversed.[51]

If our happiness is tied up in good fortune, we will too easily be made to suffer by life's travails. But if we learn to restrict what we care about only to what is under our control, then we will never fail in our pursuit of happiness. Most importantly, having practiced negative visualization, when the universe does take things from us, we will be prepared and will not view it as a loss.

Nevertheless, while we need to undergo rigorous self-examination, some negative thinking – rumination – is very unhealthy. Rumination involves needlessly and obsessively thinking about the events in our lives. Thus it is different from ordinary negative thinking. While we may generally believe that thinking about our feelings and actions is a good thing, too much thinking about them can actually be quite bad. For instance, many of us feel great anxiety over all the things we could have accomplished with

---

50 Epictetus, *Enchiridion* c. 11.
51 Seneca, *De Consolatione ad Helviam* v.2–6.

our day but did not. Such rumination does not contribute to our happiness or to anything that can change our lives for the better. In fact, it is more likely to lead to a pessimistic perspective on life rather than yielding greater meaning and insight. Not only does rumination bias us toward negativity, but it also impairs our ability to solve problems and interferes with our concentration and motivation. We can counteract our rumination by replacing our excessively negative thoughts with more realistic thoughts.[52] We need to remember that even when we are faced with problems, excessive rumination and anxiety do not do us much good.

Finding Meaning in Suffering

Even if we cannot completely eliminate our experience of suffering, we can try to find a greater meaning in it. To be sure, while we are in the midst of suffering, finding meaning in it is a difficult task. Yet, as Dr. Viktor Frankl, a neurologist and psychiatrist, and also a Holocaust survivor, notes: "Man is ready and willing to shoulder any suffering as soon and as long as he can see a meaning in it."[53] Frankl believes that our main drive in life is not pleasure or power, but to find meaning and a reason to live — everything else is merely secondary. He founded the school of logotherapy, which is a form of psychotherapy directed at helping a person find meaning for his life. Many of Frankl's insights are a reflection of what he witnessed during his three years imprisoned in several Nazi concentration camps during World War II. Frankl lost nearly everyone he loved: his mother, father, brother, and pregnant wife were all killed by the Nazis. Yet he asserts that even though the Nazis could take away nearly everything from a person, they could not take away "the last of the human freedoms, to choose one's attitude in any given set of circumstances, to choose one's own way."[54] In other words, each prisoner had the choice over what type of prisoner they would become, and over whether they could find meaning in their experience. Frankl noticed that those prisoners who had lost all hope died quickly, while those who appeared to have a sense of control over their environment survived longer or were eventually freed.

Frankl is quick to add, however, that there is not one objective meaning applicable to all; rather, meaning is subjective to each person. One

---

52 Lyubomirsky (2007), ch. 4.
53 Taken from Dalai Lama and Cutler (1998: 199).
54 Frankl (1984: 86).

implication of this is that each person is then fully responsible for her own choices and for discovering her own meaning. He explains: "To live is to suffer, to survive is to find meaning in the suffering. If there is a purpose in life at all, there must also be a purpose in suffering and in dying. But no man can tell another person what this is. Each must find out for himself, and must accept the responsibility that his answer prescribes."[55] Thus each person is responsible for discovering and actualizing his own meaning in life. Frankl terms this the "self-transcendence of human existence," referring to the fact that "being human always points, and is directed, to something or someone, other than oneself – be it a meaning to fulfill or another human being to encounter."[56]

Frankl is careful to note that meaning is possible without suffering; it is just that meaning is also possible in the face of unavoidable suffering. Frankl quotes Nietzsche in this regard: "He who has a *why* to live can bear with almost any *how*."[57] According to Frankl, we can find meaning in three main ways: "(1) by creating a work or doing a deed; (2) by experiencing something or encountering someone; and (3) by the attitude we take toward unavoidable suffering."[58] Many of the prisoners in the concentration camps found meaning through thinking about something greater than themselves, whether it might be a work of some kind they needed to finish, someone who was waiting for them outside, acts of resistance, or even a duty to help other prisoners survive, as in Frankl's own case.

As another example of finding meaning in suffering, prisoners kept in solitary confinement separated entirely from others have nonetheless found ways to transform their horrible conditions into something manageable and sometimes even enjoyable. This is certainly a difficult thing to do when one is completely isolated from all human contact. Eva Zeisel, for instance, while in solitary confinement in a Soviet prison, played chess against herself in her own head, engaged in imaginary conversations, and composed and then memorized poems. There are many such stories involving prisoners in solitary confinement, including a pilot who imagined playing a round of golf every day, or those who imagined sophisticated travels throughout the world. Activities like these not only help them hold on to their identity

---

55 Ibid., 11.

56 Ibid., 133.

57 Ibid., 97. This appears to be a translation from Nietzsche's *Twilight of the Idols*, "Maxims and Arrows," Section 12: "If we have our own why in life, we shall get along with almost any how."

58 Frankl (1984: 133).

and sanity, but also offer them an opportunity to invest their psychological energy into a meaningful goal.[59]

Suffering in extreme conditions such as these might even allow for personal development and growth. Our experience of suffering can make us more aware of what we take to have value and of how we want to shape our lives. Consider the story of Bob Shumaker, a Navy fighter pilot during the Vietnam War. While on a mission, his plane was shot down and he was captured by the North Vietnamese. He remained a prisoner of war for eight years.[60] Throughout his internment he suffered many forms of torture, including long periods in solitary confinement, being forced to kneel for days on broom sticks with boards stacked on his back, and what he calls the "rope treatment," which involved ropes being tied around him and then ratcheted so that he was folded forward until his head met his knees. To prevent him from screaming, his captors would force a metal rod down his throat.[61]

Despite being held in isolation, Shumaker and the other prisoners developed an elaborate tap method for spelling out words so that they could communicate. According to Shumaker, they would discuss everything from how to fix a television to offering each other French and biology lessons. Shumaker also occupied his time by painstakingly designing in his head the house he would build upon his release, going so far as to calculate the exact number of nails it would take to build. All of this kept his mind active and sustained a human connection to his fellow prisoners. In fact, Shumaker says that not only did these activities provide meaning that helped him to remain resilient, but they led to other positives as well. As a result of communication with one another, the prisoners were able to share humor that helped to distract them from their negative circumstances. They also developed deep and abiding friendships with one another. Finally, Shumaker says that he got to know himself better as a result of the experience, and that because of it he grew as a person.

So even though suffering is bad or intrinsically disvaluable, it can be extrinsically valuable to a good life. As a final example, philosopher Friedrich Nietzsche believed that his own suffering was essential to his work and his central life projects. He thought suffering was sometimes necessary for

---

59 Csikszentmihalyi (1990: 90–93).
60 Bio of Robert Shumaker from POW Network (http://www.pownetwork.org/bios/s/s097.htm).
61 See the PBS documentary *This Emotional Life* (2010).

great human achievement. Additionally, an experience of suffering can make one more capable to handle future adversity, captured by Nietzsche's famous adage from *Twilight of the Idols*: "What does not destroy me, makes me stronger."[62] All of these examples reinforce that one way to maintain our equanimity even in the face of deep suffering is to find some value in it. In fact, interestingly enough, when asked whether, if they could, they would erase the events of their captivity from their lives, all of the POWs in Shumaker's block said they would not.[63] If it was possible for these prisoners to create meaning out of such horrific conditions, to see their situation as a catalyst for growth and self-knowledge, the rest of us should be able to find no shortage of resolve to do the same in our daily lives.

One final technique for creating meaning out of suffering is to use our suffering to strengthen our compassion for others. In this way, our suffering provides an opportunity for practice in compassion and spirituality. This is captured in the Buddhist practice of *Tong-Len*, in which we use our own suffering as an opportunity to take on another person's suffering and give them our resources in return. It is sometimes referred to as a "giving-and-receiving" visualization. Using *Tong-Len*, you can think to yourself: "May I, by experiencing this pain and suffering, be able to help other people and save others who may have to go through the same experience."[64] Furthermore, in becoming aware of our pain and suffering, we can develop a greater closeness to others by recognizing that they experience the same suffering. We are not alone in our suffering, and when we reach out to others compassionately, we can find meaning in our shared experiences. Moreover, the more positive states of mind we cultivate – such as compassion, love, patience, tolerance, and forgiveness – the easier it is to deal with our negative states of mind. Compassion, patience, and tolerance are natural antidotes to anger and hatred. So with the cultivation of these positive states of mind, we can work to eliminate our suffering.

Also, consider that when we focus on others, we tend to worry about ourselves less. Sometimes our suffering is self-created through too much focus on ourselves; but when we worry less about ourselves, the experience of our suffering is less intense. This is a very tangible way in which a concern for others can promote one's own happiness and decrease one's suffering. This was the case for Jacques Lusseyran, a founder of a resistance

---

62 Nietzsche (1889), Maxim 8.
63 *This Emotional Life* (2010).
64 Dalai Lama and Cutler (1998: 204–05).

group in World War II who was captured by the Germans and sent to the Buchenwald concentration camp. During his internment experience, he came to realize that unhappiness "comes to each of us because we think ourselves at the center of the world, because we have the miserable conviction that we alone suffer to the point of unbearable intensity. Unhappiness is always to feel oneself imprisoned in one's own skin, in one's own brain."[65]

The Dalai Lama emphasizes that our own happiness is intimately connected with that of others and with our environment. This also follows from the doctrine of interdependent arising, according to which nothing exists by itself, but everything is interdependent and mutually self-creating. When we understand this about the world, our whole perspective changes. As the Dalai Lama explains, "We begin to see that the universe we inhabit can be understood in terms of a living organism where each cell works in balanced cooperation with every other cell to sustain the whole. If, then, just one of these cells is harmed, as when disease strikes, that balance is harmed and there is danger to the whole."[66] This then implies that each of our actions has an impact not only on us, but also on all others. For philosopher Derek Parfit, adopting this view had the effect that "the walls of my glass tunnel disappeared. I now live in the open air.... Other people are closer. I am less concerned about the rest of my life, and more concerned about the lives of other people."[67]

All of these considerations suggest that one cannot become happy without also promoting the happiness of others, for one's happiness is fundamentally tied up with the happiness of others. Contrary to one common way of thinking, other-regarding interests do not work against self-regarding interests. It may seem a bit paradoxical, but once we realize how much our interests are tied in with the interests of others, we begin to see that promoting our own interests necessarily involves concerning ourselves with others. This can easily be illustrated through the example of how the happiness of parents seems to rest so completely in the success and happiness of their children. Of course, showing this sort of concern for our children is one thing, but we can also expand on this outward to others. When we are able to realize that the interests of all others are integrally tied to our own, then we will come to see that the pursuit of our own private happiness requires that we act in other-regarding ways. So focusing less attention on the self and focusing more attention on others can improve our equanimity.

---

65 Ibid., 153.
66 Dalai Lama (1999: 41).
67 Parfit (1984: 281).

In summary, Epictetus, the Dalai Lama, and many contemporary psychologists maintain that we can train our mind for equanimity. It requires a process of learning and action. The first step in training the mind and achieving happiness is to identify the positive and negative states of mind by way of learning which states of mind are harmful and which are beneficial to our own happiness (and perhaps as well to the happiness of others and society in general). The second step is to learn how to change them by way of identifying their causal conditions: we need to identify which factors contribute to those positive states of mind and which contribute to those negative states of mind. From this knowledge, we then develop the conviction and determination to change our ways of thinking. Finally, we transform this determination into making a sustained effort to implement these changes in action. We learn specific strategies and techniques for acting so as to cultivate those alterable causal conditions that lead to positive states and eliminate the ones that contribute to negative states. We then repeatedly apply these strategies, which requires discipline, perseverance, and practice.

Naturally, then, the question we will turn to in the next chapter is whether we should promote the happiness of others, and if so, how? In addition, it seems clear that our development as a fully flourishing person can be assisted by our society. In other words, the eudaimonists we have examined are all alike in their conviction that living in the correct kind of society can help one to achieve happiness. For Aristotle, this is a rather direct conclusion from the fact that being happy requires externals. But even for Plato, Epictetus, and the Dalai Lama, a society can help to train persons for virtue and happiness. And we need to be educated in order to develop our reason and understanding of nature. We also need genuine connections to others. Thus happiness seems to be a social achievement. Societies can make people better or worse, happier or unhappier. Perhaps the proper function of a nation is to ensure the happiness of its citizens. After all, if we can structure our social institutions to aid and encourage the full development of our human capacities and thereby ensure that all persons fulfill their potential, don't we owe it to each other to do so? What more or better could be said about a nation than that it produces fully developed, happy, healthy, people who are living nothing short of excellent lives? The just state, therefore, might very well be the one that functions to make the lives of its citizens as good as they can be.

Then again, insofar as this eudaimonist advice does not fit with your values or your nature, you may not find its advice personally compelling.

You might think that living in such a way would not yield contentment, but only frustration. If, then, a society were to implement an initiative to increase eudaimonic happiness, you might well feel that it is an intrusion on your happiness. Isn't a program for national happiness a worry if you find yourself living in a society that is promoting values very different from your own? Might not that cross over into a form of unwarranted paternalism? These are the questions we will turn to next.

Part V: Applications and Further
            Questions

Chapter 11:   Justice
and National Happiness

THE KINGDOM OF BHUTAN is a small Himalayan country sandwiched between two behemoths: China and India. Yet, despite its small stature, the country has made a large impact on the world. Since 1971, and at the direction of Dragon King Jigme Singye Wangchuck, Bhutan has been using Gross National Happiness (GNH), rather than Gross National Product, as the yardstick for measuring its prosperity and development as a nation. Every policy decision must be assessed according to its impact on the happiness of the Bhutanese people. The aim of this program is to modernize the nation while avoiding the pitfalls of materialism that characterize societies focused only on increasing their national wealth. In order to accomplish this goal, the country developed a sophisticated survey instrument that measures the general level of happiness within the nation in order to use it to rate the impact that social policies would have on GNH.

The GNH Index treats happiness as complex and multidimensional. According to the measure, happiness is not solely a function of the experience of pleasures and satisfactions, but includes other constituent elements as well. The first elected prime minister of Bhutan puts it this way:

We have now clearly distinguished the "happiness" ... in GNH from the fleeting, pleasurable "feel good" moods so often associated with the term. We know that true abiding happiness cannot exist while others suffer, and comes only from serving others, living in harmony with nature, and realizing our innate wisdom and the true and brilliant nature of our own minds.[1]

Hence, for the purposes of the GNH Index, although it includes the subjective experience of a pleasant and satisfying life, happiness goes beyond this to include other eudaimonist elements. In total, there are nine domains that include some 33 indicators, as illustrated in Figure 11.1. Each of the nine domains is equally weighted in happiness. It includes both self-regarding and other-regarding values. Happiness even requires a harmony with nature, something noticeably absent from most Western accounts of happiness.

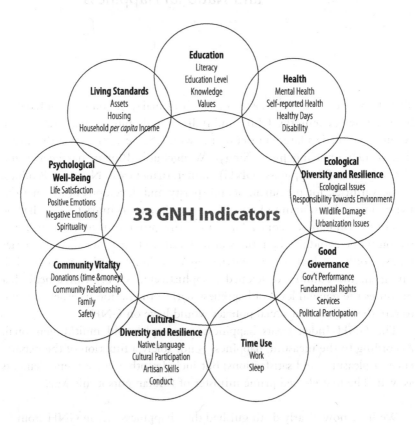

Figure 11.1: Bhutanese GNH Indicators[2]

---

1   Helliwell, Layard, and Sachs (2012: 112).
2   Ibid., 115.

Using the Index, Bhutan has undertaken efforts to increase education, transition from a monarchy to a democracy, and begin massive infrastructure projects. The goal is to modernize the country without sacrificing what is important to the Bhutanese people. Although using GNH is a relatively recent development in Bhutan, it grows out of a long cultural history. Its 1729 legal code declares: "if the Government cannot create happiness (*dekid*) for its people, there is no purpose for the Government to exist."[3] This statement voices a rather common sentiment about the purpose of social institutions: to increase the happiness of its people.

Despite starkly disagreeing over the nature of happiness, thinkers as varied as Jeremy Bentham, Richard Layard, Ed Diener, Martin Seligman, Martha Nussbaum, Amartya Sen, and even the king of Bhutan agree with the sentiment that one central purpose of government is to increase the general happiness. For instance, the hedonist Bentham explicitly declares that the sole criterion according to which we should evaluate "every action whatsoever; and therefore not only of every action of a private individual, but of every measure of government" is the potential impact on general happiness.[4] Similarly, psychologists Diener and Seligman assert that happiness "should become a primary focus of policymakers, and that its rigorous measurement is a primary policy imperative."[5] However, the policy initiatives that a nation adopts are going to heavily depend upon how they conceive of, and consequently attempt to measure, happiness.

As a quick illustration of this point, consider the Gallup-Healthways Well-Being Index. Like the Bhutanese GNH Index, the Gallup-Healthways Index accounts for domains beyond the psychological experience of life. Specifically, it includes the following six domains: life evaluation, emotional health, physical health, healthy behaviors, work environment, and basic access. In selecting these indicators, the Gallup-Healthways Index adopts a particular account of human happiness. According to the 2012 report, Massachusetts ranks as the tenth state overall in happiness.[6] Yet its residents rank near the bottom (forty-third) specifically with reference to emotional health. In other words, people living in Massachusetts are low in enjoyment, interest, and laughter, while scoring high in depression, stress, sadness, anger, and anxiety. To claim that Massachusetts is the tenth happiest state overall, then, seems deceptive to those who think of happiness only

---

3   Ibid., 111.
4   Bentham (1789), Chapter 1, Section II.
5   Diener and Seligman (2004: 1).
6   *2012 State of Well-Being Report* (http://cdn1.hubspot.com/hub/162029/file-21855213.pdf).

in terms of psychological health. If we understood happiness in this more limited sense, we would reach very different conclusions about whether those living in Massachusetts are actually happy. And, presumably, we would also undertake different public initiatives in response. After all, the Gallup-Healthways Index score potentially obscures a serious underlying need for mental-health resources in Massachusetts. Our choice of how to conceive and measure happiness and well-being, therefore, makes all the difference with regard to the data generated and the public-policy recommendations that might result.

It appears, then, that before beginning a large-scale pursuit of national happiness, the first task must be to determine what exactly matters to happiness. Should we favor something like the Bhutanese GNH Index, which promotes a eudaimonist account of happiness? Or does the GNH Index include domains that we would find to be objectionable, such as promoting spirituality, environmental responsibility, or cultural participation? Perhaps if we understand happiness only to be the conscious mental state of pleasure or satisfaction, we might want to limit our happiness program only to the elimination of pain and suffering or dissatisfaction and discontentment.

Even after we decide what happiness is, we still need to reflect on what to do with the information our measures will generate. Should we make it publicly available so that individuals can make more fully informed choices about how best to live? Or should we use the information to shape public policy in a way that more directly supports, encourages, or even enforces behaviors that increase national happiness? On what grounds is the government justified in coercing us in the name of our own happiness? We must ensure that interventions aimed at increasing national happiness are not unwarranted intrusions into the private lives of individual citizens. We do not want to violate an individual's right of self-determination in the name of her own increased happiness.

Of course, we also need to resolve the question of whether it is even possible to measure the happiness of an entire nation. After all, as we have already seen in previous chapters, quantifying the happiness of a single person is tricky enough. What, then, is our degree of confidence that we can successfully measure happiness for an entire population? Though we might reach agreement on what happiness is, we might find that collecting reliable measures of it is so fraught with error that we would do better to steer clear of using such data to set public policy. The risks of using false information are too great to go forward without being sure that our chosen happiness index accurately reflects general happiness. We need to determine whether and how to meaningfully aggregate individual happiness scores in order to quantify national happiness.

Can National Happiness Be Measured?

To be successful, a measure of national happiness will have to aggregate over and summarize the individual happiness level of a large number of people. It will then most likely offer a per-capita happiness score, what is sometimes called a "happiness index." If our happiness measure is a single-item measure, such as the intensity of a felt experience or a rating of life satisfaction, then the indexed score will likely be an average of the happiness of the individuals surveyed. On the other hand, if we use a multi-item measure as the Bhutanese do, then the index score will not only reflect the average across the different items, but it will also have to appropriately reflect the weight of each item with regard to its impact on total happiness.

Currently, there are at least three recognized methods for cataloguing national happiness. They can be arranged according to their scope: how many domains they account for in building a national index of happiness. The first, and most simple, reports happiness according to various economic measures, including per-capita income. These are indirect measures of happiness because they infer happiness levels from amounts of wealth: it is assumed that greater purchasing power means that we can secure a greater number of pleasures and satisfactions, and so we can infer that the more wealth a person has at her disposal, the happier she will be. Notice that this approach accounts only for psychological well-being. Fastening happiness to economic measures has the two major advantages of simplicity and objectivity. First, it concerns only a single domain of life that can be computed according to easily accessible data. Second, economic data is objective and not subject to distortion in the way that self-reported measures of satisfaction or pleasant experience are. On the other hand, being indirect opens the door to the possibility of error; sometimes economic measures might fail to accurately track happiness.

A second index of national happiness relies on measures of subjective well-being. Subjective well-being (SWB) is a hybrid between hedonism and desire satisfactionism. It understands happiness to involve satisfaction with life and with important domains thereof (such as work, leisure, and relationships), as well as high positive emotionality and low negative emotionality. Diener and Seligman, two strong advocates for creating an SWB index, hasten to add that such measures are intended to supplement, not replace, economic measures. Nations could use both when making policy decisions, and could thereby draw on a fuller picture of the impact that such policies would have on the financial and psychological well-being of the nation. Doing so has the advantage of determining in a more direct way how public policies affect happiness, while at the same time also accounting for their financial impacts. Yet, as we have seen in previous chapters (especially Chapters Four, Five, and Six), measures of happiness that rely on self-reported data are far too sensitive to misremembering, bias, and framing effects, and are also too frequently influenced by irrelevant features of context. So, although using an SWB index has an advantage over economic measures in that it is direct, it suffers from subjectivity.

A third approach to compiling national happiness utilizes a multi-item measure, of which the GNH Index of Bhutan provides a nice example. This strategy, sometimes referred to as an "objective list" approach, might have the best of all worlds in that it relies on both objective and subjective measures and takes into account many more elements of a good life. Objective lists typically include not only psychological well-being and material wealth, but also other important values such as degree of political liberty and participation, educational level, and physical health. By accounting for so many domains, objective lists are able to carefully determine the full impact that a particular national program would have on the lives of the population. Because every domain captures at least one of our practical interests, it matters how each is separately affected when deciding on a proposed policy initiative. Despite providing a comprehensive account of national happiness, the inclusivity of such multi-item objective list measures comes at a cost. First, the more inclusive a view of happiness is, the more complex and cumbersome it becomes to determine the impact of a policy on national happiness. Multi-item measures lose the advantage of practicality enjoyed by economic and SWB indices. Second, although there is something intuitively appealing about the GNH approach, there is also something about it that is deeply worrisome: once we move beyond financial and psychological metrics to include other elements in our concept of national happiness, we are necessarily making judgments about what is good for all persons, regardless of whether they recognize or value these aspects of life. Thus, the use of an objective list index could be potentially oppressive.

Before moving forward in our investigation, it is important to pause and take note of the fact that the above indices of national happiness do not map cleanly onto the three theories of happiness: hedonism, desire satisfactionism, and eudaimonism. In other words, we should not automatically conclude that economic measures are the preferred method according to hedonists, SWB for desire satisfactionists, and objective lists for eudaimonists. To be sure, objective list indices such as the GNH Index and the Gallup-Healthways Index do seem to more naturally fit with eudaimonist theories of happiness. However, economic indicators have adherents from within both hedonism and desire satisfactionism. In part this is because, as Plato notes, "money is the chief agent in the gratification of such appetites."[7] An SWB index also appeals to both hedonists and desire satisfaction theorists, since, after all, a pleasant emotional experience is highly satisfying and correlates strongly with subjective well-being.[8] Hence the particular view of happiness that is endorsed does not directly entail which national index will be adopted as relevant to setting public policy, if any at all. Given this, let's turn our attention to the three measures of national happiness in order to more fully explore their respective strengths and weaknesses. After that, we can move on to the more critical issue of the proper role of government in increasing national happiness.

Measuring Happiness in Terms of Wealth

Economic measures are the dominant national and international strategy for assessing public-policy recommendations. Every country keeps an accounting of its GNP and seeks to increase it when possible. Potential policy decisions are evaluated according to their effect on different economic indicators. For instance, in the United States, the non-partisan Congressional Budget Office is legally required to produce a formal cost estimate for nearly every bill under consideration. The estimate is meant to more fully inform Congress when considering approval or disapproval of the bill. At the international level, the International Monetary Fund monitors the economic and financial state of the world and is charged with providing advice to nations concerning how the policies they pursue will impact worldwide wealth. The justification for focusing on the economic impact of particular programs rests on the assumption that the wealthier a nation is, the happier its people are.

Using economic measures to index happiness is an example of the utilitarian social-welfare formula. Public-policy decisions are justified according to whether and how much they increase general happiness.

---

7   Plato, *Republic* IX.
8   Schwarz and Strack (1999: 77).

Maximizing total overall social well-being in terms of increased national wealth is the aim. To many, the connection between increased wealth and increased happiness appears obvious. Economist and philosopher Erik Angner explains why: "The fundamental idea is that greater output makes it possible to satisfy our wants and needs – that is, our preferences – to a greater degree; on the assumption that we are rational, this implies that we will."[9] In other words, those who think of economic measures as indirect measures of happiness emphasize that increased wealth results in increased choice. Having more resources at your disposal means you will be able to do and have more of what you want, whether that is to indulge in hedonistic binges, like Hugh Hefner, or to give time and money away for charitable purposes, like Warren Buffett. Moreover, the more choices a person has open to her, so it is assumed, the happier she will be, since she will choose to actualize the options that best serve her private interest. More wealth translates into more personal choice and more power to actualize those choices. Provided that people choose to do what they believe will make them happier, then increased wealth should track increased happiness. Moreover, poverty is a form of suffering, and escaping it yields increased enjoyment and satisfaction with life. Consequently, income can serve as a nice proxy for national happiness, because a person's wealth reflects the degree to which she can avoid the sufferings of poverty and purchase enjoyments and satisfactions.

Though indirect, economic measures have the major advantages of being both objective and relatively simple to calculate. First, such an approach allows us to compare many different domains of life on a single scale. There is no need to catalog a variety of different facts about each person in order to determine whether she is happy. All we need to know is the amount of material resources she commands; from that, we can infer her relative level of happiness. Such simplicity is powerful: it allows us to catalog a large amount of information in a format that is relatively easy to assess. Furthermore, because they are based on mathematical calculations and empirically observable behavior, economic measures achieve a valued form of objectivity, since they are not subject to the same degree of prejudice and bias as are more subjective measures of happiness. Finally, all the information required for indexing national wealth is empirically observable: we can measure the amount of resources open to a person and observe the choices she makes with those resources. As a result, we can infer what preferences

---

9   Angner (2009: 155).

she has, as well as their relative intensity. This allows for a scientific approach to indexing happiness.

Problems for Economic Measures of National Happiness

Even though economic measures are the most broadly used method for approximating national happiness, they are inadequate. There is now a large body of evidence establishing that even as nations become wealthier, national happiness plateaus, especially in those countries that have reached a level of economic prosperity such that necessary goods and services are widely available. As psychologist Mihaly Csikszentmihalyi notes:

> Inhabitants of the wealthiest industrialized Western nations are living in a period of unprecedented riches, in conditions that previous generations would have considered luxuriously comfortable, in relative peace and security, and they are living on the average close to twice as long as their great-grandparents did. Yet, despite all these improvements in material conditions, it does not seem that people are so much more satisfied with their lives than they were before.[10]

This is true in the United States, Britain, continental Europe, and Japan. As a case study, consider that in Japan between 1958 and 1991, per-capita income increased six-fold and yet life satisfaction remained flat.[11] In the United States, real per-capita income has more than doubled since 1960, but life satisfaction has remained unchanged here too.[12] Moreover, in the same period depression rates have increased tenfold, and rates of anxiety are on the rise as well.[13] These negative psychological effects are true even of affluent children, who are less happy and suffer from lower self-esteem and higher rates of depression and anxiety than children from less affluent families.[14] Not only does increased wealth correlate with higher rates of negative emotionality, but it also brings with it other ills of modern life such as higher rates of obesity, smoking, and diabetes. All of these negative health outcomes affect happiness and well-being and are particularly prevalent in wealthy nations.[15] These findings suggest that focusing policy efforts only

---

10 Csikszentmihalyi (1999: 822).

11 Frey (2008: 38–39).

12 Layard (2005: 29–31).

13 Diener and Seligman (2004: 3).

14 Csikszentmihalyi (1999).

15 Helliwell, Layard, and Sachs (2012: 3).

on improved wealth will not always achieve an increase in general happiness, and it may, in fact, work against it.

Despite the fact that increasing national wealth does not tend to secure sizable gains in national happiness, if we look *within* a country and compare the happiness of a wealthy individual with that of his less wealthy neighbors, there seems to be evidence indicating that wealth *does* increase happiness. This implies that it is not so much how much wealth one commands that makes one happy, but how much one has *relative to others* in one's community or nation. We tend to compare ourselves with those around us, trying to "keep up with the Joneses," and so when we are doing comparatively well we are happier. To illustrate, would you rather be in a situation where you earn $50,000 a year and everyone else earns $25,000? Or would you prefer to earn $100,000 a year while everyone else earns $250,000? If you chose the first situation you are not alone. Most people would rather earn more than those around them, even when doing so would mean they sacrifice more absolute wealth. Thus, as H.L. Mencken wryly observed, "A wealthy man is one who earns $100 a year more than his wife's sister's husband."[16]

However, data from the Bhutanese GNH Index seems to indicate that even increased relative wealth within a country does not always lead to increased happiness. Thimphu, the district housing the capital city, is the wealthiest in Bhutan. In US dollars, residents earn an average yearly salary of roughly $1,140. This is over twice as much as the poorer district of Dagana, where residents earn an average annual salary of about $475. Despite the difference in income, residents of the poorer district slightly outscore their wealthier counterparts in terms of happiness. The overall total GNH Index score is .783 for Dagana and only .773 for Thimphu.[17]

So those in one of Bhutan's poorer districts are happier than those in the wealthiest. This conclusion holds true even when we look further into the distinct elements measured in the GNH Index. As previously outlined, the GNH Index includes elements beyond life satisfaction and positive affect. One might assume that these *other* aspects explain why there is no strong connection between relative wealth and happiness in Bhutan. Maybe if we were to look only at the psychological well-being of citizens living in Thimphu and compare it with those living in Dagana, we might expect the data to reveal that increased relative wealth does correlate with increased life

---

16 As quoted in Layard (2005: 41).

17 Data from Gross National Happiness website (http://www.grossnationalhappiness.com/wp-content/uploads/2012/10/An%20Extensive%20Analysis%20of%20GNH%20Index.pdf).

satisfaction and positive affect. Yet this is not borne out by the data. If we look only at the psychological well-being of those in Thimphu compared to those in Dagana, it turns out the poorer district is still doing better. Dagana residents experience far less stress and anger than those in Thimphu, and they experience states of mental calmness and contentment far more.[18] For example, a full 91.1 per cent of Dagana residents report feeling contentment often (31.2 per cent) or sometimes (59.9 per cent), whereas only 62.4 per cent of Thimphu residents report the same (15.2 per cent and 47.2 per cent, respectively).[19] This suggests that even when one commands fewer resources relative to others in the same society, one can still be far better off in terms of psychological well-being. Then again, such data might be explained away as an anomaly, given that those living in Dagana are generally isolated from the more populated area of Thimpu, so their comparison class is still very small. In such a case, psychological well-being would be affected only by one's wealth relative to his immediate community and not the nation at large. Nevertheless, it seems that, at least at the level of nations, it is not always true that more relative wealth translates into more happiness.

A further worry with using economic measures to index happiness focuses on the assumption that each unit of wealth secures a proportional unit of happiness. Every additional dollar is supposed to produce the same amount of happiness, no matter who earns it and regardless of that person's already existing wealth. Yet this supposition is widely off the mark. As economist Richard Layard notes: "An extra dollar increases the satisfaction of a poor person by 10 times as much as it increases the satisfaction of a person who is 10 times richer."[20] This is explained by the "Law of Diminishing Marginal Utility," which describes the fact that each unit of wealth we gain affects our happiness less than the previous unit: as one accrues more and more money, the additional happiness a person derives from each additional dollar will continue to decrease. In fact, at some point, the pursuit of more wealth leads to negative utility, or a loss in happiness.

The Law of Diminishing Marginal Utility can be easily illustrated by imagining what the effect of receiving a large sum of money (such as $10,000) would be on the psychology of Bill Gates, compared to a person

---

18 Here are the specifics: Self reported stress: Dag: 57.8 not at all, TPU: 46.5 not at all; Experience of Anger: Dag: 40.0 never, TPU: 25.8 never; Experience of Calmness: Dag: 83.2 often (25.0) or sometimes (58.2), TPU: 69.0 often (24.2) or sometimes (44.8).

19 Data from Gross National Happiness website (http://www.grossnationalhappiness.com/survey-results/index/).

20 Helliwell, Layard, and Sachs (2012: 60).

living at the poverty line. Gates, who is worth roughly $79 billion, would likely not even notice another $10,000; it would increase his total wealth by only 0.00013 per cent (or roughly one-ten-thousandth of one per cent).[21] On the other hand, the federal poverty line in 2014 for a single person is an annual income of roughly $11,700, so the above sum would nearly double the impoverished individual's income.[22] This would certainly have a large impact on that person's quality of life.

The Law of Diminishing Marginal Utility then undermines the assumption that every dollar yields the same amount of happiness regardless of who earns it; those who have less money are affected more with respect to happiness through increases in wealth. This law also implies, then, that the most effective monetary policy for increasing general happiness would be to distribute wealth more evenly among the population. According to Layard, this is precisely the conclusion we should draw. He writes that we have enough evidence to conclude that "a country will have a higher level of average happiness the more equally its income is distributed."[23] Contrary to the underlying assumptions of traditional economic measures, money seems to contribute unevenly to the happiness of different economic classes. In fact, how wealth is distributed affects happiness, yet this obvious truth is overlooked by economic measures.

Beyond distributional concerns, another major worry with measures of wealth is that they do not reveal how such gains were made. In other words, what sorts of trade-offs were required in order to achieve ever-heightening opulence? If, for instance, the gains came at the expense of environmental damage, then the appearance of monetary gain may hide severe damages to the health and environment of the population, which may well mean that their happiness is harmed rather than helped by national economic growth. Happiness has as much to do with the means whereby we increase material well-being as it does with how much of an increase we enjoy. However, economic measures seem to treat the goal of increased material wealth as the sole criterion for national well-being. This ignores the fact that not all methods of increasing wealth have the same effect on our happiness. Some are better than others and, in fact, some are clearly bad for our happiness.

For all of these reasons, traditional economic measures have come under increasing scrutiny, even by economists themselves. Layard writes, "I am

21 http://www.forbes.com/profile/bill-gates/.
22 http://aspe.hhs.gov/poverty/14poverty.cfm.
23 Layard (2005: 52).

an economist – I love the subject and it has served me well. But economics equates changes in the happiness of a society with changes in its purchasing power – or roughly so. I have never accepted this view, and the history of the last fifty years has disproved it."[24] At the very least, we should conclude that measures of national wealth fail to provide a complete account of national happiness. In addition to those problems already mentioned, economic measures also suffer from the inability to accommodate other elements central to well-being, such as educational opportunities, health care, life expectancy, infant mortality, the presence or absence of political liberties, mental health and disability, and the extent of racial or gender inequality. Accordingly, we need to refocus our attention on things other than increasing wealth. But what should we focus on? What would a more accurate index of national happiness look like?

Indexing Subjective Well-Being

Ed Diener and Martin Seligman propose that we augment economic measures with more direct measures of happiness. Diener refers to happiness as "subjective well-being" (SWB) and defines it as follows:

> There are a number of separable components of SWB: life satisfaction (global judgments of one's life), satisfaction with important domains (e.g., work satisfaction), positive affect (experiencing many pleasant emotions and moods), and low levels of negative affect (experiencing few unpleasant emotions and moods).[25]

According to this definition, happiness combines feelings and attitudes, both local and global. An index of subjective well-being would thus compile data from self-reported measures of life satisfaction, domain satisfaction, and positive and negative affect. Among the most important benefits of a national SWB index is that it would "focus the attention of policymakers and the public specifically on well-being, and not simply on the production of goods and services," and add "a valuable perspective beyond a cost-benefit market analysis," the most ubiquitous measure currently used to evaluate policy.[26] Diener and Seligman argue that by taking this alternative

---

24 Ibid., ix.
25 Diener (2000: 34).
26 Diener and Seligman (2004: 21).

approach, we can overcome the shortcomings of economic measures and more directly promote national well-being.

Still, proponents of economic measures will argue that economic indicators are capable of capturing central elements of well-being. For example, they claim that mental health problems are already reflected in market changes. More specifically, those with higher subjective well-being are more productive – performing better at work and earning higher incomes. Accordingly, high subjective well-being correlates with increased productivity, and low subjective well-being correlates with decreased productivity. They thus question the need for a separate measure of subjective well-being.

Diener and Seligman counter that economic measures do in fact fail to capture information vital to national happiness. For example, lower economic output caused by mental-health disorders is measured only in terms of lost workdays and the cost of treatment. On the other hand, this appears to overlook those who suffer from depression and are miserable, yet nevertheless continue to work, rather than seeking treatment. Moreover, framing the relationship between work and happiness in terms of economic output fails to account for other practical interests we have concerning our jobs, such as what makes for an enjoyable career, or what sorts of work best utilize one's talents or align best with one's values. By relating work and happiness only in terms of productivity, we have not yet fully appreciated the ways in which our happiness is entangled with our work. And this is not the only domain in which measures of subjective well-being and market indicators offer conflicting advice for how to improve general happiness. Economic measures, therefore, do not paint a full picture and need to be complemented by more direct measures of national happiness. That is precisely the aim and the advantage of an SWB index.

Problems for the Economy of Subjective Well-Being

Though put forward as an alternative to economic measures, a national index of subjective well-being unfortunately suffers from some similar shortcomings. Specifically, it is unable to accommodate distributional concerns and it ignores the means whereby an increase in happiness occurs. This can be explained in part by the fact that both economic and psychometric measures assert that public-policy decisions should be determined according to the degree to which they enhance or diminish general happiness. In other words, though they utilize different approaches, both traditional economics and the economy of subjective well-being nevertheless share a common commitment to the utilitarian social-welfare formula: the aim is to increase aggregate social totals. Since it does not catalog the relative distribution of happiness or the impact of policies on particular persons, an index of subjective well-being may well obscure unequal distributions of happiness and even serious exploitation.[27]

How resources, goods, services, liberties, rights, responsibilities, and other such items are distributed among citizens is central to any theory of justice. It is not enough to justify a particular public-policy measure to claim that it will raise the national happiness by several percentage points. We need to know more: How is that extra happiness spread throughout society? How was it achieved? And, finally, is the increase in general happiness merely the result of people adapting to what are objectively horrible circumstances – people making the best of a bad situation? If so, we must worry about whether the fact of adaptation mentioned previously is masking underlying problems.

The phenomenon of people reporting overall satisfaction with life even despite only mediocre or even horrible objective life circumstances is pretty extensively documented. Consider, for instance, Figure 11.2. Respondents were asked to indicate their agreement with the statement "I am satisfied with my life," using a seven-point scale where seven is complete agreement and one is complete disagreement. One would imagine that *Forbes*'s richest Americans would be quite satisfied, and, in fact, they are. Yet one would not expect the Maasai people of East Africa to be equally as satisfied with their lives. Located primarily in Kenya, the Maasai are a traditional herding people. They live in small huts made of mud, sticks, grass, cow dung, and cow urine. Often the entire extended family occupies a single hut.[28] Despite their subsistence living, the Maasai report a level of life satisfaction that is almost as high as the wealthiest people the world has ever known. This seems to suggest that living in luxury matters little when it comes to experiencing high levels of happiness. In fact, even Calcutta slum dwellers report themselves as moderately satisfied. Does this mean that we need not seek to remedy the conditions of their lives since everything seems to be going well from their perspective? Hardly. The fact that those living in slums report being satisfied may well be the result of adaptation. Perhaps we come to be satisfied with what is familiar and only report a loss of satisfaction when things are going worse relative to what is normal.

---

27 Angner (2009: 162).

28 http://www.maasai-association.org/maasai.html.

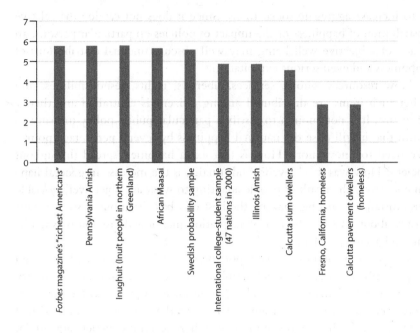

Figure 11.2: Life Satisfaction for Various Groups[29]

Nussbaum and Sen show that adaptation can occur even at the level of physical health: "women who are chronically malnourished and who are taught that they have no right to demand anything following the death of a husband report their health status as good or fair, despite the evident presence of many diseases."[30] Because these women have learned to become accustomed to a low level of physical health and are acculturated into believing they deserve little because they are worth little, they report themselves as healthy even when they clearly are not. These effects are particularly pronounced when a woman is forced to internalize the social demands and values that deny her very own self-respect. In fact, people who are brought up in an environment that treats them as unequal citizens will not report dissatisfaction with the fact that they are denied the full range of citizens' rights. They report being quite satisfied with the inequality: "Empirical work on women shows that they often report satisfaction at having less education than males, because that is what they are brought up

---

29 Figure constructed from data cited in Diener and Seligman (2004: 10).
30 Nussbaum (2012: 350).

to think is right and proper.... So deferring to the subjective experience of pleasure or satisfaction will often bias the social inquiry in the direction of an unjust status quo."[31]

We are quite capable of altering our expectations to fit terrible circumstances so as to be satisfied with very little. Yet if public policy were aimed only at increasing a nation's SWB index score, then there would be no need to adopt public-health policies to aid unhealthy widowed women, or to restructure the basic access and distribution of material resources for Calcutta slum dwellers. There would be no need to offer all persons the rights of equal citizenship or to encourage equal education for both sexes. Everyone is, after all, happy, so nothing needs fixing. And yet, obviously, this would be quite an absurd conclusion to draw.

In addition to the worries of distribution and adaptation, the idea of subjective well-being also suffers from conceptual ambiguity and normative naïveté. Conceptually, it is unclear what we mean when we ask (as does one popular instrument): "Taking all things together, how satisfied are you with *your life as a whole* these days?"[32] What does satisfaction refer to here? Some will see it as a kind of feeling closely akin to pleasure; others will interpret the question as concerning a cognitive attitude or appraisal with no associated affective component. Further, how are we sorting positive from negative emotions? It seems that most of psychology does so according to whether or not the emotion feels good, but this overlooks ways in which emotions that feel good can be negative and, conversely, those that feel bad can be positive. Finally, subjective well-being itself is a rather imprecise and nebulous concept. How do the separable components of subjective well-being fit together? Which are most operative in the concept of well-being? Must the cognitive appraisal of life satisfaction be suitably linked to the experience of positive and negative affect? Suppose a person suffers from deep bouts of depression and anxiety, but also reports high levels of life satisfaction. Do they qualify as being well off?

Most worrisome are the normative concerns surrounding subjective well-being. Why think subjective well-being is at all valuable as a social end? Nussbaum criticizes Diener and Seligman for this very reason. She notes that they diagnose Americans as too anxious and unhappy – experiencing too many emotions that feel bad to us. In turn, they propose public policies directed at alleviating our negative emotionality. However, this

---

31 Nussbaum (2012: 350).
32 Kahneman and Krueger (2006: 7).

ignores the possibility that we *should* feel these ways; maybe we should feel anxious or angry. Is being satisfied or experiencing positive emotionality the sort of thing more worthy of being promoted than something like public service or moral sacrifice? Maybe people should be aggrieved, upset, or angered at injustice in their own situation or in the world around them. Perhaps it is good to feel this way. Seeking to promote pleasant states or satisfaction might be a bad thing insofar as it undermines motivation and discourages behaviors conducive to social change.

For example, as a species we are acting in ways that are destroying our planet and making massive global unrest more likely, with the possible result being a devastating loss of life and well-being. It seems that anxiety is quite a natural emotional response to such a future. By emphasizing policies that reduce our negative emotions and enhance our positive emotions, we may only be altering ourselves in ways that are detrimental to our overall well-being. Maybe this is not the right focus. After all, feeling emotions like anger, anxiety, and fear often acts as a catalyst, motivating actions aimed at remedying our distress. Hence, rather than focus our efforts on cosmetic fixes for our unhappiness, Nussbaum suggests that we tackle the root causes of our anxiety and unhappiness: poverty, violence, inequality, and concerns of basic access. To do this, however, we need to put forward a list of goods that includes more than material wealth and psychological well-being. We need a list that details all the ways in which a citizen's life can be better or worse off. This is precisely what objective list approaches to indexing national happiness aim to do.

Building a List for Happiness: A Capabilities Index

Objective list approaches assume that to be happy is to flourish as a human person. But what does it mean to flourish as a person? The answer will obviously differ among nations. It will depend on the particular components a nation chooses to include as central to human happiness, as well as the relative weights of those elements.

For example, consider again the capabilities list offered by Nussbaum in Chapter Nine. As a quick refresher, "capabilities" are capacities to do and be certain things that are central to human well-being, while "functionings" are particular actualizations of capabilities. In other words, capabilities specify a range of possible ways from which one chooses a certain functioning. So, for example, with respect to the capability of having material control over one's environment, which involves employment, there are various forms this might take – various particular functionings of this capability. One can choose to pursue a vocation in medicine, business, the arts, and so on. The same is true of the capability of control over one's political environment, where one might choose to participate in political decision-making by attending town meetings, becoming a community organizer, running for office, or perhaps just by voting. The goal is to increase functioning by promoting capabilities, thereby giving a person more capabilities from which to choose her own way of functioning. Each capability corresponds to a sphere of human existence within which we can fare well or poorly, and so be more or less happy as a result. The capabilities approach thus seeks to promote a complex and multidimensional account of happiness. There are ten capabilities: life; bodily health; bodily integrity; senses, imagination, and thought; emotions; practical reason; affiliation; other species; play; and control over one's environment.

An objective list index based on the capabilities approach, therefore, better accounts for the many elements of a life well lived than does wealth or psychology. As a result, assessing general happiness means collecting information on the central human capabilities. The capabilities index has another advantage: as Nussbaum argues, rather than settling the question of happiness by asking how satisfied people are or by asking how much in the way of resources they command, it is better to focus instead on what people are actually able to do and be. After all, just because a person commands a certain amount of resources does not mean that she will be able to put them to work in enabling her to live a happy and full life, and just because she is satisfied does not mean that her life is objectively going well. Under certain social dynamics, there are other obstacles to pursuing opportunities, such as institutionalized hierarchies and prejudices.

As a case study, consider the opportunity that American citizens have to participate in the political process through voting. Although legally all citizens have the equal opportunity to vote, if we concern ourselves with what citizens are actually able to do, rather than merely with what the law states, we see that not everyone is equally well positioned to exercise this opportunity. When we account for the facts that voting occurs on only one day of the year (a Tuesday in November during normal working hours), that you have to be physically present at some location to vote (you cannot do it through a secure Internet connection), that you must show proof of residency after having registered months in advance, and that absentee voting is increasingly restrictive, it becomes clear that the appearance of equal distribution is just that: an appearance.

The truth is that many working-class citizens are disproportionally disenfranchised from their vote. They cannot afford to take off time from work, especially when they are paid by the hour, and barely above subsistence wages at that. Clear evidence of this can be found in the US Census Bureau data concerning the November 2012 national election. People earning over $150,000 in yearly income were far more likely to vote than were those who were earning less than $20,000. The affluent group had a turnout rate of just over 80 per cent, whereas the poorer group turned out at barely 50 per cent. In fact, data from the election held in 2012 confirms that there is a tight correlation between level of income and voter turnout (see Figure 11.3). Although every citizen has the opportunity to vote, we do not all take advantage of this opportunity. Moreover, it seems that those who have most to gain from exercising their right to vote are disproportionally alienated

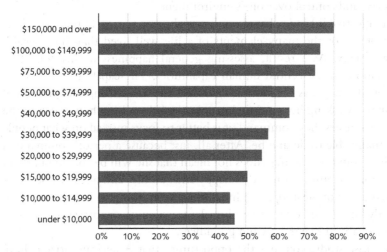

Figure 11.3: Voter Turnout by Income[33]

from their political power. And this is even before the introduction of voter ID laws that are further disenfranchising eligible women and minority voters from exercising their due political power. As another example, in some societies, women may have a formal legal right to work, but they are not able to actually *exercise* that right on account of being systematically denied work by employers and harassed while outside the home. Thus they do not

33 Source: U.S. Census Bureau, Voting and Registration (http://www.census.gov/hhes/www/socdemo/voting/publications/p20/2012/tables.html).

really have the capability for employment. Merely offering an opportunity to someone faced with such institutional prejudice may not solve the problem. Due to social pressures, a person may not be willing or able to take advantage of the opportunities she has been given.

According to Nussbaum, examples such as these teach us that in measuring the level of national happiness and setting public policy accordingly, we cannot rest on formal legal equality and opportunity alone. Instead, Nussbaum argues, we need to focus on the capabilities people have to achieve and do what they want:

> If we operate only with an index of resources, we will frequently reinforce inequalities that are highly relevant to well-being. An approach focusing on resources does not go deep enough to diagnose obstacles that can be present even when resources seem to be adequately spread around, causing individuals to fail to avail themselves of opportunities that they in some sense have, such as free public education, the right to vote, or the right to work.[34]

The capabilities approach is different. The goal is to be concerned not only with what opportunities have been extended to people, but to ensure that people have been positioned to capitalize on those opportunities. In this way, we will not obscure or otherwise overlook critically important factors in happiness.

In adopting the capabilities index for the purpose of increasing general happiness, however, we do not want to coerce an individual into particular functionings. To do so would violate a person's individuality. The whole point of the list is to foster the development of the individual, not to force conformity to a model of happiness imposed from without. Even *if* there were a large amount of data showing that those who go kayaking are happier than those who play golf, or that those who are religious are happier than those who are non-religious, we should not set public policy in ways that push or compel the particular functionings of kayaking and religiosity. To do so would be to violate individuality and the right of self-determination.

Still, the capabilities index recognizes what other indices miss. Namely, that true liberty cannot exist independent from material and social conditions. In other words, being in the right sort of society is what makes choice, liberty, and the pursuit of happiness possible. Hence, if we care

---

34 Nussbaum (1997: 285).

about a person's ability to choose for herself her own conception of the happy life and act on it, we must put in place the right sorts of policies and institutions to support such choice and activity. This includes, among other things, material conditions, educational conditions, the conditions of both mental and physical health, and political power.

Problems for the Capabilities Index

Even though Nussbaum views the multidimensionality of the capability index to be a strength, it does come at a cost. The more variables an index aims to accommodate, the more cumbersome and complex it becomes. The separate capabilities are not commensurate, and so each must be accounted for on its own terms. In other words, none of the capabilities can be reduced to any other; every capability is an important, independent measure that is not explainable in terms of another. Thus, although the capability index has the advantage in terms of not overlooking important elements of the good life, collecting samples on all ten of the capabilities presents a logistical challenge. To be sure, it is not impossible to overcome, as Bhutan has proven. Then again, the country of Bhutan is relatively small, with around only 725,000 residents. Imagine attempting to carry out the same style of project in a country the size of India, with a population of 1.25 billion people. In order to get a truly representative sample within such large populations, the capability index would require an army of surveyors and social scientists. This might well make such an endeavor prohibitively complex and expensive.

Furthermore, once we include in our account of well-being something beyond wealth and positive psychology, we are necessarily making judgments about what is good for all persons, regardless of whether they recognize or value these things for themselves. This could be potentially oppressive, depending on how it is utilized by those in power. Related to this worry, it is important to note that with so many distinct domains, conflicts between them are surely guaranteed. Perhaps, for example, a proposed policy would affect one domain for the better but another for the worse. In such cases of conflict, a nation would have to set priorities concerning which domains are more or less important compared to others; it would have to rank which of the two should give way – which would be weighted more heavily. The formula devised by a nation to calculate the relative weights of the separable domains of happiness depends on choices regarding the value of those domains. For example, should wealth or psychological health be given priority in our index? This means that two nations could collect data on the same items and yet reach different conclusions about the level of happiness among their citizens, as well as the best policy initiatives to increase general happiness.

For instance, the Organization for Economic Co-operation and Development (OECD) is an association of 34 member countries. One of its goals is to explore ways in which policy could increase general happiness and well-being. To that end, the OECD has developed a "Better Life Index" that counts 11 domains as central to happiness. Interestingly, part of the process includes surveying citizens of different countries to see how they would weight each of the eleven domains in terms of their own happiness. According to the US sample, Americans rank life satisfaction as the most important element and civic engagement as the least important; in Uruguay, on the other hand, education is most important and community is least important, with life satisfaction falling all the way to the sixth position.[35]

Given the different weightings that people in the US and Uruguay give to various elements of happiness, it seems likely that the respective policy initiatives of each nation will reflect a different focus based on their own people's stated values. This raises the following questions: How should a state decide which form of happiness to pursue? And how should we determine the relative weights of distinct but important ingredients of the happy life? For instance, Bhutan decided on the domains of GNH and their weighting within the government itself, rather than by means of a democratic vote of its people. Instead, the US might decide to do so in a way similar to the OECD, having people vote on a ranking and then going with what the greatest number of people value. Then again, the OECD limited people's choice to ranking among 11 pre-selected domains; but what if an importantly valued domain is missing from the pre-selected list? Either way, this is a highly political and value-laden choice that has real-world impacts on the lives of individual citizens. It is, therefore, a decision that should be made only after a great deal of reflection and public discourse.

The Greatest Happiness for the Greatest Number?

There is a deeper concern that has yet to be thoroughly addressed: is a socially institutionalized pursuit of increased national happiness just? Though it might be true that we *can* collectively do something to increase national

---

35 If you want to view an interactive world map and add your own voice to the Better Life Index ranking of values, you can do so here: http://www.oecdbetterlifeindex.org.

happiness, the more pressing question to ask is whether we *should*. Recall from earlier the problems inherent with accepting the utilitarian social-welfare formula. Any attempt to increase national happiness will have to deal both with issues of distribution as well as with problems in how increases in happiness are obtained. Beyond this, however, there is a more general worry with thinking that one goal of governments should be the greatest happiness for the greatest number. In particular, what is included in the elusive concept of "happiness"? A program of national happiness building will necessarily rely on measures of happiness, and such measures will, in turn, assume a theory of what matters in life. This is potentially paternalistic.

So what if the account of happiness assumed by a chosen national index is at odds with an individual's private conception? What if public policy aimed at increasing national well-being forces conformity to an ideal that we do not accept for ourselves as valuable or worthy of our pursuit? For instance, the widely touted Bhutanese GNH Index specifically counts spiritual practices such as prayer and meditation as part of happiness. Should a government therefore encourage spiritual practice? Bhutan does. At one point in its history, after discovering that too much television interfered with its citizens' time spent in prayer, the Royal Government instituted policies limiting the number of channels on television.[36] But isn't the choice of spirituality and prayer a highly private enterprise, one central to the very notion of self-determination and liberty of conscience? If so, then maybe governments that attempt to increase general happiness are overstepping their proper authority. Perhaps it is not the job of government to make people happy.

Coercing a person in the name of his own good to act in ways that he does not choose is referred to as *paternalism*. Paternalism occurs whenever a person or group of people controls the behavior of another in order to increase his well-being. Such coercion is justified, it is argued, because the controlling parties know better what is and is not in the interest of the

---

36 See the 2006 BBC Two documentary "The Happiness Formula: Happiness in Bhutan" (http://news.bbc.co.uk/2/hi/programmes/happiness_formula/4809828.stm). However, according to a 2013 *Bhutan Information and Media Impact Study* issued by the Department of Information and Media in the Ministry of Information and Communications in the Royal Government of Bhutan, only approximately 10 per cent of Bhutanese citizens report television as having an impact on their time for prayer. Even so, the number of channels on television is still heavily regulated. This might in part be due to the fact that the study links increased watching of foreign television to the depletion of cultural values and the violation of cultural norms, as well as other social ills. (See http://www.doim.gov.bt/category/publications/. Also available at http://www.bhutanfound.org.)

governed individual. Governmental paternalism, therefore, treats the relationship between the state institutions and the citizen as similar to that between a parent and a child, claiming to know best what will and what will not lead to the happiness of each citizen. The question is whether it can ever be acceptable for a government to treat a grown adult in full control of his cognitive abilities as a child. On what grounds can this be justified, or would it be a direct violation of his right to self-determination and a threat to his individuality?

Protecting individuals against the paternalistic tendencies of governmental power is one of the driving forces behind *liberalism*. Liberalism is a political theory best characterized by its commitment to two values: liberty and neutrality. Liberties are socially recognized and protected abilities to act according to one's own deliberations. According to liberalism, respecting individual liberty ought to be the norm. When it comes to restricting an individual's liberty to do as she chooses with her life, the burden of proof always falls on those who would limit her freedom. In the absence of any good reasons, liberty should be upheld.

The commitment to neutrality recognizes the obvious fact that people differ with respect to their understanding of the good life. That is, through neutrality, liberalism respects value pluralism. It seems obvious that your idea of what a good and happy life includes might very well be different from that of your neighbor. And even though you disagree with each other about what happiness is, you still have to cooperate with each other in order to achieve your collective social aims. This means that we will have to devise social policies that are sensitive to this diversity. Neutrality requires that political institutions and policies remain impartial with respect to competing conceptions of the good life. Therefore, liberalism maintains that no policy initiative can be legitimately justified by appeal to a particular conception of the good. Rather, only reasons open to all persons regardless of their independent accounts of well-being can be used to support political programs. The American ideal of separation of church and state is but one example of how this commitment shapes national politics.

One of liberalism's most avid defenders is philosopher John Rawls. Rawls argues that determining the content of a good life is not the purpose of public institutions. He points out that even reasonable people who deliberate sincerely and carefully about a happy life can disagree with each other. Rawls then argues that "the state is to ensure for all citizens equal opportunity to advance any conception of the good they freely affirm," and that "the state is not to do anything intended to favor or promote any particular comprehensive doctrine rather than another, or to give greater assistance to those who pursue it."[37] According to liberalism, determining whether you or your neighbor has the better theory of well-being is not a legitimate project for national government. Deciding what our moral, religious, and other values ought to be is an entirely private matter best left up to each of us to decide. It is, therefore, not open to public regulation. To regulate it would be to violate the moral agency, liberty of conscience, and right of self-determination that are the foundations of the dignity and respect that we owe to each other as human persons. So if we truly respect a person's right to pursue happiness, and if reasonable people can disagree concerning the nature of happiness, then it would be unjust for a government to set policy according to a singular conception of it.

Before Rawls, John Stuart Mill warned us to always be on guard against what he refers to as the "tyranny of the majority." Tyranny of the majority is a form of tyranny that can take place even in democratic governments. It occurs when the majority is able to enforce its values on a minority that does not accept them. In fact, Mill's concern here is a worry about applying the utilitarian social-welfare formula to issues of national policy. To impose a particular conception of the good life through national policy is a particularly pernicious form of the tyranny of the majority. Because it prevents a person from acting according to her conscience and instead enforces a set of values that are not her own, it prevents her from being a self-defined individual: it prevents her from being a *person*. Instead, it reduces her to a sort of machine that can be built according to a socially acceptable blueprint and made to do those things that prevailing opinion prescribes. Therefore, Mill argues, we need to be vigilant so that popular opinion about what is right and valuable does not become entrenched as institutional dogma.

This is even more pressing given the methods used in the social sciences. Social science generalizes from a sample, and the results it generates are empirically verifiable statistical regularities. From these we derive models of typical outcomes. Those who propose national happiness programs suggest using a model of the happy person to shape public policy. Such a model would describe what makes the typical person happy. Yet who among us is typical? The conclusions of science must generalize the human condition to the point of being detached from particular differences. But in every sample there are outliers, and thus for every conclusion science reaches concerning the typical causes of happiness, there will be people who are caused to be

37 Rawls (1993: 192–93).

deeply unhappy by the very same thing. They will be in the minority, of course, but does that make their happiness any less valuable? Mill therefore concludes that a person "cannot rightfully be compelled to do or forbear because it will be better for him to do so, because it will make him happier, because, in the opinions of others, to do so would be wise, or even right."[38] Respect for individual differences means that it is always wrong to coerce an individual to act against his will, provided he is not harming others through his conduct. According to Mill, increasing an individual's happiness is never sufficient reason for coercing his behavior, even in cases where science has shown that living in one way rather than another is correlated with increased happiness.

Rather than overlook our differences in the pursuit of a scientific model of well-being, we should encourage and celebrate them. To this end, Mill writes:

> Human beings are not like sheep; and even sheep are not undistinguishably alike. A man cannot get a coat or a pair of boots to fit him unless they are either made to his measure, or he has a whole warehouseful to choose from: and is it easier to fit him with a life than with a coat, or are human beings more like one another in their whole physical and spiritual conformation than in the shape of their feet? If it were only that people have diversities of taste, that is reason enough for not attempting to shape them all after one model.[39]

We are not all the same; we differ at least as much in our characters as we do in our size and shape of feet. Hence, to believe that we could put forward a model for the happy life fails to recognize our differences and treats us all as the average person. Far from advocating for a "narrow theory of life," we should rather promote "experiments in living" based on originality, individuality, and eccentricity – we should, therefore, favor strong institutional protection of individual liberty. Only then will the minority be protected from being forced to conform to prevailing opinion.

Mill offers the example of freedom of speech. He says that even if all of society wants to silence you, and even if we democratically take a vote to do so, this still cannot justify our censoring your freedom. Just because a majority, even if it is an overwhelming majority, thinks it is right to silence

---

38 Mill (1859), I, 9.
39 Ibid., III, 16.

one among them, this does not make it so. Rights are aimed precisely at protecting the minority from just these sorts of encroachments. As another contemporary case study, consider our current conversation around the institution of marriage and whether democratically adopted referendums banning same-sex marriages are unjust. On the one hand, such policies are the result of prevailing public opinion, having been adopted through popular vote. On the other, it seems obvious that the desire to ban same-sex marriages relies on a particular set of moral and religious beliefs over which reasonable people can and do disagree. Therefore, the democratic decision procedure in this case allows for a majority to impose its moral view on a minority. Doing so, however, fails to respect the minority as persons and violates the commitment to neutrality at the heart of liberalism. Such bans, therefore, are rightfully understood as rights-violating. These examples also nicely illustrate that there are some things that cannot be justifiably decided according to democratic vote. Democracy does not, once and for all, remove the threat of tyranny, notes Mill.

While perhaps seemingly innocuous, programs promoting the general happiness can also run afoul of liberty and neutrality. For example, it has been reported that Bhutan has increased its GNH score by achieving a high level of cultural homogeneity. This, in turn, was the result of systematically confining ethnic Nepalese residents to refugee camps. In fact, close to 100,000 Nepalese say they were forced out of Bhutan as a result of ethnic and political repression.[40] Or consider the law passed in 2012 by the Board of Health in New York City limiting the size at which a retailer could legally sell soft drinks. Such a policy was adopted because evidence from behavioral science suggests that mandating smaller containers would lead to less consumption and therefore fewer ill effects on the physical well-being of the population of New York City.[41] Such a policy is paternalistic, since it effectively ignores the public's clear preference to the contrary. As philosopher Antti Kauppinen writes, "well-being is irrelevant to public policy, because either people prefer a well-being promoting policy, in which case it is the preference that does the normative work, or they don't, in which case well-being considerations should be given no weight, because doing otherwise would be paternalistic, and inconsistent with respect for persons."[42]

Can the capabilities approach offer policy recommendations without assuming any particular account of the good? Nussbaum believes so. It is

---

40 See the Bhutan Profile at http://www.bbc.com/news/world-south-asia-12641778.

41 Kauppinen (2012).

42 Ibid.

important to note, she claims, that the capabilities index does not dictate any particular model of the human life, but rather articulates a set of basic abilities that every human needs in order to actively lay down a plan for life. For example, she notes the clear difference between choosing to forgo food (fasting) and being forced to go without (starving). Fasting is a choice, while starving is not. Liberty of choice is central to any view of the good. Hence, we cannot force-feed citizens and thereby impose on them a certain functioning, just as we cannot force people into a particular sexual functioning. Nevertheless, we can be sure to arrange our social institutions in such a way that each has the capability to function in the ways she chooses, and to thereby construct for herself a life that aligns with her own conception of the good – she can build for herself a happy life. This encourages living *actively*, a core component of happiness for thinkers as diverse as Aristotle and Mill.

Still, there could be at least two possible ways in which the capabilities approach might fail to be sufficiently neutral. First, if promoting a capability required also enforcing a particular functioning, then even on Nussbaum's own account this would be paternalistic.[43] In fact, it seems that operationalizing the capabilities for measurement purposes requires specifying a set of functionings. In this way, these indices measure actual functionings; and if those functionings are too narrowly construed, the policy recommendations based on them risk being oppressive. For example, as noted earlier, Bhutan's spirituality component is measured by the amount of time spent in prayer or meditation; but these are not the only ways to be legitimately spiritual. Or consider that the Gallup-Healthways Well-Being Index lists under healthy behaviors eating vegetables, and under work environment having a boss that is a partner; again, these are not the only ways for such capabilities to function. This might also lead us to worry about the capabilities approach's ability to respect liberty of choice. One should then make sure that other functionings are also measured for a more accurate representation of people's capabilities.

Second, resolving conflicts between capabilities might be a potential source of paternalism. Nussbaum states, "The central capabilities are not just instrumental to other pursuits: they are held to have value in themselves, in making a life more fully human."[44] This seems to suggest that each of the capabilities is understood as an intrinsic good. Yet, because the

---

43 That this is necessary in a wide number of cases is argued by Claassen (2014).
44 Nussbaum (1997: 287).

capabilities are all independent and incommensurate intrinsic values, we must determine what to do in cases of conflict. Which should take priority, for instance, when the capability of "other species" comes into conflict with that of "material control over one's environment," as they surely will? At least sometimes, protecting our ability to enjoy nature will conflict with our private entitlements to own property. Or when a town decides to build a new community art center that will support the capability of "sense, imagination, and thought," they might well have made a choice to funnel their small resources away from other capabilities, such as promoting "play" by building a new outdoor sports center on the same land. In making such a choice, the town, whether through democratic means or through the zoning board, prioritizes one capability as more important to well-being than another, and this choice is one over which reasonable people may disagree. Hence, allocating resources according to such a scheme might well impose a particular conception of the good. One answer is to make sure that each capability is at least minimally promoted. Indeed, Nussbaum is quick to add that since all of the capabilities are intrinsically valuable to full human functioning, "we also conceive of the capabilities as a total system of liberty, whose parts support one another. Thus ... there is something bad about not securing any of the items. The precise threshold level ... remains to be hammered out in public debate."[45] However, assuming we can specify a reasonable threshold, after it is met, how then should we make further choices?

We might be able to solve the above problem by deciding at the outset which of the capabilities should take priority in any potential case of conflict according to which is of greater intrinsic worth. In fact, Nussbaum seems to do just this: "Of course there will be circumstances in which we cannot secure to all the citizens the capabilities on my list ... political liberties and liberties of conscience should get a high degree of priority within the general capability set."[46] Nussbaum explains that this is because these particular capabilities are necessary to the pursuit of the others. But there are plenty of nations that do not place these specific capabilities at the top of their list. Alternatively, one could prioritize the capabilities through democratic vote. What if, however, people generally rank their priorities of capabilities in a way very different from you? This seems by and large true in the United States, which is a very polarized country. It certainly seems

45 Ibid., 300.
46 Ibid.

possible that a citizen could reasonably prioritize the capabilities differently from her society. And if so, the paternalism charge looms again.

No matter how we resolve the conflict – whether we *a priori* priority rank capabilities as part of the full elaboration of our index, or whether we decide according to prevailing opinion about what matters to life, or even whether we decide on a case-by-case basis according to public discussion – in order to resolve the conflict we will have to make a value judgment about which capability is more important to well-being. And this prioritization will impose on some a value they do not endorse. Reasonable people will be able to disagree with each other concerning which capabilities should be sacrificed in the name of the others in order to best promote general happiness. Insofar as the state allocates resources according to one priority ranking over the other, they seem to be promoting one theory of happiness over another. So just how capable is the index when it comes to adhering to the liberal commitment to neutrality? If it cannot successfully remain neutral in cases of conflict, then it seems to impose on individual citizens values that are not their own. Furthermore, why should an individual value each and every one of the capabilities? Can we not determine for ourselves our own conception of the good and act according to it? It seems that national policies aimed at promoting particular values carry with them the risk of an unjust form of paternalism.

Although we have focused our attention on the capabilities index, it should be noted that similar sorts of concerns could be raised with regard to an SWB index, since it also prioritizes a particular account of the human good. By defining happiness as life satisfaction, satisfaction with certain domains, frequent positive affect, and infrequent negative affect, an SWB index, too, will have to decide which to promote in cases of conflict. Therefore, it will face the same worries as those just mentioned with regard to the capabilities index. Additionally, why *should* someone hold the particular values of life satisfaction, domain satisfaction, and positive affect to be part of their conception of the good life? Insofar as a person does not value such ends – perhaps because she thinks positive affect is too shallow a pursuit for life or because she disagrees with Diener and Seligman that one should prioritize satisfaction with work or leisure time, deciding instead only to concern herself with doing right by her family – then any policies built on such an account of happiness will be alienating from her point of view.

On the other hand, economic measures are not open to the same charge of paternalism, since increasing one's wealth is a proxy for increasing one's choice to do as one wants, whatever that may be. Hence economic measures, though they do not capture a robust account of human well-being, avoid assuming a particular account of what is good and valuable in life, opting instead to increase freedom of choice. This leaves each person to decide for herself what is important to her well-being. However, as noted earlier, economic measures do still overlook potential distributional concerns and worries of exploitation.

Insofar as indices of happiness fail to make room for individual differences, and instead aggregate over the common person, any recommendations they make concerning human happiness will be problematic. Moreover, any institutional program designed as a result of such information will fail to make *all* of us happy and may well instead make many of us deeply unhappy. This is due in large part to the fact that what makes a person happy depends on the expression of her individuality. Furthermore, this self-expression of her own individual character requires that she be afforded the liberty to act as she wants according to her own conception of the happy life, provided that her actions do not harm others. To deny her this is to fail to respect her as a moral agent with the right of self-determination. As such, we should be quite skeptical and cautious about unreflectively accepting the recommendations of national happiness indices when it comes to directing social policy.

Then again, policy decisions need to be made as a matter of practical exigency. Insofar as our current policies are based mostly on economic measures, utilizing subjective well-being or objective list indices are a step in the right direction, provided appropriate caution is taken. After all, using economic measures alone seems to create its own set of problems, as we have already seen: in addition to the worries over distribution of wealth and the potential for exploitative practices to be overlooked, it is also clear that economic measures fail to track national well-being. Hence, policies aimed to promote wealth often directly harm citizens' happiness. Far from being neutral, a single-minded pursuit of increased wealth is positively bad for well-being. At least the capabilities index employs a normatively adequate account of well-being. It also takes pains to include only those elements that are ubiquitous to human experience, and in that way it is broadly applicable cross-culturally to many diverse societies with different views about the good. So while there may be some normative worries about the possibility of an oppressive implementation of the model, sticking with the economic status quo seems clearly worse.

Of course, even if we think that using happiness data to set public policy is sometimes paternalistic, this does not mean we should stop caring about the science of happiness. There might still be good reason for a society to continue to engage in this research, even if the aim is not to support a national program for increasing happiness. It seems clear that the information that such a science would generate could be tremendously valuable for individuals who are pursuing well-being. So as a society we might think that developing the science of well-being is a valuable collective end, as it has the possibility to help each of us achieve well-being more fully, even while acknowledging that we ought to exercise serious caution when using such values to set public policy. Conducting scientific research on the causes and correlates of happiness and providing citizens with that information enables individuals to make more informed choices about how best to live given their relative system of values. Of course, this is only true if the information provided is accurate and if it is presented in a way that does not mislead, as in the case of the Gallup-Healthways Well-Being Index declaring Massachusetts as among the happiest US states. Therefore, we also need to exercise care in the ways in which the information is disseminated. In particular, the components of happiness measured by the survey instrument need to be explicitly outlined. Otherwise, we might mislead people if we lump everything under the general category of what increases "happiness."

Chapter 12:   Concluding Reflections

WE'VE COME A LONG distance from where we started. At this point in the book, we hope you have found that you are more aware of what you think about happiness, including its nature, causes, and value. Initially, you may have had only a rough understanding of happiness, but after having reflected carefully on the arguments for and against each theory, you are probably now able to formulate a more considered view of your own happiness. The key, now, is to remind yourself of the arguments and criticisms of these positions in the previous chapters. For a subject matter so practically important to our lives as happiness, it is essential that you evaluate the arguments carefully and make up your mind only after you have been sufficiently thoughtful. In this final chapter, we would like to remind you of the main ideas, issues, and arguments we have explored throughout the book.

When we begin to think carefully about happiness, we immediately notice that we have hazy, and sometimes inconsistent, intuitions about happiness. In particular, the case of Truman Burbank from *The Truman Show* brings to the fore that we seem to think *both* that happiness is about our experience of life *and* that it is about more than this. This reminds us how important it is to clarify for ourselves what exactly happiness might be. Moreover, any adequate theory of happiness ought to address certain crucial questions. For instance, is happiness only a state of mind, or is it something more? Can we be wrong about our happiness? Is it the same for everyone, or do we each decide for ourselves what is a happy life? Is happiness under our control, and if so, to what extent? It is also important to clarify the relationship, if any, between a happy life and a good life. How do happiness and well-being relate? Indeed, one central concern we should have is to determine just how valuable happiness is in our lives. Is it the only thing of value, and therefore the same as well-being? Or perhaps happiness is just one value among many. If the latter, should it give way when it conflicts with other things of value? In particular, in cases in which our pursuit of our own private happiness conflicts with our moral obligations to others, which should we prioritize? What exactly is the nature of the relationship between the moral life and happiness? Any theory of happiness should respond to these questions, and how a given theory does so helps us to test them against our own intuitions and settled beliefs.

Thus, it is important for us to explore the various theories of happiness in depth, identifying their strengths while also subjecting them to critical scrutiny. Throughout the book, we examined views that identify happiness with: pleasurable experience; positive emotionality; satisfaction of our desires; satisfaction with life as a whole; and flourishing to our fullest potential where this might consist primarily in being morally virtuous, achieving a state of equanimity or mental calm, living in an active way and possessing a range of goods, or exercising certain fundamental capacities. More generally, each of these views of happiness falls into one of three main categories of theories: hedonism, desire satisfactionism, and eudaimonism.

To summarize the views, hedonism is the theory that happiness is the experience of pleasurable mental states. The more pleasure we experience, the happier we are. This view captures a common intuition: being happy feels good. It also makes it possible to empirically measure happiness according to the intensity and duration of the pleasurable experience. From the outset, however, we might worry about whether such a view can account for the value we place on our happiness. After all, it seems like the experience of pleasure might be too shallow, fleeting, and trivial to really matter to life. Some versions of hedonism are sensitive to this worry and so divide pleasures into higher and lower kinds, where the higher-quality pleasures are those that contribute most to our happiness. Although this has the advantage in terms of explaining the normative authority we tend to place on happiness, it makes measuring happiness or comparing the level of happiness between two people highly difficult.

Additionally, all versions of hedonism face the challenge of bad pleasures and good pains. There are at least two ways in which we might think a pleasure to be bad. First, it might come about as a result of immoral activity, such as the pleasure Ted Bundy felt at killing his victims. This makes the pursuit of pleasurable experiences deeply morally problematic. If pleasure can result from such immoral conduct, and therefore happiness can result from living in vicious ways, then perhaps happiness is not a worthy end at which to aim in life. Second, pleasures can be bad for us in the sense that they might not function properly to serve our overall interests. Sometimes, feeling pleasure can reinforce desires and behaviors that harm us, as in cases of addiction.

Desire satisfaction views of happiness also take happiness to be a mental state, though not necessarily one that feels any particular way. Rather, happiness is an attitude: a cognitive appraisal of our life or some aspect of it. The more satisfied we are that our lives are going as we want them to, the happier we are. The primary advantage of such a view is the fact that it broadens the scope of what affects our happiness. Unlike hedonism, which thinks happiness can only be affected by feelings, desire satisfactionism makes room for valuing things for reasons other than how they feel. This can explain why something like writing poetry positively affects our happiness. The art of writing is vexing, and it requires high levels of concentration, skill, and patience, yet many people claim that writing makes them happy. The idea that happiness is about whether or not we approve of how things are going can make sense of these kinds of cases better than the view that happiness is about pleasurable experience only. Additionally, desire satisfaction views better explain the fact that sometimes we are made happy by a reduction in pain, or made unhappy by a diminished amount of pleasure. In other words, desire satisfaction views do a better job at explaining the ways in which our anticipations can affect our happiness. The life satisfaction version of desire satisfactionism has the added benefit of capturing the notion that happiness is global: it is about our lives as integrated wholes. We value some of our desires more than others, and we can be made happy by satisfying our most important wants in life. To be happy means that we have thought about what is valuable to us and that we have successfully set about getting those things.

At the same time, we might worry that an attitudinal account of happiness strips it of its feel-good qualities. More than that, it also means that we cannot be happy unless we have actually reflected on our life and thought about what we value most. This requirement might then preclude a large group of people from claims to happiness. Yet even for those who have undergone the work of reflection, there is a serious worry that those judgments of life satisfaction may be trivial and erratic. Given the ways in which arbitrary features of context (such as the weather or finding a dime) can influence our judgments of satisfaction with life overall, we might worry that there is no reliable way to evaluate life satisfaction. More troublesome still is whether being satisfied with life is even good for us. After all, when we are satisfied, we rarely feel motivated to improve our situation, and given that we can quite easily adapt to dire circumstances, it should worry us that we might be living objectively bad lives despite high levels of satisfaction.

Furthermore, considering cases of radical deception illustrates that perhaps we are misguided to think that happiness is a psychological state and nothing more. Instead, given that we can be completely deceived about our lives and yet experience pleasure and satisfaction, we might be inclined to believe that happiness includes elements beyond our first-hand experience. But what would these other elements be? Eudaimonism answers this question by filling in a list of other values that make up our happiness. Eudaimonism connects happiness with flourishing or fulfilling our positive potential. It also directly links happiness with well-being, arguing that they are the same. Hence the happy life is, according to eudaimonism, the life that lacks nothing that would make it better. Such things as authenticity, autonomy, genuine relatedness to others, and moral virtue, among others, are values according to which life might be going better or worse, and so are included as among the constituents of happiness. Additionally, when we are pursuing a life of flourishing, we should not fall into the trap of focusing only on the positive; we should also tackle the sources of suffering in our lives. Suffering cannot be superficially treated through just the cultivation of positive mental states; it requires its own set of practices to eliminate those conditions that cause our negative mental states. Eudaimonist views bring greater clarity to the question of why we think happiness cannot just be given to us, as by an Experience Machine or drugs, but instead, why it has to be earned or achieved. Eudaimonism also best justifies the tremendous value we place on happiness in our lives and why we wish happiness on others.

Nevertheless, the very same attributes of eudaimonism that allow it to explain the pre-eminent value of happiness also make it troublesome. Eudaimonism specifies a set of universal or objective standards for evaluating happy lives, which may or may not fit with your individual preferences or values. Insofar as you are not drawn to the values endorsed by the view, then you really have no reason to accept its advice. As a result, eudaimonist views of happiness have the potential to seem a bit prescriptive and imposing.

In this vein, there are also potential hazards in basing public policy on national happiness. First we might question whether it is even possible to measure national happiness, given that it is already difficult to accurately quantify happiness at the individual level. There are several different measures we might use in measuring national happiness, each with its own strengths and weaknesses. While economic indices are simple and objective, they can at best only indirectly approximate happiness. Subjective well-being indices are more direct, but they suffer from errors related to self-reporting. Furthermore, insofar as both economic and subjective well-being measures utilize a social-welfare formula that aggregates and summarizes the individual happiness scores of millions of people, they may ignore serious distributional concerns and exploitation. Objective list indices, on the other hand, focus on quality-of-life indicators as part of a more robust account of human welfare, but they are open to the charge of paternalism. Insofar as an objective list index includes in its account of happiness values that you do not endorse, setting policy according to such factors could be oppressive.

In fact, these very concerns might lead us to question whether the government even ought to be in the business of happiness building in the first place. Is increasing national happiness a proper role for government to play in our lives? In choosing to pursue national happiness, a government will have to adopt a particular conception of happiness and thereby encourage or enforce a specific view of the human good. This might then violate the liberal commitments to liberty and neutrality, as a nation may impose on some citizens a theory of the happy and good life that they do not accept. On the other hand, doing nothing – offering no policy recommendations whose aim is to increase national happiness – is potentially much worse than paternalistically pursuing one particular account of human happiness.

After you have determined what you take happiness to be, you must then decide what its value is to you. Do you think that happiness is the *only* valuable thing in life? Or are there other values that are more important? Is happiness even valuable at all? Answering the question of value is essential because it is hard to know what practical advice you should follow unless you understand where happiness fits in your system of values. Perhaps what you have discovered is that happiness is not the most important thing in life. You should then search for what else has value to you and research how best to go after it. On the other hand, maybe you think that happiness is the pre-eminent value in life, taking priority over all or most others. If so, then you should set out a plan for achieving it.

The key, now, is to take your considered responses to these questions and put them to work in living your life. After deciding on a view, you also need the conviction to alter your plan of life and live by it. After all, there is no point in embarking on this journey if you are unwilling to change the way you live as a result of your newfound knowledge. Just having the knowledge without action seems a waste. What sorts of general plans or strategies should we develop in order to more effectively pursue happiness?

It would be wise, first of all, to learn about what sorts of conditions promote or interfere with your happiness. Before you set out haphazardly trying activities to see what effect they have on your happiness, you can learn lessons from empirical science about the causes and correlates for each of the above possible views of happiness. Part of this will include learning which among the causal conditions you can willfully manipulate. You need to direct your focus toward the proper techniques and strategies, and not waste your time trying to change things that are not within your power to change. Then you can follow specific strategies to cultivate and eliminate those alterable conditions. This is important so that you are best able to encourage and bring about the conditions for happiness.

We suggest that when you are planning for a happy life, you review the empirical causes and correlates of pleasure, satisfaction, and eudaimonia, as well as the recommendations they seem to imply, since many of them hold promise for increasing your level of happiness, regardless of your particular view. That is, many of the strategies suggested to increase one type of happiness are applicable to the others. So you might find that following a suggested strategy will increase your level of happiness no matter your particular conception. In part, this is due to the fact that there is a great deal of overlap among the main views of happiness. Typically, eudaimon lives are pleasurable and satisfying, and we usually find pleasant lives satisfying and satisfying lives pleasurable. Therefore, attempting to increase one conception of happiness will usually have the effect of increasing the others. For instance, one important insight shared among all the views is that much of our happiness resides in our ability to train our mind. Through inner discipline and mindfulness training, we can come to experience a more pleasurable, satisfying, and meaningful life.

Certainly, though, there are some critical differences among the views concerning what causes happiness. This is especially true when dealing with whether our mental states are the result of deception or immorality. Accordingly, the best way to increase your own level of happiness will vary to some extent depending on your view of the nature of happiness. Specific advice relevant to increasing one's pleasure will vary from the advice suggested by satisfaction accounts, and the same will be the case with different forms of eudaimonism. This suggests, too, that when reading reports or books on what will lead to happiness, you should be cautious. Whenever someone, whether it is a psychologist, economist, sociologist, philosopher, or self-help guru, advertises some strategy for making you happier, you need to be sure to ask what they mean by "happiness." Investigating beforehand what exactly the suggested techniques are designed to increase will help to prevent you from wasting time on strategies that are not aimed at getting you to where you want to be.

After discovering the causes and correlates of happiness and strategies for cultivating the conditions for happiness, the final step is to actually live according to the knowledge you have gained. This will take some measure of resolve, as building a life of lasting happiness is not easy. In fact, you should be skeptical of any view that claims there is some easy secret to happiness. Those who say this are dealing in half-truths, at best. Happiness is not something you can come by effortlessly. It will take some work, but it will be worth it. If we take seriously the idea that the *purpose* of our life is happiness, it can profoundly change the rest of our lives. Thinking about this simple idea alone can influence the choices we make in our lives, and it can help us in solving our daily problems. It can help to generate the will and resolve to become happy. It also helps us to focus our minds on what things are truly valuable to us. We can then concentrate on discarding those things that will not bring us happiness and obtaining those things that will. In fact, here is a simple exercise that you can try. Before making any decision, ask yourself this question: "Will it bring me happiness?" Just asking this simple question helps to shift our perspective so that we focus on what it is we are really seeking: ultimate lasting happiness. And in so doing, it aids us in making more careful decisions and helps us to skillfully conduct our lives.

We must incorporate what is learned into the living of our life. Indeed, Epictetus advises us not just to think appropriately about our lives, but to *act* appropriately – otherwise we have gained little in our quest for happiness. Happiness will not simply come to us if we wait. Rather, we must work, and work diligently, to attain it. In our pursuit of happiness, we should be unwavering. We must approach this project with a sense of urgency. As Epictetus advises, "remember that the contest is *now* and the Olympic games are *now* and you cannot put things off any more and that your progress is made or destroyed in a single day and a single action."[1] So decide right now that you are worthy of happiness and that you will dedicate your life to being the best version of yourself that you can be. Life is valuable; do not waste it.

We hope you have found this book enlightening, and even motivational, and that you are now more prepared in your pursuit of the happy life. In the end, we hope you have come away a bit wiser and more effective at pursuing happiness. We will close with some thoughts from the Dalai Lama on happiness. We hope these words may be of some benefit to you in your own pursuit of happiness:

> Sometimes when I meet old friends, it reminds me how quickly time passes. And it makes me wonder if we've utilized our time properly or not. Proper utilization of time is so important. While we have this body, and especially this amazing human brain, I think every minute is something precious. Our day-to-day existence is very much alive with hope, although there is no guarantee of our future. There is no guarantee that tomorrow at this time we will be here. But still we are working for that purely on the basis of hope. So, we need to make the best use of our time. I believe that the proper utilization of time is this: if you can, serve other people, other sentient beings. If not, at least refrain from harming them. I think that is the whole basis of my philosophy.
>
> So, let us reflect on what is truly of value in life, what gives meaning to our lives, and set our priorities on the basis of that. The purpose of our life needs to be positive. We weren't born with the purpose of causing trouble, harming others. For our life to be of value, I think we must develop basic good human qualities – warmth, kindness, compassion. Then our life becomes meaningful and more peaceful – happier.[2]

---

1 Epictetus, *Enchiridion* c. 51.
2 Dalai Lama and Cutler (1998: 63–64).

References

Angner, Erik. 2009. "The Politics of Happiness: Subjective vs. Economic Measures as Measures of Social Well-Being." In *Philosophy and Happiness*, ed. Lisa Bortolotti, 149–66. New York: Palgrave Macmillan.

Annas, Julia. 1998. "Virtue and Eudaimonism." *Social Philosophy and Policy* 15 (1): 37–55.

Annas, Julia. 2004. "Happiness as Achievement." *Daedalus* 133 (2): 44–51.

Aristotle. 1925. *Nicomachean Ethics*. Trans. W.D. Ross. Oxford: Oxford University Press.

Aristotle. 1935. *The Eudemian Ethics*. Trans. H. Rackham. Cambridge, MA: Harvard University Press.

Bentham, Jeremy. 1776. *A Fragment on Government*. In *The Collected Works of Jeremy Bentham*, ed. J.H. Burns and H.L.A. Hart. London: The Athlone Press, 1977.

Bentham, Jeremy. 1789. *An Introduction to the Principles of Morals and Legislation*. London: T. Payne & Son.

Bentham, Jeremy. 1825. *The Rationale of Reward*. London: John and H.L. Hunt.

Bok, Sissela. 2010. *Exploring Happiness: From Aristotle to Brain Science*. New Haven, CT: Yale University Press.

Brickman, Philip, and Donald T. Campbell. 1971. "Hedonic Relativism and Planning the Good Society." In *Adaptation Level Theory*, ed. M.H. Appley, 287–305. New York: Academic Press.

Brickman, Philip, Dan Coates, and Ronnie Janoff-Bulman. 1978. "Lottery

Winners and Accident Victims: Is Happiness Relative?" *Journal of Personality and Social Psychology* 36 (8): 917–27.

Burkeman, Oliver. 2012. *The Antidote: Happiness for People Who Can't Stand Positive Thinking.* New York: Farrar, Straus, and Giroux.

Butler, Joseph. 1726. *Fifteen Sermons Preached at the Rolls Chapel.* London: J. and J. Knapton.

Cahn, Stephen. 2004. "The Happy Immoralist." *Journal of Social Philosophy* 35 (1): 1.

Cash, Johnny, and June Carter Cash. 1962. "The Legend of John Henry's Hammer." *At Folsom Prison* [CD]. New York: Sony Music Entertainment.

Claassen, Rutger. 2014. "Capability Paternalism." *Economics & Philosophy* 30 (1): 57–73.

Csikszentmihalyi, Mihaly. 1990. *Flow: The Psychology of Optimal Experience.* New York: Harper and Row.

Csikszentmihalyi, Mihaly. 1999. "If We Are So Rich, Why Aren't We Happy?" *American Psychologist* 54 (10): 821–27.

Dalai Lama, His Holiness. 1999. *Ethics for the New Millennium.* New York: Riverhead Books.

Dalai Lama, His Holiness, and Howard Cutler. 1998. *The Art of Happiness.* New York: Riverhead Books.

Diener, Ed. 2000. "Subjective Well-Being: The Science of Happiness, and a Proposal for a National Index." *American Psychologist* 55 (1): 34–43.

Diener, Ed, and Robert Biswas-Diener. 2008. *Happiness: Unlocking the Mysteries of Psychological Wealth.* Malden, MA: Blackwell.

Diener, Ed, R. Lucas, and C.N. Scollon. 2006. "Beyond the Hedonic Treadmill: Revising the Adaptation Theory of Well-Being." *American Psychologist* 61: 305–14.

Diener, Ed, and Martin Seligman. 2004. "Beyond Money: Toward an Economy of Well-Being." *Psychological Science in the Public Interest* (5) 1: 1–31.

Dunn, Elizabeth, and Michael Norton. 2013. *Happy Money: The Science of Smarter Spending.* New York: Simon & Schuster.

Easterlin, Richard. 1974. "Does Economic Growth Improve the Human Lot? Some Empirical Evidence." In *Nations and Households in Economic Growth: Essays in Honor of Moses Abramovitz,* ed. Paul A. David and Melvin W. Reder, 89–125. New York: Academic Press.

Easterlin, Richard. 2003. "Explaining Happiness." *Proceedings of the National Academy of Sciences* 100 (19): 11176–83.

Epictetus. 1993. *Enchiridion*. Trans. Nicholas White. Indianapolis: Hackett Publishing.

Epictetus. 2008. *Discourses*. In *Discourses and Selected Writings*, trans. and ed. Robert Dobbin. London: Penguin Classics.

Feldman, Fred. 2010. *What Is This Thing Called Happiness?* New York: Oxford University Press.

Foot, Philippa. 1958. "Moral Beliefs." *Proceedings of the Aristotelian Society* 59: 83–104.

Frankl, Viktor. 1984. *Man's Search for Meaning*. Boston: Beacon Press.

Frey, Bruno. 2008. *Happiness: A Revolution in Economics*. Cambridge, MA: MIT Press.

Gilbert, Daniel. 2006. *Stumbling on Happiness*. New York: Vintage Press.

Gilbert, Daniel, and Timothy Wilson. 2000. "Miswanting: Some Problems in the Forecasting of Future States." In *Feeling and Thinking: The Role of Affect in Social Cognition*, ed. Joseph Forgas, 178–97. New York: Cambridge University Press.

Greene, Joshua. 2013. *Moral Tribes: Emotion, Reason, and the Gap Between Us and Them*. New York: Penguin Press.

Griffin, James. 1986. *Well Being: Its Meaning, Measurement, and Moral Importance*. Oxford: Clarendon Press.

Hanh, Thich Nhat. 2009. *Happiness: Essential Mindfulness Practices*. Berkeley, CA: Parallax Press.

Haybron, Daniel. 2001. "Happiness and Pleasure." *Philosophy and Phenomenological Research* 62 (3): 501–28.

Haybron, Daniel. 2003. "What Do We Want From a Theory of Happiness?" *Metaphilosophy* 34 (3): 305–29.

Haybron, Daniel. 2005. "On Being Happy or Unhappy." *Philosophy and Phenomenological Research* 71 (2): 287–317.

Haybron, Daniel. 2008. *The Pursuit of Unhappiness: The Elusive Psychology of Well-Being*. New York: Oxford University Press.

Helliwell, John, Richard Layard, and Jeffrey Sachs, eds. 2012. *World Happiness Report*. New York: The Earth Institute, Columbia University.

Hughes, William, and Jonathan Lavery. 2004. *Critical Thinking: An Introduction to Basic Skills*. 4th ed. Peterborough, ON: Broadview Press.

Irvine, William. 2009. *A Guide to the Good Life: The Ancient Art of Stoic Joy*. New York: Oxford University Press.

Kahneman, Daniel. 2000. "Experienced Utility and Objective Happiness: A Moment-Based Approach." In *Choices, Values, and Frames*, ed. Daniel Kahneman and Amos Tversky, 673–92. New York: Cambridge

University Press.

Kahneman, Daniel. 2011. *Thinking, Fast and Slow*. New York: Farrar, Straus, and Giroux.

Kahneman, Daniel, J. Knetsch, and R. Thaler. 1991. "Anomalies: The Endowment Effect, Loss Aversion, and Status Quo Bias." *The Journal of Economic Perspectives* 5 (1): 193–206.

Kahneman, Daniel, and Alan Krueger. 2006. "Developments in the Measurement of Subjective Well-Being." *Journal of Economic Perspectives* 20: 3–24.

Kauppinen, Antti. 2012. "Schmucks and Philosopher Kings: A Dilemma for Well-Being Policy." *PEA Soup*. Web. http://peasoup.typepad.com/peasoup/2012/10/schmucks-and-philosopher-kings-a-dilemma-for-well-being-policy.html.

Keats, John. 1993. "Ode on Melancholy." In *The Norton Anthology of English Literature*, 6th ed. Vol. 2, general ed. M.H. Abrams, 794–95. New York: W.W. Norton and Co.

Kekes, John. 1982. "Happiness." *Mind* 91 (363): 358–76.

Kraut, Richard. 1979. "Two Conceptions of Happiness." *The Philosophical Review* 88 (2): 167–97.

Lamb, R.J., K.L. Preston, C.W. Schindler, R.A. Meisch, F. Davis, J.L. Katz, J.E. Henningfield, and S.R. Goldberg. 1991. "The Reinforcing and Subjective Effects of Morphine in Post-Addicts: A Dose Response Study." *Journal of Pharmacology and Experimental Therapies* 259 (3): 1165–73.

Layard, Richard. 2005. *Happiness: Lessons from a New Science*. New York: Penguin Books.

Long, George, trans. 2004. Epictetus's *Enchiridion*. Mineola, NY: Dover Publications.

Lykken, David, and Auke Tellegen. 1996. "Happiness Is a Stochastic Phenomenon." *Psychological Science* 7 (3): 186–89.

Lyubomisrky, Sonja. 2007. *The How of Happiness: A New Approach to Getting the Life You Want*. New York: Penguin Books.

Marcus Aurelius. *Meditations*. Trans. George Long. *The Internet Classics Archive*. http://classics.mit.edu/Antoninus/meditations.html.

Maslow, Abraham. 1943. "A Theory of Human Motivation." *Psychological Review* 50 (4): 370–96.

Michaud, Stephen G., and Hugh Aynesworth. 1983. *The Only Living Witness: The True Story of Serial Sex Killer Ted Bundy*. Irving, TX: Authorlink Press.

Michaud, Stephen G., and Hugh Aynesworth. 1989. *Ted Bundy:*

Conversations with a Killer. New York: Signet Publishers.

Mill, John Stuart. 1859. *On Liberty*. In *The Collected Works of John Stuart Mill, Volume XVIII – Essays on Politics and Society Part I*, ed. John M. Robson, 213–30. Toronto: University of Toronto Press, 1977.

Mill, John Stuart. 1861. *Utilitarianism*. In *The Collected Works of John Stuart Mill, Volume X – Essays on Ethics, Religion, and Society*, ed. John M. Robson, 203–60. Toronto: University of Toronto Press, 1985.

Monk, Ray. 1990. *Ludwig Wittgenstein: The Duty of Genius*. New York: Penguin Books.

Moore, Andrew, and Roger Crisp. 1996. "Welfarism in Moral Theory." *Australasian Journal of Philosophy* 74 (4): 598–613.

Nettle, Daniel. 2005. *Happiness: The Science Behind Your Smile*. New York: Oxford University Press.

Nietzsche, Friedrich. 1889. *Twilight of the Idols*. In *The Portable Nietzsche*, trans. Walter Kaufmann. New York: Viking Press, 1967.

Nozick, Robert. 1974. *Anarchy, State, and Utopia*. New York: Basic Books.

Nozick, Robert. 1989. *The Examined Life*. New York: Simon and Schuster.

Nussbaum, Martha. 1993. "Non-Relative Virtues: An Aristotelian Approach." In *The Quality of Life*, ed. Martha Nussbaum and Amartya Sen, 242–69. Oxford: Clarendon Press.

Nussbaum, Martha. 1997. "Capabilities and Human Rights." *Fordham Law Review* 66 (2): 273–300.

Nussbaum, Martha. 2012. "Who Is the Happy Warrior? Philosophy, Happiness Research, and Public Policy." *International Review of Economics* 59: 335–61.

Parfit, Derek. 1984. *Reasons and Persons*. Oxford: Oxford University Press.

Plato. 2005. *The Republic of Plato*. Trans. J.L. Davies and D.J. Vaughan, with revisions by Andrea Tschemplik. New York: Rowman and Littlefield.

Pojman, Louis J. 2003. "The Case against Moral Relativism." In *The Moral Life: An Introductory Reader in Ethics and Literature*, ed. Louis J. Pojman and Lewis Vaughn, 166–90. New York: Oxford University Press, 2007.

Rawls, John. 1993. *Political Liberalism*. New York: Columbia University Press.

Ricard, Mattieu. 2003. *Happiness: A Guide to Developing Life's Most Important Skill*. New York: Little, Brown, and Co.

Scanlon, T.M. 1993. "Value, Desire, and the Quality of Life." In *The Quality of Life*, ed. Martha Nussbaum and Amartya Sen, 185–200. New York: Oxford University Press.

Schwarz, Norbert, and Fritz Strack. 1999. "Reports of Subjective Well-Being: Judgmental Processes and Their Methodological Implications." In *Well-Being: The Foundations of Hedonic Psychology*, ed. Daniel Kahneman, Ed Diener, and Norbert Schwarz, 61–84. New York: Russell Sage Foundation.

Sen, Amartya. 1993. "Capability and Well-Being." In *The Quality of Life*, ed. Martha Nussbaum and Amartya Sen, 30–53. Oxford: Clarendon Press.

Seneca. 1917. *Moral Letters to Lucilius*. Trans. Richard Grummere. Cambridge, MA: Harvard University Press.

Seneca. 1932. *De Consolatione ad Helviam*. In *Seneca: Moral Essays*, vol. 2, trans. John W. Basore. Cambridge, MA: Harvard University Press.

Seneca. 1932. *De Consolatione ad Marciam*. In *Seneca: Moral Essays*, vol. 2, trans. John W. Basore. Cambridge, MA: Harvard University Press.

Siderits, Mark. 2007. *Buddhism as Philosophy: An Introduction*. Indianapolis: Hackett Publishing.

Tatarkiewicz, Władysław. 1966. "Happiness and Time," *Philosophy and Phenomenological Research* (27) 1: 1–10.

Taylor, Richard. 2002. *Virtue Ethics*. Amherst, NY: Prometheus Books.

This Emotional Life: In Search of Ourselves ... and Happiness. 2010. Hosted by Daniel Gilbert. Corporation for Public Broadcasting. DVD.

Tiberius, Valerie. 2003. "How's It Going?: Judgments of Overall Life Satisfaction and Philosophical Theories of Well-Being." Presented at Minnesota Interdisciplinary Workshop on Well-Being. Unpublished.

Tiberius, Valerie. 2006. "Well-Being: Psychological Research for Philosophers." *Philosophy Compass* 1 (5): 493–505.

Tiberius, Valerie, and Alicia Hall. 2010. "Normative Theory and Psychological Research: Hedonism, Eudaimonism, and Why It Matters." *The Journal of Positive Psychology* 5 (3): 212–25.

Tversky, Amos, and Dale Griffin. 1991. "On the Dynamics of Hedonic Experience: Endowment and Contrast in Judgments of Well-Being." In *Subjective Well-Being*, ed. Fritz Strack, Michael Argyle, and Norbert Schwarz, 101–18. Oxford: Pergamon Press.

Williams, Redford, and Virginia Williams. 1993. *Anger Kills*. New York: Harper Books.

Yang, Stephanie. 2014. "5 Years Ago Bernie Madoff Was Sentenced to 150 Years in Prison – Here's How His Scheme Worked." *Business Insider* July 1, 2014. http://www.businessinsider.com/how-bernie-madoffs-ponzi-scheme-worked-2014-17.

Index

Page numbers in italics refer to figures.

From the Publisher

A name never says it all, but the word "Broadview" expresses a good deal of the philosophy behind our company. We are open to a broad range of academic approaches and political viewpoints. We pay attention to the broad impact book publishing and book printing has in the wider world; for some years now we have used 100% recycled paper for most titles. Our publishing program is internationally oriented and broad-ranging. Our individual titles often appeal to a broad readership too; many are of interest as much to general readers as to academics and students.

Founded in 1985, Broadview remains a fully independent company owned by its shareholders—not an imprint or subsidiary of a larger multinational.

For the most accurate information on our books (including information on pricing, editions, and formats) please visit our website at www.broadviewpress.com. Our print books and ebooks are also available for sale on our site.

broadview press
www.broadviewpress.com